Acclaim for Karen Tintori's

Trapped: The Cherry Mine Disaster of 1909

"*Trapped* is everything that such a book ought to be, and much more: A gripping narrative, powerful in its language and extraordinarily well-constructed. A portrait of elemental human strengths and frailties. . . . A reminder of the terrible price paid by immigrants to establish themselves in America. Karen Tintori's account of the Cherry Mine Disaster is a classic of its kind."

—Frank Viviano, author of *Blood Washes Blood* and *Dispatches from the Pacific Century*

"The author's writing skills are evident; she crafts . . . a very accessible and gripping account of a human tragedy that elicited both the best and worst from those involved. Highly recommended."

—*Library Journal*

"Tintori's graphic account of this tragedy is a sad but gripping story."

—*Booklist*

P9-DDL-772

TRAPPED

The 1909 Cherry Mine Disaster

Karen Tintori

ATRIA BOOKS
New York London Toronto Sydney Singapore

ATRIA BOOKS
1230 Avenue of the Americas
New York, NY 10020

ISBN: 978-0-7434-2195-9
0-7434-2195-7 (Pbk)

First Atria Books trade paperback edition September 2003

10 9 8 7 6 5 4 3 2 1

ATRIA BOOKS is a trademark of Simon & Schuster, Inc.

Manufactured in the United States of America

For information regarding special discounts for bulk purchases,
please contact Simon & Schuster Special Sales at 1-800-456-6798
or business@simonandschuster.com

Front cover: Cherry miners, left to right: Attilio Corsini, Adam Galletti,
Bobby Corsini; seated: Louis Galletti

For my family,
especially Lawrence, Mitchel and Steven
and for miners,
and their families

A little fire is quickly trodden out,
Which, being suffer'd, rivers cannot quench.

William Shakespeare,
King Henry the Sixth, Act IV, Scene VIII

Fire is the test of gold; adversity, of strong men.

Seneca, *De Providentia*, 5,9

And after the fire, a still small voice.

I Kings, 19

In the crisp postdawn hours of Saturday, November 13, 1909, four hundred and eighty Illinois coal miners dropped down into a mine touted to be the safest in the country. By midday more than half of them were living their worst nightmare, trapped in an inferno raging nearly four hundred feet below ground. Cut off from exit routes, these men and boys battled for their lives, driven back by smoke, ferocious heat, walls of flames and the deadly invisible gas miners call "the black damp."

By nightfall the mine was sealed, burying—dead and alive—more than half of the miners. No one could have guessed it would be March and beyond before rescuers could retrieve and bury most of those still trapped below.

Death touched nearly every home in Cherry, Illinois. Hundreds of women were widowed. Nearly five hundred children were orphaned. Just weeks before Thanksgiving they were plunged into despair and destitution, with no food or fuel in homes suddenly robbed of men.

Cherry's tragedy was a national one that dominated headlines for weeks. In a time before radio and television, newspapers devoted page after page to detail the continuing relief and rescue efforts and the investigation that ensued. Foreign governments dispatched their consuls to Cherry to look after their bereaved nationals, troops arrived to maintain order and Americans everywhere reached deep to answer appeals from the Red Cross and *The Chicago Daily Tribune*.

The catastrophe stands as the worst coal mine fire in U.S. history and the country's third-worst coal mine disaster. Only the December 6, 1907, Monongah, West Virginia, explosion which claimed 362 at Monongah Numbers 6 and 8 and the October 22, 1913, Dawson, New Mexico, explosion at Stag Canon Number 2, where 263 died, surpass it for loss of life.

It was a tragedy that precipitated sweeping changes in child labor practices and in the coal industry, and was the catalyst for the first worker's compensation laws enacted in the United States.

It was also a tragedy that never should have happened.

Considered to be the largest coal shaft in the U.S., Cherry was the epitome of modernity and safety both in construction and equipment. Completed in 1905, it was one of the only mines in the country outfitted throughout with electricity. Built of steel, concrete, brick and stone, and with a tipple its engineer rated the safest in the world, the St. Paul Mine was declared fireproof—a designation that would be the first of the ironies to haunt Cherry just four years later.

I never knew my Grandpa Tintori, but I grew up in Detroit in his home, a two-flat house heated by radiators that were steamed by coal. I can still hear the slush of those sooty lumps sliding down the chute at the side of our house into the coal cellar, hear the scrape of the shovel as my dad heaped another load onto the fire in the coal furnace.

Grandma Tintori, my dad's widowed mother, lived in the upper flat. On Sunday mornings, she'd invite me up for tea and whole wheat toast and stories about her hard life as the child of a coal miner who died in his forties of black lung disease. My parents, my sister, JoLynne, my brother, John, and I lived downstairs.

In January 1948, with her pregnancy just a hunch, my mother, Joanne, had stood beside her father-in-law's hospital bed and told him she was carrying his first grandchild. "I won't live to see the baby," he told her. He died the next day. I have always felt a strong connection to this grandfather thanks to the gift of my mother's announcement. What I've learned of him has come from photographs, a couple of legal documents and far too few family stories.

John Tintori was born in Fanano, Italy, and in his early twenties came to join relatives in Illinois to mine coal. He became a citizen, shipped out to France with the U.S. Army in World War I, came back to earn his miner's license, then worked in mines throughout Illinois until he and other relatives succumbed to the lure of the assembly line. He packed up his young wife, Catherine, and my father, Raymond, and headed for the auto plants in Detroit.

Aside from the bittersweet story that he knew about me before he died, what burns in my mind most vividly about him is the sentence I remember first hearing when I was about seven, a pronouncement Grandma Tintori gave to me throughout my childhood like a recurring gift.

"Your grandfather survived the Cherry Mine disaster."

That was all she'd say—one unembellished statement that filled a little girl with such awe I never pressed her for more.

Ten years ago, I began to trace my Tintori genealogy and the Cherry disaster clue was the first I followed. Any firsthand account of the horror my grandfather witnessed was lost to me, and by the time my writer's curiosity was hungry to know it, both my grandmother and father were also dead. I turned to my mother, who told me my grandfather had survived the disaster not by heroism, but by a quirk of fate. Though he was noted as a winemaker, taught well by the priests who'd raised him in Italy, he wasn't much of a drinker. It was an uncharacteristic hangover that kept him home from work the Saturday of the fire, when four hundred and eighty miners dropped down into the bowels of the St. Paul Mine that morning instead of four hundred and eighty-one.

My next visit was to my dad's cousin, Lester Corsini. His father, Attilio, was one of the last to escape the burning mine, his mother's eighteen-year-old brother, my grandfather's first cousin, Johnny Galletti, perished. Lester told me about Cherry and, together, we pored over his collection of picture postcards taken in the aftermath of the disaster and the firsthand account written in Italian by Antenore Quartaroli, a family friend who survived. My search went on.

My quest to know my father's father, to learn his place in the Cherry story, to find his name in some news account or union ledger or census roll, consumed me. As I pored over the letters, articles, photos and reports I'd collected looking for him, I found instead a story that engrossed me.

As the details and the ironies of the disaster unfolded, I became obsessed with the life-and-death struggle of the miners below ground and the terror of the women and children thronged at the entrance to the mine, praying for the men and boys they loved.

Over the years, in addition to my research on coal mining at the turn of the last century, I have collected an abundance of material on the disaster that includes firsthand accounts of survivors, government inquiries and reports, legal correspondence, photographs, newspaper accounts, pamphlets, both court reporters' transcripts of testimony taken at the coroner's inquest, commemorative programs and memorabilia. In addition, via phone, letter and e-mail, many descendants of the Cherry miners have generously shared with me their family stories and mementos. My thanks to them and others appear in the acknowledgments.

I finally placed my Grandpa Tintori at Cherry, spotting his face peeking from the back row in a photo of Johnny Galletti's funeral. My grandfather survived the Cherry Mine disaster, and because he had I was here to recount the tale. My journalist's head and my novelist's heart fought over the best way to do so. In the end, with thousands of pages of dialogue from inquest transcripts, letters, E. P. Buck's 1910 account, *The Cherry Mine Disaster*, and newspaper reports before me, I decided on the immediacy of a straightforward, nonfiction, you-are-there recounting of the story.

With the exception of the initial conversations between John Tintori and Johnny Galletti, the conversation at the Galletti breakfast table, and Charlie Galletti's questions about his family at the mine shaft—three incidents I derived from family stories—all of the dialogue in this book is exact. In a few instances where phrases like "there is" or "we are" read too stilted, I have taken the liberty of using their less distracting contractions. In a few other instances, where I thought the actual dialogue too convoluted, I have paraphrased instead.

The ordeal of the twenty-one miners entombed in the second vein is taken from two sources—an account dictated by miner Thomas White, and the diary of Antenore Quartaroli given to me by my cousin Lester and translated from the Italian by my late friend, Sandra Sonnino. I have tried to be faithful to the cadence and drama of Quartaroli's native tongue, and the thoughts italicized in those chapters attributed to him and Thomas White are their own.

With every survivor dead by the time I began my research, the biggest challenge was to breathe life into characters whose history I did not know, when all I had to draw from were their own words, the inquest testimony, newspaper accounts and, if I was lucky, photographs. In instances where I've referred to "a miner," "an Italian" or "one of them," it is because the records gave no name.

As family genealogists know, surnames at the turn of the last century were usually spelled the way the writer heard them. I have done my best to use the most consistent spelling contained in the numerous sources, or those given me by descendants. Likewise, I have done my best, checking and crosschecking the numerous accounts, to bring this story accurately to its wider audience.

In September 2000, ten years after I began to research the disaster, I visited Cherry, Illinois, for the first time. Although my father's Parochetti cousins still live near the coalfields our ancestors once worked, it was the first time my husband, Larry, or I had been there. It was impossible to finish this book without a trip to the town, the mine site and the cemetery. We spent five days researching and interviewing, building up to and saving the actual visit to the mine site for the last. While Larry climbed the slag pile with Charlie Bartoli, who now owns the property, with Ed Caldwell and with Dave Philippe, the latter a descendant of other Cherry miners, I stood at the sealed mine shaft and tried to evoke another time and the men, women and children whose story I am about to retell.

The story of the Cherry Mine disaster is a human drama rife with heroism, cowardice, supreme sacrifices and twists of fate. Ultimately, though, it is a triumphant tale of survival against all odds. Eight days after the mine ignited, with the fire barely controlled, twenty men who'd been trapped in the deepest recesses of the mine miraculously emerged alive. Today, November 21, 2001, is the ninety-second anniversary of their rescue and, by coincidence, the day I completed this final draft.

This is their story—and the story of the all the victims, survivors, widows, orphans, townspeople and mine owners, every one of them trapped by the disaster at the Cherry Mine.

CHAPTER ONE

Standing like a twin-peaked hill, a spoils dump lush with vegetation throws shadows across the farmland that buries the St. Paul Mine. Cornfields wave at jutting remnants of the hoisting shaft and other mine buildings, and chunks of coal, shale and rock lie scattered among weeds and wildflowers. Nature and nearly one hundred years have reclaimed what was once the most prosperous coal mine in the Midwest.

At the village's southern edge, tiny Holy Trinity Miners Cemetery abuts a curve in Highway 89, barely revealing its towering stone monument to passing motorists. Dedicated to the two hundred and fifty-nine men and boys who perished there in one of the most tragic coal mine disasters in U.S. history, the monument's bowed and weeping woman grieves over the final resting place of many of them.

Their little-known story is preserved in the tiny Cherry Library, where mine artifacts and photos line the walls alongside poignant missives penned by entombed miners as they waited for smoke, flames and poisonous gases to overtake them.

From a vibrant community of twenty-five hundred in its heyday,

Cherry has dwindled to a village whose five hundred residents either farm the land or earn their livelihood in neighboring Ladd, LaSalle, Mendota, Ottawa, Peru and Spring Valley. Many live in the original company houses, most of them renovated or expanded, some with water pumps still standing in the backyard.

Cherry was born on rolling prairies roughly one hundred miles southwest of Chicago in 1904. Mining experts called to the heart of Bureau County's rich coal region by the St. Paul Coal Company discovered a vast, inexhaustible vein of bituminous coal almost unequaled in quality. The company, licensed to mine coal in six Illinois counties, instantly began to sink the state's largest coal mine, certain that within two years the black diamonds buried there would make it a principal coal center in the Midwest.

Forty years before, 62 percent of the world's energy came from wood. By the 1910s, coal had supplanted wood. It owned that 62 percent pinnacle and accounted for 80 percent of America's fuel right before the dawn of electricity while the Wright brothers were still perfecting the airplane and the world traveled by coal steam-powered rail and ship. Today, coal still generates 25 percent of the world's energy, and nine of every ten tons used in the U.S. go to produce electricity.

In 1909, the coal industry was booming. The U.S. mined out four hundred and thirty-one million tons a year, but production was seasonal, tied to winter's heavier heating demands in homes and offices. Families spent about $35 of their average $651 yearly income for fuel, and in 1904, only 3 percent of them used electricity. The first electric range, vacuum cleaner and iron would not appear until later in the decade. Beating and mixing, dishes and laundry were all done by hand. Women cooked on wood- or coal-burning stoves, buying blocks of ice twice weekly to preserve the food in their wood-and-metal iceboxes.

The steadiest call for coal came from industry, shipping and railroads, and Cherry's entire output—estimated then at upward of twenty-five hundred tons per eight-hour day, three hundred and sixty-five days per year—was already earmarked for the Chicago, Milwaukee and St. Paul Railway Company, which immediately built a spur track from Ladd. As the northernmost coal deposit in the state, Cherry was the end of the line, both for coal and the railroad. From there, train cars had to travel the three miles back to Ladd in reverse.

Word of the astounding find spread quickly to surrounding mining communities and even to Europe, as immigrant miners alerted friends and relatives to the opportunity for steady work. Unlike most mines, which shut down in summer leaving miners with no income, Cherry would operate constantly to furnish coal for the locomotives, machine shops and offices of the giant coal company.

Cherry was incorporated in April 1905, and by June the St. Paul Coal Company had sunk $200,000 into developing the mine and the town born to house its workers. It christened both after James Cherry, former Seatonville mayor and the region superintendent of mines put in charge of sinking the hoisting shaft. To ensure lively commerce between the new town and the rich farming community surrounding it, the coal company constructed the largest grain elevator in the vicinity. The Illinois farmers were conflicted about the mining communities springing up in their midst. They welcomed the economic opportunities mining brought with it, but looked down their noses at the foreigners mine companies had to import because few farmers could be lured to the dangerous work. They refused to mine, yet hated the foreigners—most of whom had been farmers themselves—for earning more working underground than they could eke from their land.

Farmers saw the foreigners as a threat to the country's character and "Eyetalians" were the most disliked, both by the native farmers and other English-speaking immigrants. One farmer interviewed for Herman R. Lantz's study, *People of Coal Town*, called nine out of ten foreigners "no good." "We would have been a heap better off if they had never been brought here."

The few Americans who did mine were threatened by the immigrants as well. To survive, the foreigners were willing to work harder, longer and at more dangerous mine jobs than the Americans. An American miner told Lantz, "No American would work as hard as they did because the foreigners didn't have any sense."

The mine company's plan for the new town was charming, calling for a park, a school, a bank and several general stores. Expecting Cherry to be its crowning jewel, the railroad built a first-class railway station two blocks from the main business district.

Promising "Money in a New Town," the coal company offered one hundred and twenty acres of land for sale as home and business sites on June 21, 1905, announcing reduced rail fares to Cherry that day and parking a special dining car there to serve lunch. The six-page pamphlet advertising the 10:30 A.M. auction of town lots predicted they would sell out by noon.

The coal company built a fifty-room hotel and fifty modern model homes, and while work on the mine continued day and night under the supervision of experts from across the country, a town grew across the prairie.

Touted to be the largest coal shaft in the U.S., the Cherry Mine was the epitome of modernity and safety both in construction and equipment. The engineer who built the tipple rated it the world's safest, and it was one of the only mines in the entire country outfitted with electricity. Even the darkest areas of any mine, the mule stables and pumping room, were strung with incandescent light. With a tower of steel, a foundation of concrete and its engine, boiler and fan houses all made of brick and stone, the men who built it declared the Cherry Mine fireproof.

CHAPTER TWO

T hey came from Austria, Belgium, Germany, Greece, Ireland, Italy, Lithuania, Poland, Scotland, Sweden, Yugoslavia and from mining towns across the U.S. From around the world they flocked to Cherry seeking a better life, even if it meant trading daylight for a future. It was a time of peace, prosperity and progress. America had gone two full generations with no major wars, and the U.S. Treasury swelled with a $46,380,000 surplus.

With nearly five million people, Illinois was the third most-populous of America's forty-six states, right behind New York and Pennsylvania. Each year, one million immigrants paid about twelve dollars to sail to America in steerage, where farming was the leading occupation, employing eleven million of the country's seventy-six million people. Mining, with seven hundred and sixty thousand workers, ranked seventh.

Bituminous coal miners had been organized nationally since the Civil War started in 1861. Pennsylvania anthracite miners followed suit seven years later. From six unions in the late 1880s, U.S. organized labor had swelled to one hundred and seventy-one unions with more than two million members by 1909. Though accepted grudgingly by some coal operators, the nineteen-year-old United Mine Workers of America was a potent force in the coalfields. The UMWA sought to bring order to a competitive industry, extending its influence to reduce unfair competition among the various regions of the state and country by promoting a fair wage scale.

"Their power reduced the ability of any company to cuts its costs, wages, to gain unfair advantage over competitors," said Illinois labor historian Richard Joyce, whose mother's ancestors left Fanano, Italy, to mine in Illinois.

In 1910, life expectancy averaged 47.3 years, with diphtheria, malaria and typhoid leading the causes of death. The only vaccination available was for smallpox, and colds often turned to fatal pneumonia. Babies were born at home, parents doctored their children with cod liver oil and sewed their cuts with sterilized needles and cotton thread. There were no vitamins, just tonics and patent medicines that claimed to cure a variety of ills. There were also no antibiotics. People either got well or they died.

It was a time when women wore long skirts, corsets to cinch in their waists and never left the house without gloves and something on their heads. Usually it was a hat, and the bigger the better. They wore their hair long, piled atop their heads to emulate the Gibson Girl, the paragon of beauty immortalized in the sketches of Charles Dana Gibson. The *Ladies Home Journal* sold a million copies each month, and the Sears, Roebuck Catalog was America's "wish book," with rockers for $2.95 and wood-burning stoves, $17.48. A woman's skirt cost four dollars, a shirtwaist three dollars, and a man's suit set him back nine dollars. Boys wore knickers and girls wore crinolines. There were no zippers, only buttons, hooks or snaps.

It was a dressier time for men too. They wore suits and hats to the office and on Sundays. Haircuts were short and males sported beards and mustaches, shaving with a straight razor after lathering up with a special stubby brush and soap sold in mugs.

Housewives boiled the laundry, scrubbed it by hand and hung it out to dry. Everything had to be ironed. They baked their own bread and canned fruits and vegetables for the winter. Eggs were twelve cents a dozen, canned vegetables a dime, and per pound, sirloin ran twenty-four cents, and chicken or turkey, seven cents.

William Howard Taft had just succeeded Teddy Roosevelt, Pius X was the pope and Nicholas II was still the Russian czar. In April 1909, after eight attempts in twenty-three years, Robert E. Peary finally reached the North Pole. Antiliquor crusader Carrie Nation was smashing up saloons with her hatchet and women were championing for the right to vote. It was the year the NAACP, the National Association for the Advancement of Colored People, was founded, and twenty thousand New York garment workers went on strike.

Barbershop quartets entertained on Saturday nights. Americans sang "Shine on Harvest Moon," "Meet Me Tonight in Dreamland" and "I Wonder Who's Kissing Her Now," and reading by kerosene lamp filled the evening hours. Novels outsold nonfiction two to one, with stories like *The Virginian* wildly popular just as the Old West was disappearing. Cinema was in its infancy. Ten-minute movies chased the heels of the first connected story on film, 1903's eight-minute *Great Train Robbery*. Ford introduced his Model T in 1908, and while Sunday drives became a pastime of the wealthy, many doubted the horseless carriage novelty would last. America had 193,368 miles of railroad track and only ten miles of paved road. In bad weather, horses and buggies got mired in muddy ruts.

No one had a radio. Only eighteen in a thousand owned a phone. The world communicated by post, telegram and telegraph. Trains brought the mail, and many cities delivered it three times a day. Often, relatives in Ladd would send a postcard three miles to Cherry midweek just to say they'd be coming for Sunday supper.

While Italians and Slavs predominated Cherry's growing population, a cacophony of languages filled the air. Miners worked alongside men they could not understand, and neighbors communicated with nods and gestures.

With the influx of a primarily young population quickly swelling the town to twenty-five hundred, the public schoolhouse was one of the first buildings up and running. A barber shop and other businesses followed. So did two churches, one small and Catholic and the other a Congregationalist offering both services and regular Sunday school classes. But it was the saloons, which excluded women and numbered seventeen of Cherry's thirty-five businesses, that flourished. Prayer fortified the miners' spirits on Sundays and spirits kept them fortified the rest of the week. A whiskey or three to cap off a day below ground was as important to the average miner as his dinner, and the saloons made certain no man went home parched. Yet tippling in Cherry was modest by standards in Westville, population one thousand, whose men supported sixteen saloons.

Protestant missionaries preaching temperance among the Illinois coal miners met deaf ears. "A saloon," said one Westville miner in a 1902 issue of *Missionary Review*, "is the only decent place we fellows have to go. We have a newspaper to read, another fellow to argue with, and we can put our feet on the table and eat all the free lunch we want. We have a blooming fine fiddler who plays for us—say, wot's a fellow livin' for, all work?"

Miners everywhere drank hard because they worked hard. Their labor was tough, tedious, dirty, backbreaking. And it was dangerous. Miners were regularly maimed and killed. Accidents were common, mainly from the dynamite they used to blast coal from the seams. Poisonous gases claimed their victims slowly, and explosions took lives the instant a spark ignited the undetectable methane so pervasive in a mine. Odds of an Illinois miner dying on the job in the early 1900s were about one in four hundred, still better than in other states where miners lacked a union.

Families worried more than the miners. Women and children lived in constant dread of the piercing shriek of the mine alarm whistle. Explosions, cave-ins, slides and other accidents occurred so frequently that one Illinois miner's wife remarked, "A natural death is such a strange thing here that when one hears that So-and-So is dead, they ask at once, 'When was he killed?'"

Coal mining, like war, made camaraderie, friendship and concern for one another an unwritten law among miners. With danger ever present down in the depths, miners had only each other to save them. Many made lifelong friends of their mining "buddies."

Most miners, by necessity, adopted a fatalistic attitude toward their work, but one sixty-seven-year-old Illinois miner quoted in Herman R. Lantz's study, *People of Coal Town*, said if he had to do it over again he'd choose another occupation. "You never step on that cage without wondering if you're going to come back or not. Being a miner is just like going into battle. There is always this fear of the mine."

Some miners feared injury more than death because there were innumerable ways of getting maimed. Chest and other permanent injuries were the most feared, and poor health was a given.

"To do this work results in the degrading of a man," Lantz quoted one sixty-year-old Illinois miner. "Many people get sick because of lots of dust. The lungs fill up with asthma. People die. They become discouraged, hopeless."

Working in pairs in total darkness illuminated only by the thick grease called "sunshine" burning in their helmets, miners had to depend for their livelihood on their own strength, their own tools and their work partner. They rose before dawn to head for the mine, carrying deep dinner pails their wives or landladies packed with sandwiches and water. Often they crouched for hours, hacking coal from tight spaces with ceilings so low they could not stand upright. In this darkest place on earth, their only company was the nearby sound of dripping water and scurrying rats and the distant, muffled noise of hammering and explosions.

Faces smeared black, the men and boys worked in the pits like the mules they harnessed to the coal cars by day and stabled near the shaft overnight. For eight hours at a stretch, miners breathed in a variety of noxious fumes and a coal dust so silty it coated their lungs and embedded itself in their clothing. Despite soap and water at the end of the day, their skin and fingernails remained stained with a dark patina that never quite scrubbed off.

Coal superintendents and their bosses in the pits had considerable influence in the coal towns. "They were feared, if not universally liked or respected, due to their power to control the economic well-being of miners, their families and the towns they had created," Richard Joyce said. When the owners decided to close mines, especially in smaller, one-industry towns, they created ghost towns as miners moved away to find work elsewhere.

Coal bosses often showed favoritism in assigning workplaces, giving choicer areas to men who were "loyal" to them. "These were also the men who supported the mine superintendents at the polls when they ran for public office," Joyce added. "Superintendents often had the largest, nicest homes in the coal towns, along with the ability to purchase such frills as pianos and automobiles.

"Coal superintendents were sometimes viewed by miners as uncaring tyrants," he said. "Other coal owners and bosses, however, were paternalistic benefactors who helped build the communities they had often created. They donated money and/or land for parks and churches, helped finance the purchase of land and homes by miners, started banks and seemed to care about their men. Others, however, were viewed as heartless manipulators of men whose purpose was solely to increase the companies' profits. The miners usually had more respect for local men who had risen up through the ranks to positions of authority, while they often resented those who were sent in by the coal companies from the outside."

Technically, a "miner" was a digger or blaster who dislodged large blocks of coal from the seams, the top tier in a young slate picker's progression up the ranks. "Miners" were artisans who never handled the coal, but left their daily production for the laborers to shovel.

Small boys who started out picking rock from coal moved up to trapping, spending their days standing guard at mine ventilation doors and opening them only long enough to let mule drivers through with full or empty coal cars. Timbermen and spraggers kept the roofs shored up, trackmen kept the rails in shape and examiners searched for lurking dangers. Miners were Illinois's highest-paid mine workers, with wages tied to output. Depending on how much they produced in a shift they could earn an average of $2.50 a day, roughly $45 in today's dollars. It was forty cents a day more than the rock men, timbermen, cagers and trackmen earned, and more than double the set wages paid to young trapper boys and slate pickers. All miners, from the boys to the men, had to supply their own lamps, oil, wicks and tools and pay the company to keep them sharpened.

With year-round work and a choice of stores, Cherry's miners had it better than the average miner, whose life and town was run by the mine company, had work only one hundred and eighty-one days out of the year and was always in debt, forced to purchase necessities on credit from the company store. Pay came on the first and sixteenth of the month in wage vouchers from which the mine company had already deducted grocery purchases, heating coal and six to ten dollars monthly rent in the drab houses it typically slapped up for mine families, one on top of the other.

Unlike other "company towns," where identical shabby dwellings stood side by side, five different styles of architecture made each of Cherry's three hundred and seventy-five homes different from the one next to it. The mine company built one hundred and twenty-five of these designs, the rest were privately contracted. Only Steele Street, which four years later would be dubbed Widows' Row, was lined with thirty interchangeable houses.

Some of the company houses, plucked from other mining towns, rode into the state on flatbed cars. Split in two for their journey and reassembled in Cherry, most were one and a half stories. Each could house ten to fifteen people in three small downstairs rooms and two slope-ceilinged upper rooms cramped beneath the eaves. The kitchens were tiny, the closets sat under stairwells, and chickens, cows, thirty-foot surface wells and outhouses took up most of the minuscule backyards.

The town was seven blocks long and five shorter blocks wide, bisected by the railroad track and its modern depot. The park graced an entire square block opposite the schoolhouse at the north end of town. Main Street's thirty-five, all-brick buildings comprised the attractive business district that boasted wide curbed streets and concrete sidewalks.

The mine company offices and buildings, fashioned of brick and stone, sat clustered immediately northwest of town near the huge gray rock dump or slag pile. The eleven buildings consisted of carpenter, machine and blacksmith shops; the power, fan, boiler and storehouses; engine rooms for each of the two veins and an emergency hospital. All were dwarfed by the massive eighty-five-foot steel tower rising into the air from the mouth of the mine. Visible for miles around, it was the hub of topside activity as hoisting cages brought their coal loads through the center of the tower and ran them out onto the tipple where they were dumped—first into hoppers for weighing and then into the coal chutes. It was state-of-the-art, with a shaker, screens, crossover dumps, steam pushers and steam transfers and a boxcar loader that, alone, cost $10,000. A conveyor system across the length of the tipple sent the scrap rock and waste materials to the nearby slag pile.

Like most coal deposits in Illinois, the rich one beneath Cherry consisted of several semihorizontal veins, or seams, separated by shale, clay, rock and mineral. Typically, the uppermost vein was ignored. Areas were cut away by glacial drift or were too narrow and irregular to be of any commercial value. Cherry's second vein, nearly three hundred and twenty feet below ground, was four to six feet thick with better quality coal but less favorable working conditions than in the third vein.

Throughout Illinois, that third vein was uniform and extensive, yielding the most profitable product, often referred to as "black diamonds." And glistening four hundred and eighty-six feet below Cherry was a seam three and a half feet thick with enough high-grade coal to keep the mine running at capacity for at least fifty years.

Initial plans were to mine out this bottom vein first. But when the second vein proved so bountiful, with a rich coal ore that could be mined immediately and easily, officials reversed their decision and concentrated their operations on the second vein.

There were only two passageways in or out of the mine—two vertical shafts, sunk three hundred feet apart and plunging nearly five hundred feet from the surface to the bottom of the third vein. (Refer to mine map, Appendix A, Figure 1.) The hoisting shaft ran cages of men or coal between the surface and second vein only, while the air shaft operated its cages only between the second vein and the third. The hoisting shaft was the larger of the two and the mine's main entrance, with its mouth centered below the giant steel tipple. Sixteen feet long by twelve feet wide, the shaft had a five-foot-thick top crest of concrete and was lined with eight-by-twelve-foot pine timbers set lengthwise to divide the shaft into two cageways, or elevator shafts. Each cageway contained a six-by-sixteen-foot steel cage, one a counterweight for the other.

The eight-by-twelve-foot air shaft, half the size of the main shaft, was also divided. With a wooden stairway in one compartment running from the third vein to the surface, it was also called the escapement shaft. Partitioned off in a separate compartment between the second and third veins, a single smaller cage brought up either men or single full coal cars from the bottom. Its counterbalance ran up and down the shaft's ventilation compartment and all bell signals to hoist were sent by the third vein cagers to the air shaft engineer at the controls in the topside engine room.

The ventilation compartment provided fresh air to the mine via a strongly built, double inlet Clifford-Capell fan connected to a high-speed engine. Six feet wide and made of steel plate casing, its huge blades spanned sixteen feet and could push an air current seven hundred feet per minute. Although it was reversible, the fan ordinarily propelled a constant stream of fresh air down the air shaft, forcing oxygen through the mine, up the hoisting shaft and out again. At up to one hundred and eighty revolutions a minute, it could circulate one hundred and eighty thousand cubic feet of air in sixty seconds. The air intake split at the second vein, with the larger volume flowing through the workings there while the remainder blew down the air shaft into the third vein works before upcasting through the hoisting shaft.

Incandescent electric lights were strung in the topside buildings and underground along the shafts, main passageways and stables. Miners still blasted entries open and dug out coal in pitch darkness brightened by the light of oil lamps.

The two veins in the mine contained an irregular square of tunnels, each approximately six feet high, seven feet wide and three hundred feet long, joined like streets outlining a city block. These runabouts were laid with a double track system of steel rails, along which mules hauled full coal cars to the hoisting shaft. Branching out from these runabouts was a labyrinth of mine entries that snaked through the coal block to the "rooms" worked by the miners.

Beneath the cages at the bottom of the second vein was a sump, or marshy bottom, boarded over with flat wooden doors and a perforated iron screen, all removable. A pump room, the large lengthwise fresh air tunnel and a mule stable situated opposite the sump completed the second vein.

Work in the third vein had begun only a year before the disaster. Although a large coal pillar surrounding the shaft had been blocked out, most of the coal here was dug in a circular route, with miners starting from two set points and meeting at the middle. By November 1909, approximately ninety such third vein areas were being worked.

From the four-hundred-ton, first-day yield on December 11, 1905, to the fifteen-hundred-ton daily average flowing down the chutes just four years later, the mine and town prospered. By 1909, Cherry was putting out four hundred thousand tons annually, at an average of thirty thousand tons of high-grade coal per month.

And there was no limit in sight. The St. Paul Coal Company owned 7,217 acres at Cherry and had worked only three hundred and sixty of them.

CHAPTER THREE

Friday, November 12, 1909
Cherry, Illinois

The mine shaft disgorged its groups of weary miners, one cageload after another, in the steady rhythm marking day's end. Like alternating pistons, one cage shot up the tower, struck the landing and triggered the gate, raising it so the men could exit, while the other zipped down for another load. They stopped only to check in their tools as they hurried through the chill autumn air in search of something to warm their bellies. Some headed for home. Others, family men, boarders and loners alike, made a straight shot for a tavern and a drink or three to help them forget the hours they'd just spent crouched and cramped and listening for cave-ins.

"Adam, tell your mother not to save me any dinner tonight," John Tintori called to his cousin. "I'm going to the tavern."

Adam Galletti's eyebrows went up. Sure, the priests who'd raised John in Italy had taught him to make a fine bottle of wine, but Adam couldn't call his older cousin much of a drinker. In the months since twenty-two-year-old John had come from Italy to board with them, Adam had never seen him down more than an occasional glass of wine. Something in that pit must have gotten to

John today—his square face looked pale beneath a coal dust veneer nearly as black as his sweeping mustache and wavy hair.

Saturday, November 13, 1909

Johnny Galletti rose before dawn to eat a hurried breakfast of biscotti dipped in strong coffee, same as he had every day since he was a kid. Before morning could swallow the fading glimmer of moon from the sky, he, his brother and brother-in-law would be swinging their pickaxes down in the inky caverns of the Cherry Mine.

He watched over the rim of his coffee mug as his mother, Beatrice, and sisters, Mary Corsini and Olinda Galletti, packed the men's lunches into deep covered metal pails. Beatrice glanced over her shoulder, taking note of the empty chair beside Johnny.

Her nephew, John, was still in bed, sleeping off a hangover. She sliced up his chunk of cold polenta and added it to the one already in Johnny's lunch pail. John wouldn't have the stomach for it and Johnny would have to dig twice as fast today to offset his digging partner's absence. The miners were paid by the ton, and the rock they hacked out along with the coal didn't count.

Cold polenta was the same lunch his father and grandfather had carried out to the mountains in Italy where they'd tended sheep, but Johnny liked the cornmeal mush best the way his mother cooked it for dinner, sliced thin and fried in butter. Sometimes, when they could afford it, she'd dust the top with Parmesan cheese.

In Tuscany the Gallettis and their Corsini and Tintori relatives had all been sheep herders and farmers. Until they left the fields and sloping hills for the coal mines of America, only an uncle had tried his hand at something else and became a shoemaker.

At eighteen, Johnny was the man of the house, responsible for his widowed mother and six of seven younger siblings. He'd been in charge since age thirteen, when his father was killed in a mine accident in nearby Braceville. Johnny had worked that mine too, but with production and paychecks continuous in Cherry, the family had picked up and moved there, eleven of them squishing into a tiny one-and-a-half-story company house rented from the St. Paul Mine.

The work, solitary, dirty and backbreaking, was easier for Johnny than the responsibility. He was exceptionally strong and athletic. He'd been a catcher for the Braceville White Sox baseball team in the spring and summer, and a football player for their Tigers in the fall. He was popular and would have been thinking of starting up a family of his own soon if the one he already had didn't depend on him so much.

The first whistle sounded from the mine like a sonorous rooster announcing a new day.

"*Andiamo.*" Let's go.

Chairs scraped back from the table as the miners rose for the door. Johnny downed the last of his coffee and grabbed up his deep lunch pail. His brother, Adam, and brother-in-law, Attilio Corsini, followed him down the wooden stairs. At least it was Saturday, the last workday of the week. By 3:30 he'd be on his way back home and tomorrow, he'd try to sneak in some time to rest.

Over in John and Jessie Love's home, number 83 in the Long Row, a family of Scottish miners was also finishing up their breakfast. Jessie readied lunch pails for her husband and the five brothers who shared their tiny home—Morrison, James and David on John's side, and orphans Alexander and Robert Deans on her own. Alex, almost seventeen, had barely six weeks of mining under his belt. He'd started right off as a digger, like John Love and his brothers. Bobby, twenty-two, was assistant cager at the second vein air shaft. All day long he'd help shove off each full car of coal coming up from the third vein, replace it with an empty car and ring the engineer to send the small cage back down.

Only one car a day ever went down full, the one William

McAdams always loaded high with heavy hay bales to feed the mules that lived and worked in the mine.

While the miners made the quick trek across town, bosses and top-side personnel were already at work—the whir of machinery and clang of tools echoed from the company buildings clustered near the huge gray slag pile. Second vein boss John Bundy stepped out of the company offices, hoping to spot the crates of new electrical wiring stacked on the ground. A father of eight, he was an Englishman whose own father farmed a mean and rocky patch in Herefordshire. Bundy had left farming as a young man to work the mines in Wales, then with his Welsh wife, Sarah, he'd crossed the ocean to mine coal in Illinois. Four years ago, James Cherry offered him this job while Cherry was still a cornfield.

For weeks on end he'd expected that delivery on each morning's train. The electricity had been out in the mine for nearly a month now, ever since moisture caused a breakdown in the lead-covered electric cables and sparked a short circuit. In the interim, miners had reverted to the old kerosene torch system in the main passages. Fashioned from two-by-sixteen-inch lengths of pipe, they were plugged at one end and narrowed down at the other to hold a two-inch cotton wick. The torches were hung horizontally, strung to the supports and overhead timbers by wire. As the kerosene burned off they were tipped downward to keep fuel supplied to the flame.

Everyone would be glad to have the electric lights up and running again, especially John Bundy. Twice they'd put in an order for that electric wiring. It should have been here and long installed by now. But today, Bundy was disappointed again.

Something Sam Howard had been waiting for arrived in Cherry on that Saturday's early morning train. For days the dark-haired twenty year old from France had been stopping at the post office on his way to work, anxious for the mail order engagement ring he'd sent away for, engraved with his sweetheart's initials. It was several weeks before Thanksgiving, and he planned to marry Mamie Robinson on Christmas Day. But he needed to propose to her first.

With a farewell kiss to their mother, Sam and his brother, Alfred, took their lunch pails and bounded from the tiny wood house for the short trip across town to the post office. With Alfred hovering at his elbow, Sam tore into the small parcel waiting for him and checked over the ring. *Perfect,* he thought. He rewrapped the package and asked the postmaster to hold it until after his shift. He'd pick it up on his way home and propose to Mamie that night.

Sam was glad his Italian-born mother, Celina, was fond of his girl. Their father, like Johnny Galletti's, had been killed in a mine accident and he and Alfred were all their mama had left. Now she'd have a daughter-in-law and, someday, grandchildren.

The brothers donned their safety helmets and scrambled up the tower, stopping at the little office midway up to collect their "checks" from the United Mine Workers Union's check weighman, Martin Powers. Each miner was assigned his own check number and each morning Powers doled out these metal tags by request, recording the miners' names and quantity of checks taken. The miners hung their identification number on each car they filled so that its weight would be credited to their daily output. Midafternoon, Powers would gather the weight records to begin tallying up each miner's wages for the day. The checks were also supposed to be a way for the union to track that every man who entered the mine also exited, but that was near impossible since men with checks left from the previous day wouldn't stop at Powers's station.

Check tags in hand, Sam and Alfred hurried to join the huddle of men waiting to board the hoisting cage. From 6:30 to 7:00 each morning the miners climbed the tower, piled onto the two steel cages in groups of sixteen and plummeted deep into the earth. All day long, two at a time, the two-ton cars they loaded with coal rose on those same cages to the surface.

Legally, Alfred Howard wasn't old enough to be working in the mine. Illinois law set the minimum age at eighteen, and he wouldn't even turn sixteen for several more weeks. But like most of its counterparts, the St. Paul Coal Company looked the other way for Alfred and Alex Deans and boys even younger whose families desperately needed their incomes. Trapper boys like Alfred earned $1.13 a day and besides, Cherry was the safest mine in the state—probably in the entire country. With its modern appointments and concrete and steel construction, everyone knew it was fireproof.

CHAPTER FOUR

The morning whistle wailed, calling miners to the shaft. Day-shift hoisting engineer John Cowley had begun running the steam-powered hoist at 6:30, and as quickly as a group of men in overalls and miners' helmets filled a cage, he released the levers and dropped it. In a heartbeat it fell 317 feet, swaying and creaking to the second vein while its counterweight cage shot up the shaft's opposite cageway for another load.

Semihorizontal veins of shale, clay, rock, mineral deposits and the narrow, noncommercial first coal seam whizzed by in a blur. The entire drop took only thirty to forty-five seconds. Johnny Galletti's stomach lurched as they plummeted, shoulder to shoulder and jostling one against the other in the narrow steel cage. He'd never get used to this dreadful sensation of plunging into a pit of darkness. He'd nearly peed his pants the first time he shot down.

The cage jerked to a stop and the men stepped off at the second vein bottom and put a match to the thick grease they'd loaded in their helmet lamps. Sunshine, they called the stuff. It cast a tiny trembling glow, throwing scant light and wavering shadows in their path as they left the torchlit main passageways and made their way in the darkness of low, narrow tunnels.

The shale layers directly overhead made an extremely poor roof for the rooms being mined out. Nearly continuous timbering with heavy, well-joined board shored up the roof against falling dirt and rock or cave-ins.

Breathing in the strong familiar odor that was a mixture of gunpowder residue, oil, manure and damp earth, Johnny and the others pushed forward into a total abyss, feeling their way through the maze to the rooms and entries being hacked from the solid seam of coal. They lit the handheld safety lamps, essential to augment the pale glow cast by their helmet lamps. Set on the ground, these oil or carbide lamps created eerie illuminated pockets in the enveloping darkness. Carried, they bounced light into the dense shadows as the miners trudged deeper into the mine. Here and there along the way, the lamps' rays glinted off little points of coal, making them twinkle for a moment like subterranean stars.

The two second vein miners working farthest from the shaft, Thomas White, thirty-one, and his partner and buddy, John Lorimer, thirty-two, set off in a southerly direction, walking nearly a mile to reach their work station.

A majority of the men also set off for work areas deep in the second vein, but French-born driver Andrew Lettsome and his father, Alma, and one hundred and seventy-nine others on their way down to the third vein headed instead for the air passage tunnel.

Since the two counterweighted hoisting shaft cages ran only between the second vein and the surface, and the single air shaft cage ran only from the second vein to the third, third vein workers had to walk through the second vein's three-hundred-foot fresh air tunnel to reach the air shaft and continue down one hundred and seventy more feet to the third vein.

The Lettsomes proceeded down the large tunnel, passing the forty-stall mule stable and the sump, a ditch fifteen to eighteen feet deep, to the air shaft. Instead of waiting for the single cage to return from the bottom to take them down, they dropped through a trap door set on the floor between two rails of tracks and took the stairs. They climbed first down a six-foot ladder, then the lengthy expanse of wooden stairs and finally down another ladder ten feet long, to reach bottom.

By 7:00 A.M., John Cowley had dropped the last load of workers into the mine. In a short while the mule teams would be hauling the miners' output to the shafts, and he'd get the signal to begin hoisting up the full coal cars. If today was typical, he'd bring up fifteen-hundred tons, all of it high-grade.

The clank of picks, the scrape of shovels and the creak of the pit cars' wheels against the tracks soon echoed through the black caverns as the four hundred and eighty men and boys set to work before sunrise. It would be four hours until the second whistle blew at 11:00 A.M., signaling the miners' midday half-hour break for lunch. At 11:30 a third whistle sounded and work resumed.

The miners drilled into the seam, tamping gunpowder or explosive charges into the narrow holes to blast away sections of coal from the block. Their partners loaded it onto the cars.

Up on the tipple, boys as young as ten squatted all day sorting rock from coal, glad to have entry-level jobs as slate pickers. The carloads of rock they filled formed the huge slag pile that rose behind the tipple like a growing gray mountain.

The coal cars were made of wood with steel running gearage. Filled third vein cars were lifted one by one to the second vein and shoved off the cage onto tracks at the air shaft's southwest side. Then mules hauled them down three hundred and fifty feet of steel rail track to the hoisting shaft, where they were joined to cars filled on the second vein, loaded onto the huge steel cages and hoisted in tandem to the surface.

Once emptied up top, all cars were sent back to the second vein.

Third vein cars were taken through a runaround to the air shaft and loaded back onto that cage from the opposite, or northwest, side of the shaft. At times these empties were butted against full coal cars, which they shoved from the cage and replaced for the trip back down to the bottom. Just recently, a switch track had been installed at the air shaft. Now, full cars there could be pushed off onto one branch of the Y-shaped track while the empties waiting on the other branch were pushed onto the cage from that same track.

Man cages ran to the surface that Saturday to carry miners up at midmorning, at noon, and at 1:30 P.M. Although the usual Saturday workday ran until 3:30, a number of miners quit work early that day and left the mine on the 1:30 cage run.

CHAPTER FIVE

Once a day, fresh feed for the seventy mules housed inside the mine was loaded into a wooden six-by-three-foot coal car at the tipple and dropped down the shaft. Right after lunch that Saturday, sometime between noon and 1:00 P.M., six bales of hay intended for the third vein stables were placed upright in a coal car and lowered through the main shaft to the second vein.

Charles Thorne, who drove in the east runaround, hitched his three-mule team to the feed car and drew it along the tracks and up the main passageway, bringing it to the manway a short distance from the southwest side of the air/escapement shaft. The manway was used for backswitching empty cars from the siding to the cage in order to send them down the air shaft to the third vein.

Thorne brought his mule team to a halt and unhitched the animals from the hay cart, which he left beside some empties. The small cowbells the animals wore to alert miners tinkled as he led them to the straight track where six loaded coal cars waited for the trip to the surface. One of the mules stopped to champ a bite of hay from the cart as they passed it, but before the others could imitate him, Thorne hurried them along. They knew the routine. Their days

were a series of eight- to ten-minute round-trips to and from the
hoisting shaft. Hitching his team to the loaded cars, Thorne doubled
back along the track to the main bottom. The miners commonly
called the two sides of the hoisting shaft at the main or big bottom
"north" and "south." The two sides of the air shaft at the little bottom
were dubbed "east bottom" and "west bottom."

The air shaft cage was managed by cager Alexander Rosenjack,
twenty-one, and assistant cager Robert Deans. Their assistant was fifteen-year-old Matt Francesco. Working together, Deans and
Francesco pushed empty cars through the manway and pulled
loaded cars off to the south side of the cage. There, Francesco coupled them for the trip to the hoisting shaft.

Deans and Francesco got behind the hay car and pushed it the
rest of the way up the track to the air shaft. But instead of sending it
immediately down to the stables, they left it in the air passageway
while they unloaded a car that had just come up on the cage. While
they coupled the new car to the other loaded cars waiting on the
south side, Rosenjack pushed an empty car onto the cage and rang
the signal bell, alerting third vein cager William A. Smith that it was
coming down.

Some accounts say Deans and Francesco left the hay car next to a
kerosene torch with its end blazing five to eight inches below the
top of the upright hay bales; others say the car was parked directly
beneath the torch and that kerosene dripping from it soaked
steadily into the hay while the two young men worked.

Under normal circumstances, cut, compressed hay does not burn,
a reason mine companies regularly used bales to construct partitions
in their stables. When occasional stable fires did break out, everything combustible was reduced to ashes, leaving only the hay partitions standing and intact. Cut hay, in fact, is a material so fireproof
that a blowtorch held to it will leave nothing more damaging than
some sooty scorch marks.

But the cut hay Deans and Francesco left near the second vein air shaft could not withstand the combination of open flame, a kerosene accelerant and fresh air. When the two returned to the car about 1:25 P.M., they found some of the hay ablaze. Neither of them was too alarmed. Small fires were commonplace in the mines, and were easily extinguished.

In fact, several men quitting the mine for the day ignored the fire on their way out, even though they could have put it out quickly with just their coats. They considered the blaze so inconsequential, they left Cherry without ever mentioning it to anyone else, either in or out of the mine.

With much the same nonplussed attitude, Rosenjack, Deans and Francesco set about to putting out the fire. Rosenjack pushed the car through the manway to the south side of the shaft and tossed off one of the blazing bales. Then he changed his mind.

"Bob! Lend me a hand here."

The two pushed the car back through the manway and onto the backswitch track. Just then, six men who were leaving for home came up on the cage from the third vein to catch the 1:30 cage run to the top. They had no inkling of the fire until they came upon the cage. Emil Giroz didn't think the fire amounted to much of anything since the car was billowing more smoke than flames.

"Emil, please, can you help me move this cart out of the way of the others," Rosenjack called out, enlisting the help of Giroz and James Hanney, president of the local union, to try shoving the cart away from the air shaft.

"Which way do you want it?" Giroz asked.

"Any way, as long as we can get it out of here," Rosenjack answered. "Watch out for your hand. It might burn your hand."

Rosenjack looked northwest to the sump near the mule stable. "Let's get this over to the sump so we can draw some water and put it out," he said, positioning himself to push while the others pulled.

The plan should have worked. There was plenty of water there. In one of four nearby crosscuts, an enlargement called the pump room

housed the mine's large Cameron pump. A canvas curtain hung between the pump room and the stable to prevent the moisture from
short-circuiting the stable's electric current.

Third vein sump water was discharged into the second vein sump
via a pipe in the air shaft. In turn, the Cameron pump sucked the
water from that sump and sent it to the surface via a pipe in the
hoisting shaft.

Together, the three men managed to move the flaming cart some
distance but because of the heat and flames could not make it as far
as the sump, a marshy bottom boarded over with removable flat
wooden doors and a perforated iron screen. The men got behind the
cart and pushed it the other way, toward the air shaft, until it got
stuck on something on the track and would not budge.

"We can't shove it any farther. It's a waste of time," shouted Hanney, who'd been mining for forty-seven of his fifty-six years. "We'd
better go to the big bottom and get help."

By now it was so smoky that Giroz had to walk past the car with
his left hand covering his face. He took off for the main bottom, but
just before he reached the first trap door he got his foot wedged between some pipes that were stored there. They had been stacked
across that area for a month or so, and men routinely slipped across
them in the dark while walking to or from their workplaces. Sometimes the men only temporarily lost their balance, sometimes they
went crashing to their knees.

As Giroz yanked at his foot without success, other men leaving
the mine opened the trap door nearest the exit shaft and he was suddenly overcome by heavy smoke pouring in. These two doors, situated twenty-five feet and forty feet from the corner of the main
bottom, were kept closed to prevent fresh air from escaping up the
hoisting shaft at the second level instead of circulating down to the
third vein.

Coughing and choking as he fought to extricate his foot from his
shoe, Giroz was convinced he was a goner. He struggled for the

breath to yell to a passing man to come help him dig out his shoe, then knelt down on the pipes to work at it. With that motion, the pipes rolled apart, releasing him. He jumped up and managed to get down the passage and force his way through the main bottom doors.

The burning car not only sat stuck in the draft coming down the air shaft, it caught every gust of air that whooshed through the doors at the main bottom. Fed by a fresh rush of air each time someone opened the doors to exit on the hoisting cage, or pushed through to check the progress of the fire, the flames shot even higher, licking at the overhead timbers until they ignited.

Theodore Dhesse, the driver who was Charles Thorne's counterpart and drew coal cars along a route through the west runaround, spotted the blaze as he pulled up to the shaft with a load of empty cars. Yelling "Fire!" he took off to get water, with Matt Francesco at his heels, echoing the cry.

Albert Buckle, a boy almost fifteen and barely four feet, six inches tall, sat playing near the main bottom. The light-haired, light-eyed boy had been trapping in the mine just three months. Hour after hour he stood guard at the outside door on the straight north runway, keeping it closed to ensure proper ventilation in the mine. He opened it only to let Charlie Thorne or Domenico Cresto drive through. He'd opened it just a while ago to let in the car of hay.

Buckle had just gone back to work after finishing his midday meal with his sixteen-year-old brother, Richard, when Matt Francesco ran by, telling him of the fire. Mule boss Dave Johnston ran up and sent him charging after Matt Francesco.

"Bring your pail and we'll run for water."

They ran north, passing the shaft and the burning car, hurrying through the air passageway and the two trap doors outside the main bottom.

Dhesse and Francesco grabbed up the first pails they saw at the main bottom and raced to the stable for water. But in the short time it took them to rush there, the smoke was already too thick for them to retrace their steps through the main air tunnel. Instead, they had to run to the end of the bottom, then through the west runaround and past the shaft to reach the burning car and throw their pails of water at it.

But two deep pails of water were no match for the onslaught of oxygen streaming down the air shaft and fanning the blaze.

The fire had intensified enough to prevent Buckle and Johnston from getting anywhere near the stables or the pump with their pails. They tried running from the other direction to reach water, but the burning car was standing too close by, throwing intense heat at them. They gave up.

"We'll send the car down to the third vein," Rosenjack shouted. He picked up the pipe phone and called down to third vein cager William A. Smith.

"We've got a hay car on fire up here. Can you take it?"

"Let 'er come."

Meanwhile James Hanney, his brother-in-law, James Flood, and the others made their way through the smoky air tunnel and caught up with Giroz at the main bottom. They sounded the bell and caught the 1:30 cage out. The minute he reached the surface, Hanney ran to alert assistant mine manager, Alexander Norberg. Concern immediately flashed in Norberg's deep-set eyes. Despite a receding hairline, he was a young-looking thirty-seven, with a big, sweeping mustache, light Swedish coloring and an open, square face. Quickly, they hunted down the mine's head mechanic, John Chedister, who decided to slow down the fan to starve the fire of oxygen.

"The flames are floating out to the big bottom," Hanney told him. "Shut the thing down altogether."

Chedister rushed into the fan house and threw the switch. The mine's giant Clifford-Capell fan ground to a halt at about 1:35 P.M.

Chapter Six

Wᴵ ith fire spreading along the support timbers, Alex Rosenjack jumped on the empty cage and rang three bells for John Raisbeck up in the air shaft engine house to lower him to the third vein. He told Deans he'd tell the men below about the fire, then wait for Deans to send down the burning cart so they could put it out with the hose.

Dhesse signaled one bell to let Raisbeck and Smith know Rosenjack was ready to descend. He lifted the plunger on the pneumatic bell, sending the signal reverberating simultaneously to the top, the bottom and the engine house. Deans waited with Theodore Dhesse for Rosenjack to send back the empty cage, but Matt Francesco decided he wasn't waiting around for anything. He fled through the east runaround and left the mine on the hoisting cage.

Charles Thorne took off as well. When his mules stopped dead in their tracks as they approached the air shaft, he had walked around them to see why they were refusing to budge. Ahead he saw fire and three men he couldn't make out for all the smoke. In the few minutes he'd been gone, the hay cart had been moved through the runaround and was now sitting on the north side of the shaft.

"Halloo," he shouted.

Someone called back, asking Thorne to go to the main bottom to have the fan stopped. Abandoning his mule team in the middle of the passageway while the crazed animals reared and brayed in fear, he beat a path back to the hoisting shaft to ask after second vein foreman, John Bundy. He learned Bundy was in the mine, but instead of attempting to locate him, Thorne decided to get himself up top.

At the surface, a thin curl of smoke rose from the air shaft. Raisbeck, twenty-four, at the throttle in the engine house, first noticed it about 1:30. Before long it began to billow. Ever alert to such signs of disaster, women and children began running to the mine, shouting, "Oh, God, the mine is on fire!"

John Chedister, who'd been chief mechanic for two and a half years, was in the mine yard working on a cage. He told Williams, the top foreman, to call down the speaking tube to find out what the problem was. Confirmation came from the pipe telephone below.

"Boys, Billy Richards says a car of hay is blazing down there near the air shaft at the second vein," top cager John Quimby said.

Richards, the main shaft cager, first noticed smoke snaking down the main road toward the escape shaft about 1:20 P.M. and didn't give it much thought. Ten minutes later he rang to send up the 1:30 cage filled with men. Minutes after that, with smoke blowing thicker all the while, he sent up two cars of coal followed by another cageload of miners.

Realizing his decision to stop the fan had backfired, Alex Norberg pushed through thick smoke to the shaft. In an effort to dissipate some of the pillowing clouds and give the men breathable air, he sent Richards up top with a new set of orders—start the fan again, slow. In the time it took him to relay the message and ride back down, the smoke had quickly gotten much worse. Richards could only stand it for a few minutes before he had to get out.

The thirty-five year old was about to ride up again when he remembered something: *Oh, God, the dynamite.* Richards took off after the explosives in the mine. Each day enough kegs for a day's work were lowered into the mine. They were stored on each side of the hoisting shaft in eight-foot-wide by ten-foot-long powder houses cut into the coal and closed up with wooden doors.

Richards and his helper boy loaded into a car all the powder and dynamite inside the small magazine off the east bottom. He grabbed up the caps, then asked if any explosives were left in the west bottom. There were none. He rang the bell for a hoist and fell onto the cage, overcome by smoke. He rode up, the caps in hand, and was revived up top where he ordered the waiting car of dynamite and powder immediately hoisted out of the mine.

Alice Mills was scrubbing off her porch after dinnertime when she saw Jimmy Flood head up the steps of the boardinghouse next door. He'd just come out on the 1:30 cage, so she asked him about the smoke she saw coming from the mine.

"That's nothing. Just some hay on fire, Mrs. Mills."

Figuring the hay was burning topside, she kept at her scrubbing, but a few minutes later she called Jimmy outside again to take another look at the smoke.

"That's pretty bad," he said.

"Where is the hay, Jimmy?"

"It's down in the shaft, Mrs. Mills."

Leaving her children, two and six, alone in the house, the young mother dropped her scrub brush and took off running for the shaft. Her twenty-eight-year-old husband, Arthur, was in the mine.

Jemima Miller, who lived next to the railroad tracks, was in her kitchen baking when her friend, Fanny Buck, telephoned to invite her over. She glanced at the kitchen clock as she left home—it was 1:45. Five minutes later, as Jemima and Fanny sat in the Bucks's kitchen, the two noticed smoke coming out of the mine six hundred feet away. They ran to the shaft, worried about Jemima's husband

and brother-in-law, but Fanny's husband said he guessed there would be no danger, the fire would soon be out. He told his wife and Mrs. Miller to go on home.

When they learned the smoke was coming from a hay fire, many women who'd hurried to the shaft relaxed. Figuring it would amount to nothing, like Mr. Buck said, they went home. But others, like Jemima Miller, stayed on through the afternoon, watching and worrying as main shaft engineer John Cowley brought two more loads of coal to the surface as late as 2:15.

"Why aren't you hoisting the men out," they chastised, "instead of the coal?"

Burned and choking on the acrid smoke, Dhesse, Deans and others struggled to get the burning car loaded onto the cage. But just as they managed to shove it part way on, someone opened the trap doors at the main bottom, creating a draft so hot the men could not stand anywhere near the burning car.

Dhesse decided to try attacking the problem from the south side of the cage. He fashioned a hook from a piece of pipe and attempted to tug the car onto the cage, but flames were shooting out in every direction, preventing him from getting near the car. So it sat, a fireball lodged half on, half off the cage.

While third vein driver Andrew Lettsome and others attached a hose to a tap in the sump, Alex Rosenjack stood nearby at the bottom of the shaft waiting for the burning car. Four long minutes passed, still no cage.

"God, why doesn't that car come!" he cried.

Seconds later, he called over to assistant manager Alexander Norberg, who'd come from deeper inside the vein to ask what was wrong. Rosenjack apprised him of the situation and told him to warn his men about the fire. Norberg hollered up the shaft for the men to send the hay down, but no answer came. He hollered again, rougher and louder. Still no response. With that, he ran up the stairway to the second vein to investigate.

In the meantime, on the second vein, Dhesse saw that Deans was staggering around, apparently overcome by the smoke. The driver abandoned his efforts to pull the burning car onto the cage and instead grabbed Deans, led him to the main bottom hoisting shaft and got him out of the mine. Dhesse spent a few minutes topside sucking down fresh air before reentering the mine and helping Norberg warn the men.

Martin Powers was tallying up columns of weigh checks when Mike Hunkle, Evan Thomas and another miner who'd quit on the 1:30 run told him there was a fire at the shaft. The union man got up and stuck his head out the window of his small office. He smelled smoke. Unnerved, he suggested they let the checking go for a while.

"You can go ahead and check up fast and let us get done," the others urged. Just then, Bobby Deans came into the office.

"Give me a drink of water. Oh my."

Powers looked up from a column of seventy-five checks on his sheet. Motioning with his left hand for Deans to go over to his dinner pail to take a drink from it, he resumed his work. He finished the column, then looked quizzically back at Deans.

"What is the matter with you?"

"Oh, they are all lost down there," he wailed. "The hay caught fire on the bottom, they are all lost."

With that, Powers threw down his pencil and everyone ran to the lower landing.

Shouts echoed down the shaft to the third vein sump, muffled by the snapping of flames. Lettsome and the others couldn't make out the words. Figuring it was Norberg trying to tell them something, Rosenjack headed toward the stairway to find out. Minutes later he was back, saying it was impossible to get up. Andy Lettsome decided to try. He turned to cager William A. Smith and said he'd tell Norberg that if he couldn't get the cart on the cage, he should shove it down the shaft and they'd take care of it.

Dave Wright and Rosenjack went back up the stairs with him, Rosenjack complaining about how hot it was in the shaft the whole time they climbed. The men managed to get out and found the car partially on the cage and completely afire. There was no one else anywhere in the vicinity.

"My God, Rosenjack." Norberg gaped at the blinding bonfire before them. The heat was so bright, so intense, it burned their hair and faces, scorching their skin right through their heavy work clothes. "You can never reach that car alive and move it. You can't get it down to the third vein. This is a dead hope."

Flames shot out as far as fifty feet, and the heavy timbers above their heads began cracking and snapping in the intense heat.

Sweat darkened Norberg's light hair. "We can't put out those flames!" he cried. "Rosenjack, we've got to save those poor devils below, and save them quick, or it will be too late!"

Lettsome and Wright braved the flames and tried pulling the car with their hands. No matter how much they struggled to budge the car one way or the other, it was useless. Rosenjack rang four bells and one to the engineer, meaning to hoist slowly.

George Richards was digging back in the third vein when he heard some of the fellows talking about fire. He went out toward the air shaft and saw smoke, then ran back to tell his father.

"All right. Come on."

The two dropped their picks and hauled out of their workplace as fast as they could go, hollering a warning to the others working nearby. But no one else followed them toward the air shaft.

There, while Rosenjack was above trying to get the cage hoisted up and out of the way so the burning car could free-fall into the sump, Smith and John Brown waited with a length of canvas hose attached to the steam pump. It was a hose normally used to wash down the mules and to fill water tanks used to sprinkle the dusty mine roads every morning after powder charges were set off.

Engineer Raisbeck got a slow bell up, four rings on the pneumatic gong, then a silent interval followed by one ring. He threw the levers, hoisted the cage about four feet, then stopped.

"Look out!" came the cry from above.

The cage fell, sparks shooting everywhere. Like a roaring orange comet, it sailed one hundred and sixty feet down the shaft and crashed into the sump's three feet of water where Brown and Smith waited. The cage floor had caught fire and one side of the roof's protective iron sheet was already glowing red hot. John Brown held onto the front of the hose. William A. Smith, the opposite cager, stood at the water column gripping the back of the hose, ready to throw the valve to prevent water from going to the second level or into the sump, keeping plenty of it flowing at the hay fire.

As Smith opened the valve, the water force hit him full in the face, blinding him and sending him staggering backward into the great clouds of smoke and steam that mushroomed the instant the water hissed into the flames.

"What's going on?" he yelled to Brown.

"I'm working down here on some timbers that took fire," the dark, sharp-faced cager shouted back. "Don't bother me."

Ole Freiburg rushed forward to grab the hose from Smith.

"Go get some air and let me have it," Freiburg shouted.

Smith gave him the hose, but refused to leave. He moved away from the smoke and stood where it didn't bother him as much. Just then, George Richards and his dad stumbled up. There was so much smoke they could barely find their way.

"The stairs are the only way out," Brown told them.

The old man wasn't in the best of health so the pair didn't wait around to see if those they'd warned were following them out.

With plenty of water streaming from the force pump, it didn't take very long to put out the fire. In minutes, they'd even cooled down the red-hot metal across the top of the cage.

By 1:48 they had completely put out those flames.

*   *   *

Herbert Lewis had been at the mine for about twenty minutes, hauling cinders, when he noticed the smoke and asked what was wrong.
Someone told him there was a hay fire in the mine he'd helped sink
five years earlier. But once Herb realized no one was too excited
about it, he kept at loading the cinders. They fell from the moving
trains and accumulated along the railroad tracks, a by-product of the
coal burned to power the steam engines. With coal supplying fuel to
the boilers, steam-powered hoisting engines and the mine offices,
there were plenty of cinders to shovel.

"How is the fire?" he asked a while later when one of the Taggert
boys came out of the mine.

"They got it all out now."

Herb went back to work. Minutes later, his brother, Isaac, came
up to ask if Herb had his team at the mine. When he answered in
the affirmative, Ike, a liveryman, sent him on an errand.

"Go over to my barn and get four or five lanterns. They need
lanterns down below."

Herb brought the lanterns back to the tipple just as Ike was
preparing to go down the shaft. He hollered over to his brother, asking where he wanted the lanterns, but Ike hurried past him and ran
to the shaft without answering.

About the time they got the hay fire out at the sump, Andy Lettsome
came down from the second vein to see if they'd succeeded. The
Frenchman took one look at William A. Smith and told him that he
didn't "look so good."

"There is still fire in the timbers up there that I don't like the looks
of," Lettsome reported, "but I hurried back to see if you got this out."

"Some of us will have to go up and see about that," Smith replied.
They belled repeatedly for a cage to take them up, but there was no answer. Up on the second vein, everything north of the shaft was on fire.

CHAPTER SEVEN

While the blaze roared through the area north of the second vein shaft, with flames shooting up the shaft itself, the only evidence of fire to the south were some ashes from the burning hay bale Rosenjack had thrown off the car.

As smoke drifted through the bottom seam, a few of the miners began to notice on their own that the air was bad. They left their rooms and headed for the third vein shaft, but when they signaled for the cage, there was no response. All they could hear was Alex Norberg shouting warnings and giving orders. William A. Smith said he would go up the escape stairs to the surface and tell John Raisbeck to hoist without signals, allowing the usual intervals between trips.

Andrew Lettsome ran up the one hundred and sixty stairs to the second vein with Smith. Pulling open the trap door, they faced flames nearly cutting off the route of escape.

"We have to get our men out," Smith yelled.

"I'm going back after my father," Lettsome said. "I'll go down and notify the men."

"Hold on, Frenchie. I guess one of us had better go down and notify the men and one go up and ask the engineer to hoist without signals, giving some regular intervals."

"You can go up, but I'm going after Pa."

"Will you notify the men?"

"Sure, I'll scare them up."

He rushed back down the stairs and warned the ten to fifteen men near the bottom to get out. He had his chance to escape, and thought the others deserved the same. After asking mule driver Thomas Hewitt to hurry along the west side and warn Lettsome's father and brother and the men around them, he ran through the east side. He could see the miners' lights glowing in their work areas and got down as far as the coal face, shouting, "Save yourselves! Save yourselves!" all the time.

These first cries to abandon the mine did not sound until the fire had raged for nearly forty-five minutes.

Lettsome ran along about one hundred and fifty feet, calling into places, hoping the men would pass the warning back deeper into the works. Before he escaped, Hewitt ran far enough in the other direction to warn Lettsome's brother.

Mine examiner George Eddy had worked through Friday night, checking the mine for pockets of gas, weakening supports and other dangers. His wife roused him from bed late that morning and he went over to the mine around 1:30 P.M. He was sitting on the steps outside the third vein engine house just as the first wisps of smoke wafted to the surface. At the first sight of smoke, Eddy sprang up and went down into the mine to investigate. He asked a driver to loan him his lamp.

"I've only got one."

Eddy's bushy eyebrows narrowed. "Well, lend me your lamp until I go to the cupboard," he demanded, reaching for it. He ran to the cupboard at the second vein bottom, grabbed up a hand torch and proceeded through the trap doors toward the air shaft, where he ran into Alex Norberg.

"George, the whole thing is on fire!"

By the time Eddy reached the burning car, the trap doors were wide open, sending air rushing at the blaze. The support timbers over his head were on fire.

"Yes, it's working on the roof," he told Norberg.

Eddy turned and took off to get men out of the mine. He found some empty cars and a team of mules near the air shaft, and hay on the other side. There was no one else around.

There was nothing on the west side of the bottom. The flames were roaring through, destroying everything in their path. Eddy grabbed his torch and went inside the works, desperate to get all the men out he could.

Nearly three hundred diggers comprised the day shift in the second vein. These men made their way on foot even to the farthest workings nearly three quarters of a mile from the main shaft.

Eddy went up on second west to notify the men and met up with drivers gathered on the parting. They asked him what was wrong.

"It's all ablaze at the air shaft. Get out just as soon as possible—just as fast as you can. Leave your mules here and everything here and run."

As the drivers all started out for the bottom, Eddy turned to go into the sixth south entry. There were twenty-two rooms turned there, the first seventeen of them finished. He ran to eighteen, the first room where men were working, and got all the rest out.

Work on a considerable percentage of rooms had been abandoned midway because of poor roof or irregularities in the second vein coal seam. Depleted and abandoned rooms were closed off with canvas tarps to prevent fresh air from flooding into empty rooms. In sections with a poor roof, not all the coal was removed. To help prevent cave-ins, strategic floor-to-ceiling pillars of coal were left standing as supports. This "pillar" system employed in the second vein accounted for nearly two thirds of the area that had been already mined and blocked off.

Eddy came out again to the main entry and met John Bundy.

"The shaft is on fire," Eddy told him.

"Where is it?"

"Between the air shaft and the main shaft. I got all the men out here."

"Go get the others to the south."

Eddy headed to the south and notified the men there, then went into the seventh and eighth rooms south where he met up with assistant mine manager Walter Waite. A popular mine boss whose brother Charles also worked in the mine, he was a small wiry man, dashingly handsome and with a direct gaze that exuded confidence to his men.

Eddy told Waite what was wrong.

"You finish this entry and I'll go in the nine and ten north," Waite told him, and the two set off.

Albert Buckle watched the commotion as mine manager John Bundy, the diggers, spraggers and cagers gathered near the hoisting shaft.

"Fire! Come out," Bundy called to him.

"Oh, there's plenty of time," young Buckle answered.

"There isn't time. Get your water pails and get water."

Buckle stalled, but when the diggers came along to get onto the hoisting cage he decided to join them. The cager tossed him off along with some other young boys.

"Get the pails and put the fire out."

Like many other teams of brothers or fathers and sons, John Donna and his sixteen-year-old son, Peter, were at work in their third vein entry as the fire crept toward them. Peter was shoveling coal into a nearby car while his father picked it out of the seam. The Donnas didn't wait for a warning to leave their posts. At the first smoke seeping underneath the canvas curtain hanging across their entry, the two dropped their tools and fled.

The Donnas clambered up the escape shaft ladder to the second vein, where fire blocked them off, singeing the hair on the side of Peter's face and head. Unable to proceed forward, the two doubled back to circumvent the blaze. They fought their way through dense smoke that veiled their familiar surroundings and threatened to overtake them as it rolled over them like an ashy avalanche. With one foot constantly on the railing that ran along the bottom of the floor, Peter led his father—and a few others who joined up with them on the way—in the direction of the hoisting cage.

The group stumbled through the darkness, unable to purchase light. One by one they lit matches that refused to burn. Finally, they were at the cage, stumbling onto it one minute and blinking hard against the strong glare of sunlight in the next.

For several seconds after he broke the surface, Peter was unable to see. He squeezed his eyes tight, waiting for them to adjust to the daylight, but when he finally looked around, his father was nowhere in sight. Terrified, Peter fought against strong men who tried to prevent him from going back down to search. Several more cars rose to the surface before Peter was able to heave a sigh of relief as his father walked off the cage with an old man he'd managed to rescue.

Meanwhile, the smoke escaping from the mine shaft blew blacker and thicker than ever. Stopping the fan had done nothing and starting it slow proved just as futile.

As third vein miners hurried to the shaft, now encircled by smoke thick as their shaving foam, panic spread. The nearly two hundred third vein miners on the day shift were spread out in approximately ninety areas, working primarily in longwall fashion due to the vein's clay floor and soapstone and shale roof.

Choking and fighting for position, they crowded against the base of the ladder, shoving to beat each other up the rungs to the exit stairs beyond. Hewitt and Brown struggled to maintain order. While Andy Lettsome lead the charge, guiding the men up the ladder through the smoke, Hewitt stood at the bottom, sending them up after the young Frenchman in rapid succession.

But they couldn't go any farther than the second vein bottom—the air shaft stairs above that were completely ablaze.

Albert Buckle loitered on the second vein, watching as five or six more loads of coal were hoisted to the surface. Through the smoky haze he made out a man with bushy eyebrows and a steep triangle of mustache drooping at his mouth. It was George Eddy, standing opposite the shaft, telling the drivers that things would soon be under control. "I believe we will get the fire out and start to work again."

One of the drivers, Richard Cullen, ran up to Billy Richards. "You'd better leave us up," he told the cager.

"No," came the reply.

"Give us a cage," the driver pleaded. "Everyone is going to die here."

Richards was adamant. "No, we are going to hoist coal and when the fire is out we are going to start up again."

CHAPTER EIGHT

George Richards held on to his father all the way down the dark, smoky passageway to the hoisting shaft, pulling the older man around the obstacles as best he could. There were mules and manure and coal cars to navigate and neither of them could see where they were going. The fire was relentless and now it was every man for himself. Just as the two reached the bottom, George's father fell, choking on the acrid smoke. Mule boss Dave Johnston, going through the middle vein bringing men out to the shaft, came upon them.

"Where's your father, George?"

"Here, on the ground."

Together, the two men hoisted the old man up and lugged him alongside the mules and toward the cage. Jittery and terrified, one of the animals struck out as George approached, kicking him in the stomach and knocking him out cold. He woke up at home, with no idea who had rescued him.

William Vickers was working with his partner at the coal face in southeast room one when he heard shouts about 2:35 P.M. from a man at the switch.

"Come out, there's a fire on the second vein!"

Vickers echoed the cry into the straight east. "Come out right away! The shaft is on fire!"

But the miners working there spoke Italian and did not understand the warning.

"What's the matter?" asked one, who understood some English.

"Fire in the second vein! Come out quick, right away!" Vickers said, shoving the Italians from the wall where they were working and onto the roadway. The third vein bottom, where Freiburg and Brown had just put out the hay fire, was three hundred feet ahead.

Vickers started for the escape shaft stairs with his partner and more than a dozen others right behind him. "Go on up," he told his buddy, stopping to shake some of the coal out of his shoes. "I'll come up after you." He turned to Ole Freiburg, who was still holding the hose. Steam rose from the sump where the hay cart had just been extinguished.

"Aren't they running the cages?"

"No," Freiburg answered. "It has been quiet for quite a while."

With his shoes cleaned out, Vickers made it up the stairs to the ladder just below the second vein bottom. Just as he got to the last step, the trap door that led to the ladder extending the rest of the way to the second vein came slamming shut on his head, knocking him all the way back down the stairs.

He dragged himself up, and with the two men behind him, crawled back up the stairs and through the trap door. It was now 2:45.

Vickers held it open until the others behind him got through. He had no idea who they were. The flames and smoke were so thick, he couldn't even blame the man who'd let the door fall on him. Ahead, nearly sixty-five men sat stupefied. Vickers couldn't rouse them. He began hollering, trying to determine which way to go. Flames were everywhere. His mind raced: *Why doesn't some boss have men stationed here to direct us? There are three roads leading to the hoisting shaft. Which one is the safe route out?*

Pandemonium reigned. Men were shouting above the screams of the mules. The coal cars were now on fire, vibrating with flame. Everyone was scared almost to death. Men at the rear wrested others out of their way in efforts to be the first to get out. Men at the front shoved back, using elbows and fists against those trying to crowd them out. Suddenly there was a bottleneck ahead. Vickers shoved his way through, reaching the first men bunched in the passageway.

"Why don't you push through?"

"There are mules here."

"To hell with the mules, push through!"

Together they drove their bodies past the animals, bearing to the left where the road branched off. Vickers knew if he followed to the left he wouldn't miss his road out. He pushed ahead, searching blindly in pitch darkness for lights to follow out. Suddenly, lights flickered before them.

"Stop! Hold up!"

They shouted for the men ahead to stop and light their way, but the men ahead kept running.

Vickers started to run too, and the faster he ran the louder he shouted for someone to stop and give him a light. Finally he caught up with the fleeing miners, and the last man turned back and gave him a light. Then Vickers turned to help the men behind him. He knew if he went back around the corner the bad air would snuff out his flame, so he stood at a corner where the air was smoky but still good enough to support fire. He remained there, signaling with his light and hollering to the men behind him.

A young man and his father ran up, and Vickers gave them each a light. Just then his own flame went out. Their air was losing oxygen.

"Come back here and give me a light, Johnnie," he called to the fleeing boy. He was weakening in the smoke by the minute. "I can't stand here any longer, this smoke is getting the best of me. Somebody else has got to stay here."

"I have two lamps," Johnnie Brovel offered.

Vickers took the second lamp and pulled at the wick to elongate it. Then he hung it on the overhead beam and yelled into the darkness that the men could come up and get a light from it. But no more voices echoed from behind them.

As the two continued down the road, suddenly Johnnie's lamp went out.

"You've got a good one there," he said, just as Vickers's flickered out too. Plunged into sudden darkness, the two put their coats together and struck a match. They managed to get both lamps relit and ran on. They stumbled across an abandoned coal car hitched to a team of terrified mules and kept running forward, running with no idea where they were.

"Where are we?" Johnnie cried. It was so dark, their eyes might as well have been closed.

"I don't know," Vickers replied, feeling around for the timbers, which he knew were square in the west bottom. In the distance he could hear Bundy's voice, but couldn't make out what the mine boss was saying. "We are on the bottom," he finally reported. The two felt their way to the cage. Bundy and several others were standing there.

"How is it?" Bundy asked.

"The men can't get out of there, because they can't see," Vickers answered. "You should have lanterns strung along the road. The lamps can't hold a light."

"All right."

A cager rang the bell, signaling to the engineer above ground to hoist the men. When he got up top, Vickers ran into his friend, Ike Lewis.

"Run home," Lewis told him. "Your wife is in pretty bad shape."

The thirty-six-year-old Vickers ran home to reassure his wife that he was safe. Then he took off his coat, changed his hat and ran back to the mine.

✼   ✼   ✼

John Stuckert, secretary of the Cherry local miners' union, had worked the mines for thirty-five years. He too was at work in the third vein when the fire broke out. At 2:30 P.M. smoke began flowing into his workplace right off the air tunnel.

"What are those fellows burning up there, anyhow?" he shouted to his partner, who was Italian.

The smoke got thicker.

"I guess we got to die like mules," his partner answered in broken English.

Stuckert at first paid little attention, until the smoke intensified. "We better try and make the bottom and investigate what is going on."

They headed toward the bottom but couldn't get through for the smoke. It only grew stronger the closer they got, rolling toward them thick as cotton. Driven back along with six or eight miners, they ended up back in their own working places, where they waited.

"I can see light on the bottom," one man said after a few minutes.

"If there's light on the bottom, it's clear," Stuckert replied. "Let's go out."

They got to the bottom and heard someone hollering down from the top. "There's no more work today. You'd better try to get out."

Stuckert climbed up the escape shaft to the second vein behind a group of others. Like Vickers and the rest, he found the second vein filled with flame and smoke. He tried to light his lamp, but with the atmosphere growing heavy with the mixture of air, carbon dioxide and nitrogen called black damp, it refused to burn. Several groups of men came climbing up behind him, but not a one of them knew which way to go—it was impossible to discern the roadways leading out. Above them, up the stairway, all they could see was flame and smoke.

"What do you think?" someone asked him.

"You have to judge for yourselves. I don't know."

Stuckert and some of the men attempted to climb up farther, but the lead man screamed back at them, "For God's sake, get back quick!"

"I'm going to make for the old east runway," Stuckert said. It was the road the men took to go up in the evening.

"Let's try."

Driven forward by the sheer will to survive, they ran blindly through the smoke. But before they could make it to the end of the bottom, the men crashed headlong into a jumble of empty coal cars. Crazed teams of mules reared at them in the narrow roadway. It was impossible to squeeze through. Terror pounding in their hearts, the men dropped to their bellies and crawled between the mules and manure and coal cars to get past them. Once clear, they made a turn to the left but the nightmare repeated itself. They were confronted by still more empty cars and braying, terrified mules. The stench of the animals' steaming dung filled their nostrils while the bitter taste of adrenaline filled their mouths. Eventually they made their way through the thick smoke almost to the bottom.

There were still the two trap doors to get through. The first was so difficult to open, Stuckert fell through it with the exertion and a man coming behind him toppled over him in the panic. The second miner picked himself up and then helped Stuckert to his feet. Stuckert stood back, waiting. His partner grabbed him and had to pull him along to the next trap door.

They'd made it onto the bottom—now they only had to make it to the hoisting cage.

The smoke there was so thick, so heavy, that every breath felt like a vise crushing the men's chests, sucking out their air. Suddenly the man ahead of Stuckert stopped dead, then tried to pull him back.

"No further, boys. We are going to die here."

"No, friend, don't go back," Stuckert pleaded. "I see only one chance for us to make the big bottom, and if we can't make the big bottom we are lost."

The miner pulled away from Stuckert and stumbled a few steps back into the smoke. It was the last anyone saw of him.

Stuckert stumbled forward as best he could toward the hoisting cage, grabbing at the railing along the right side of the wall for support. Blinded by smoke, he relied on his senses of touch and hearing. Caught in the jostling arms and legs of stampeding men, he stumbled and crawled for the exit. Just short of the cage, he collapsed.

He was spent, exhausted. Unable to go on, he lay just a few feet from survival. At last, he forced himself up, crawled a little more and made it to the bottom, where he fell on the hoisting cage. He kept his wits about him only until he made it to the surface. Then shock set in and he walked home, stupefied.

It was about 2:30 P.M. when townspeople on the street who had noticed smoke emanating from the mine began stopping mine physician Lyston D. Howe to point it out. But the surgeon had noticed it too. He was already on his way to his office to grab his medical bag. He also snatched up a jug of whiskey. Dr. Howe arrived on the scene to see Alex Norberg coming down from the tipple and heading over to the fan house. Dr. Howe went up the tower to the tipple. The men coming out were scared. As he watched their expressions while they described the extent of the fire, his concern for the men left in the mine grew.

Norberg ran up the tower to grab a cage back down.

"Can I be of help?" the doctor asked the foreman.

"You could help some of those fellows—to keep them alive on the bottom until we can get them up."

Alma Lettsome first figured something was amiss when the cars stopped coming down to the third vein. He hurried to the bottom of the hoisting shaft and saw a driver standing there.

"How is it they aren't hoisting in the big shaft?"

"Probably they are waiting for the flats."

Lettsome shrugged it off and walked back to his workplace with two other men. Twenty minutes later his son, Andy, came running up to warn them.

"The mule barn is on fire. We've been up there and it's all afire."

The second vein stable sat about sixty feet above and parallel to the one on the bottom vein. A mule feeder's passageway ran across the front of the stalls, as did a constant stream of running water for the animals.

"We must get out as quick as we can," he said.

The escape shaft was about seven hundred and fifty feet away. They shouted a warning to the men around them and began making their way out. They met up with a group of men waiting on the bottom and charged up the stairs one after the other, to the trap door above.

A man stood there, paralyzed, blocking the way. He'd lifted the door, seen the fire and flat out refused to go on through.

"We can't go through there, it is all afire."

"We can't go back, we *have* to go through there," Alma Lettsome answered.

The man was immobile, petrified. "I can't get through."

"Well, get out of the road."

Alma Lettsome and the others pushed past him. They saw everything on fire, but refused to give up. The group plunged around the east way to head south. But Thorne's and Dhesse's mule teams were bunched up in the passageway, still hitched to their trips of empties. One man was afraid to venture past them, terrified of getting kicked. But they found the west road was no better. There was a string of empties there too, still hitched to their mules. Together the men finally made it through the dark to the hoisting cage and rescue. They didn't see another soul coming out of the second vein at the time they were hoisted up.

※　　　※　　　※

William Maxwell and his family lived in Spring Valley, but also maintained a home in Cherry since for some time he and his son had been working the southwest third vein of the St. Paul Mine. About 2:30 P.M. he saw smoke coming in at the face.

"Maybe a sheet has taken afire," he told his son, walking out of the entry to see what was causing it. Maxwell made his way to the bottom, his alarm increasing with each step. The farther he went, the thicker the smoke became. It was all that he could see until he reached the bottom, where he spotted a car in the sump and a man with a hose putting out some burning hay. Maxwell started up the ladder to go home. A cry stopped him cold.

"The middle vein is on fire!"

He immediately turned back for his son, who was still working at the face of the entry. He fought a rising panic as he made his way back through the stinging smoke to reach the boy.

"The mine is afire. Hurry."

Two Italian men joined up with them. Together they groped their way, smoke searing their throats and lungs with every breath. Choking and gagging, the four staggered through to the bottom. When they arrived, no one else was there.

Mustering their strength, father and son forced themselves up the ladder and then up the stairway with the Italians right behind them. With so little oxygen in the superheated smoke, every step took enormous effort. Finally they made it to the top. There, at the second vein, they faced the next obstacle—the trap door. The climb through smoke had sapped their strength. It took both of them to lift the heavy, two-foot-square sheet-iron door to get out.

But the two Italians who had followed them were not as lucky. They collapsed on the road between the ladders and the cage in the second vein, overtaken by the smoke. Maxwell's son was the next to drop, falling about seventy feet from the cage. Helpless to drag or carry him, Maxwell left his son and went on, staggering to the cage through heat that felt to him like he was in a big furnace.

"Can you take hold of the bar yourself?" Rosenjack asked, helping him onto the cage.

Maxwell nodded. "I can. But . . . my son . . ."

Rosenjack sent him up alone on the cage, while two parties took off in search of the boy. They found him, alive. The two Italians were already dead.

The six or eight minutes until his son was brought up was an agony to Maxwell. He looked around and judged they'd been about the last to get out of the bottom vein.

The last bells engineer John Raisbeck ever got up top sounded immediately after he'd hoisted the cage free of the burning car. Whether men could not get to the pneumatic gong because of the fire, or whether it stopped working, no one would ever know.

First Raisbeck got two bells, meaning to lower down. He did, to the bottom. Then he got three bells, meaning men are coming up. He gave a one-bell return signal and got one bell in reply, meaning "All ready—go ahead." He figured William A. Smith at the bottom gave the signal, but he wasn't certain. He hoisted the cage to the second vein, then got no further signals of any kind.

Thomas Hewitt was the last to leave the bottom seam alive. He, Andrew Lettsome and John Brown were responsible for screaming the warning that saved the lives of those third vein miners who managed to escape. Hewitt and the others in that last group to leave the third vein begged Brown to come with them.

The cager stood sentry in the smoke at the bottom of the shaft and wouldn't budge.

"I won't go until every man is out of this mine."

He never made it out alive.

CHAPTER NINE

M en began to pray. They began to weep. From every direction fire charged at them like some screaming orange lo-
comotive spewing smoke. They ran, stumbling and
gasping for air, knowing that what little of it they could suck down
was most likely poisoned with the invisible black damp.

Down in the third vein, men whose escape route was now a wall
of flames succumbed to panic. They had no idea that beneath the
sump in the other shaft sat a small cage that might save them.
Newly built for emergency use, it was designed to be fastened to the
bottom of the main cage at the second vein with a length of cable
and a hook, once the wooden doors and iron screen that sat above
the sump were removed.

Although the main cage could not descend to their level, this ex-
tension could pull them from the bottom to two platforms ten feet
short of the second vein bottom. Able to accommodate four men
each, these platforms had been built into the shaft buntings to line
up opposite both open sides of the cage. When the auxiliary cage
reached its maximum ascent, the men could crawl out through an
opening at the top of the cage and shimmy over to the platforms.

From there, they'd be able to climb to the second vein bottom by way of a ladder and transfer to the main hoisting cage.

But so few of the several mine managers knew about it that not even local union president James Hanney was aware it existed. It had been hoisted only once, by the carpenter who built it.

Young trapper Albert Buckle hung around the bottom, waiting to get back to work once the fire was put out. For more than half an hour he watched cagers load on full coal cars and send them up to the surface while mule boss Dave Johnston ran around opening and closing doors as the smoke kept getting stronger.

Buckle's sixteen-year-old brother, Richard, also a trapper, was still at his own work station, manning the door. Their father, Otto, who'd been a blacksmith up top, had been dead for about three years. The two young boys supported their mother, Mary, who'd been sickly for some time, and their eleven-year-old sister, Lottie.

"Andrew Timko will go tell your brother about the fire," Domenico Cresto told him.

"You ought to notify them diggers inside that's working in there," Buckle added.

One of the men nearby turned to the boy. "*You* run and tell them."

Instead, young Buckle told Cresto to do it, and Cresto went off with Timko to tell the diggers to come out. Charlie McDonald left to run inside the second west to call a warning, while Johnston headed for the straight west, realizing it could take half an hour to forty-five minutes to notify all the diggers and drivers back there. McDonald brought out young Frank Jagodzinski, a sixteen-year-old trapper boy who was standing in the smoke, then went back in twice, saving the four drivers and two trappers he found standing in the dark behind his trip.

Meanwhile, Dhesse and Norberg stood on the big bottom, blocked by smoke and heat from getting near the air shaft. Still the twenty-three-year-old Frenchman wanted to make the attempt.

"Get back," Norberg ordered. "You can't get any farther on account of the heat."

Instead, Dhesse and another driver, Richard Cullen, hurried to the hoisting shaft with mule feeder Johnny Apple to grab the hose that had been brought down from the shed up top. Buckle watched them put something over their faces and head toward the barn. With the two drivers assisting, Norberg and Rosenjack tried in vain to attach it to a water tap in the stable.

"What is coming through that? Cold water or hot?" Dhesse asked, as the men shoved the hose over the pipe and turned on the water.

"Hot."

"How am I going to hold that? I haven't got anything on my hands. How am I going to hold that?"

No one answered him. As the three men struggled to enter the mule barn door with the hose, a blaze shot out at them, knocking Rosenjack over. As he fell backward, the nozzle flipped from his hands, striking Norberg in the temple and knocking him senseless. Rosenjack righted himself and dragged Norberg away from the fire. He was on the ground for about five minutes before he finally regained consciousness. Still dazed, Norberg got to his feet and went back into the fray.

Again the men tried to get the hose running, but the fittings didn't match up. The hose coupling was too large to screw onto the tap and although they'd managed to shove it over the pipe, they couldn't get any water flowing through it. By then the smoke was so thick that all the men were forced to flee up top to get fresh air and recover.

"If you don't give us a cage, we're all going to choke," Dhesse pleaded, but still cager Billy Richards refused.

"At least send up Toots and the other kids," Cullen said, referring to Buckle and the other trapper boys.

Richards pulled his pocket watch out and looked at it. "No. Maybe the shaft won't quit."

"If somebody gets fired, I will stand it," Cullen pleaded. "Let the responsibility be mine."

The smoke was coming strong. Finally, Richards gave them a cage.

"Notify them diggers," Buckle hollered to McFadden as the cage went up. McFadden ran back.

After a short rest up top, Dhesse, McDonald, Rosenjack and Cullen went back down the shaft to the second vein. With Rosenjack acting as cager, the others fanned out into the fire and smoke, listening for footsteps or voices and pulling men to the cage and safety. As soon as they saw any men coming, Dhesse ran to grab them and put them on the cage. Cullen guessed they managed to get out fourteen to sixteen men.

Fresh air was filtering down the escape shaft stairs as cager William A. Smith, one of the last men out of the third vein, made his way up. Usually as the men climbed, the fan's downcast air sent the blaze from their headlamps flowing down toward their faces. But halfway to the second vein, the air was suddenly gone. The fan had been stopped. Smith didn't think anything of it. The fan had been stopped before.

This new signal to stop the fan, seven gongs of the bell, was sent to the surface by Alexander Norberg. If air was not flowing into the mine, he reasoned, it could no longer fan the blaze or force smoke back into the corridors and entries.

But his plan failed. With no air current to dilute the smoke, it pillowed, thick and choking, into every crevice. Men threw themselves into the walls and tore into their skin with their fingernails, writhing in agony as they choked to death.

Not more than three minutes passed before Norberg changed his plan. He told Dhesse and Cullen and two others to return up top.

"Open the water rings and have the fan reversed."

Dhesse and Cullen went to the surface, then over to the air shaft. They had to go down the stairs about one hundred feet to open the water rings. Carpenter R. L. Daugherty directed them to the plug. They let the water sheet down the bunting timbers, soaking the shaft lining in an attempt to prevent that too from going up in flames.

In less than ninety seconds, Smith realized the fan had started up again, in reverse. The light from his headlamp was flowing straight up. Realizing that the smoke and fire would soon catch him, he climbed faster than he'd ever climbed in his life. He made it about halfway up, maybe more, choking and climbing the entire time, before the smoke overtook him. Somehow, he managed to get up the rest of the way.

Andrew McFadden ran back to the diggers, just as Albert Buckle asked him to. He was twenty-two and obedient. A foreman near the main shaft entrance called him over, issuing an order.

"McFadden, stay here with the mules. It's only a little smoke. It'll soon blow over."

He stood.

Escaping miners ran past him. Dozens of them. Every one urging him to save himself.

"Run for it! Run!"

McFadden shook his head and remained where he was, standing guard over his four-legged charges.

Within minutes, he and the bellowing animals he refused to abandon were burned to death.

It was Norberg again who'd sent up the second signal, nine gongs, ordering the fan reversed. The men up top reluctantly obeyed, but feared it was an order of death. Norberg thought otherwise. He envisioned the giant blades spinning at a blur, sucking smoke up the air shaft and improving the conditions nearest the fire.

For a time it worked. When Andrew Lettsome and his party reached the main bottom, they found the air there free of smoke.

But the plan proved a disaster. Instead of blowing fresh air into the mine, the mighty fan now drew the smoke and air from it, bringing the flames right along with it. The men who rushed to the main bottom immediately after Lettsome's group found it already clogged with thick dark smoke.

With its powerful suction, the Clifford-Capell fan drew the inferno straight out of the mine, reducing the escape ladders and stairs to cinders. Smoke and flames spewed from the mouth of the air shaft like a volcanic eruption. Now there was only one way out.

Nearby, in the fan house, the monstrous machine kept pulling. Like a mighty magnet it sucked the ferocious heat straight to itself. Within minutes, the blades of the giant fan began to glow red hot. Instantly, the fan doors burned out and the giant Clifford-Capell fan and the wooden roof above it burst into flames.

In horror, engineer John Cowley watched the blades' glowing crimson blur. At any second, he feared, the molten heat would loosen the pivots of the fans and wings and hurl the giant red-hot blades. He pictured them slicing straight into the crowds gathered around the mine.

There was only one thing he could do.

"Stop the fan!"

The women wept and wailed. The children cried, terrified and clinging to their mothers' skirts. If the fire could leap out of the earth to devour machines and buildings above ground, what hope could they hold out for their loved ones trapped below?

Just minutes later, portions of the air shaft's brick walls collapsed inward with a muffled puff. The damaged red-hot blades slowed to a stop, their babbitts—the metal antifriction liners in the bearings—melted from their boxings. With the fan and air shaft in shambles, the women realized that the only hope for fresh air to their men below was what little current might filter down the burning shaft on its own.

Meanwhile, in town, Mrs. Charles Waite walked out of the dentist's office to find Alex Norberg's wife heading down the street, crying.

"Oh, they say there is a terrible fire in the shaft," Mrs. Norberg sobbed. "They say Ike is in it," she said, referring to her sister's husband, Isaac Lewis, "and they say my man is in it too."

"Oh, it couldn't be so bad as that." Mrs. Waite wanted so much to believe her own words. She had just seen her husband at home before she left for the dentist's. He should still be there, off shift, since he worked nights as a mine examiner. But suddenly the dread that Charles was in the mine overcame her. *Oh, God! Surely he wouldn't go down in the fire.* Unable to contain herself, she flew toward the mine as fast as her feet would take her.

Deep in the mine, Bundy, Rosenjack and Norberg fought against time. For more than half an hour men had been fighting their way out. Now, in the distant corridors they could still hear cries and moans and prayers, but no more men were stumbling out to the cage.

They rang the bell, signaling the engineer above.

Hoist the cage.

Cowley cranked the lever in the engine house. In agony and suspense, the crowd watched the creaking chains as the cage made its way to the surface.

The three men jumped from the cage. Their appearance was ghastly. Their faces and hands were bleeding. The coal soot covering their skin was streaked white where sweat had left trails. Their clothes were torn and scorched and they struggled hard for breath in order to find their voices.

Norberg's voice finally croaked out, hoarse and gasping.

"Boys, that's hell down there! The men are burning to death or dying by the gas and smoke! For God's sake, do something for the poor devils and do it quick!"

Rapid-fire, the three men shouted orders for the rescue work. Some men went running to the supply house for hose coupling. Others took off in search of firefighting tools. Dr. L. D. Howe, who had been tending the injured who'd escaped earlier, gathered up an armful of first aid supplies and jumped into the hoisting cage. The men gathered around the cage and tried to dissuade him, arguing even as Bundy, Norberg and Rosenjack leapt on beside the doctor.

"It is too dangerous. You'll all die down there."

Ignoring the warnings, they signaled to Cowley.

Drop us down.

They plunged back into the crackling furnace, steeling themselves against heat fierce enough to raise blisters on their unprotected skin. The cage jerked to a stop at the second vein and the small band bolted with the two lengths of canvas hose, fighting through the smoke-clogged tunnel for the pump. Miners who were pushing one another toward the exit scrambled instead to help them drag the hose.

"Let's get this coupled up and get some water on this fire."

Working at fever pitch, the men managed to attach the hose and let water loose on the fire. The flames snapped and hissed back, mocking the feeble stream that spit at the inferno.

Bundy knew the fight was futile. "Boys," he shouted to Rosenjack and Norberg, "I'm going back into the vein and see if I can't help out those poor fellows who are dying back there!" While they kept the hose steadied on the fire, he groped his way down tunnels thick with the smell of burning tar. Shouting the warning to flee, he stumbled into chaos, buffeted in the dark by miners trampling and shoving one another in their frenzy to get out.

Running his hands along walls he couldn't see, he tripped over men felled by smoke and black damp. Many were already dead, and others lay crying, barely clinging to life.

"The cage is this way," Bundy shouted. He yelled his warnings deep into the branching tunnels, but the foreign-born miners who spoke no English did not understand his words.

"Save us," men screamed.

"I will save you," he hollered and turned back toward the hoist. Too weak to walk, the miners crawled after him, following his voice as he guided them out of the smoky maze. Working quickly, Rosenjack and Norberg helped Bundy load the gasping miners onto the cage and send them up top.

Once again, Bundy headed back into the runway to lead others out of the death trap. At the opposite end of the runway, an Italian miner named Tossetti fought hysteria on finding it smoke-filled and littered with cars and fallen mules. He succumbed to despair at the sight of prostrate miners weeping into the ground of the main passageway. "There's no hope," he shouted to the men behind him, then fell on his face and sobbed.

But Noverio, another Italian, shouted words of encouragement and hope, urging the terrorized men forward. Over dead bodies and wailing coworkers, the young miner lead them straight through the flames to Bundy's small team and rescue. His eyeballs were singed, ruining his sight, but he was alive.

"Come along. Get in," Bundy and the others urged, working against time to fill a cage and sound the pneumatic gong. While each group of half-dead men rose to the surface to be revived, the rescuers hurriedly scoured the tunnels for others to load onto the counterbalance cage already on its way down.

Men couldn't see the roofing overhead, they couldn't see the floor. They couldn't see their hands stretched out in front of them, frantically groping for a wall. They could feel their skin stretch taut over tissues swelling rapidly in the onslaught of heat. They were sweating and suffocating and lost, coughing and vomiting from panic and from smoke.

The thunder of fire, the bellow of mules, the loud staccato reports of heated cracking rock—the din reverberated from every direction. It was diminished only by the most petrifying clamor of them all, a rising crescendo of hundreds of voices shouting, screaming, crying and praying in a dozen different languages.

Through the echoing bedlam, Dr. Howe persisted. Tentatively, he kicked his way down passageways, praying his feet would strike against something soft. It was his only hope of locating fallen miners and dragging those who still breathed back to the cage.

Sobs rang out as each load of men he saved broke the surface. Anxious women and children pressed forward, praying their man was among the lucky ones plucked from the growing hell. Their sobs turned to screams, each one begging information from the burned and bruised survivors about those still below. Mrs. Waite ran back and forth about the shaft, asking everyone if they'd seen her Charles. No one had.

"My brothers, Johnny and Adam," little Charlie Galletti yelled out, "did you see them down there?" He'd been pushing through the crowd looking for them and for his sister's husband, Attilio, and his brothers. "Did you see any of my family?"

Adam had to coerce Attilio into getting out with him on the last full cage, came the answer, but no one had seen Johnny.

Up top, smoke rolled from the mouth of the mine, licked by leaping tongues of fire. Finally, the tiny band of rescuers searching for victims below could take no more. "Let's get out," Bundy shouted. "We have to get out."

He urged them toward the cage with the few men they'd been able to find. Succumbing to the smoke and heat, they fell upon the cage and Bundy rang the signal to be hoisted up. They staggered off and Rosenjack collapsed to the dirt. Too weak to get up again, he lay moaning and sobbing.

An uneasy silence fell over the crowd as Bundy and the others sucked the cool November air into scorched throats and lungs. A woman's sudden shrill cry or a father's keening moan seemed to beg them to press on. Bundy eventually dragged himself up and made his way back to the smoking shaft. The others followed. They'd regained some strength and decided to try again. Time was running out. The hoisting chains were glowing red with heat and the cables had begun to sizzle.

Nearly the entire town thronged the mine as the rescue party was lowered back down. As overhead timbers blazed and superheated rock cracked like gunfire, they crawled on hands and knees with their faces pressed against the wall railing so they could find their way out again.

Burned and spent, they rang to be hoisted up with those few they could save.

"My God, boys, we need help," Rosenjack cried. "The air down there is unbearable. It's burning out our lungs. We need strong men. Who is willing to risk it for the sake of the boys down below?"

Before he'd even finished his plea, a surge of volunteers rushed forward, each man willing to risk death to save the hundreds still trapped. There were more volunteers than places on the cage, but clothier John Flood and liveryman Isaac Lewis didn't wait to be chosen. They'd never set foot inside that mine, but hopped aboard the cage without a second's hesitation, followed by Rosenjack and Dr. Howe.

"Come on, boys," the physician called to the others. "Let's help those poor fellows below."

Among the first to volunteer was Mrs. Timko, who had rushed to the mine shaft at the first sound of the emergency alarm. Her husband, Joseph, had worked the mines for many of his fifty-one years, and now three of her six sons were down there with him. Steve and Andrew were single, but her Joseph Jr. was married with five little children under six years old. She begged, pleaded and cried to be chosen but was refused, kindly.

Ten more of Cherry's strongest men entered the cage, ignoring the frantic pleas of their families. Beside mine manager John Bundy and assistant manager Alexander Norberg stood fellow miners Robert Clark, Andrew McLuckie, James Speir, Harry Stewart and John Suhe; driver Joseph Robeza and cager John Szabrinski (Smith), who was also a town alderman. A third resident with no mining experience, grocer Dominick Formento, completed the courageous rescue party.

The signal came and Cowley let go of the brake, lowering the cage. The cable went slack as the cage hit bottom. It sat less than a minute before the frantic signal to raise it came to Cowley from below. The cable creaked and groaned as he pulled the cage to the surface, every second of its ascent stretching into an agony of suspense. Women clutched their shawls tighter about their chests and men held their breath.

The charred cage emerged and discharged its cargo—the rescue party and not another man more. Panting for air, their clothing singed and streaming smoke, they fell from the cage. Wives threw themselves at their husbands' feet, begging them to abandon the search. But their pleas fell on deaf ears.

The brave band disengaged themselves from their women and threw off the hands of the neighbors who tried to help or restrain them. They pushed their way back to the cage and signaled to the engine house. Cowley released the brake and lowered them again.

The agony above ground escalated as each minute ticked by. Finally, the signal to raise the cage sounded in the engine house and Cowley threw the switch. This time the heroic efforts were rewarded.

A shout went up that could be heard clear to the center of Cherry.

Six additional men were on the cage, several so injured they could barely stand. They hung in the arms of their rescuers. Others were unconscious on the cage floor, with blood seeping from their eyes, ears, noses and mouths. Men scrambled forward to carry the six to the triage post hastily established along the railroad tracks. Weeping family members ran after them.

Women fell to their knees, some crossing themselves, all murmuring prayers of thanks and redoubling their pleas that the next cages would return their loved ones to them.

Men still lived. There was hope.

CHAPTER TEN

Volunteers cringed at the odor of burnt flesh as they rushed the stricken miners to the makeshift hospital. The victims' wounds glared raw and angry where fire had branded their coal-grimed skin. They moaned in agony. Two of them, brothers Joe and John Bernardini, were rushed to the LaSalle hospital, burned so badly from their heads to their ankles that their bodies had swelled nearly double in size. Only their feet were spared, protected by their heavy shoes.

One crazed miner, bathed in blood, had split open his forehead while bashing it repeatedly into the coal face. Those who were luckier suffered only cuts, bruises, smoke inhalation or shock.

While Dr. Mason, a local physician, and a crew of volunteers tended to the injured and revived smoke victims, the rescue party sucked down fresh air and the courage to return to the second vein. Of the four hundred and eighty men who went down this morning, only about two hundred had made their way out.

———

Like he did nearly every morning, Italian native Antenore Quartaroli had kissed his wife, Erminia, and their six-month-old son and headed out with a smile on his face to meet his friend and partner, Francesco Zanarini, for the short walk to work. Quartaroli was a man with dark good looks and large soulful eyes. He usually walked with a spring in his step, yet today, for some reason, he thought it took forever to get to the mine.

The friends had worked themselves hard throughout the morning, pausing only long enough to eat lunch around 11:00 A.M. Typically, they ate quickly, packed up their lunch pails and got back to work. Around noon, the assistant pit boss stopped by and the two broke off to chat with him a few minutes, then started digging again the minute he left. Two hours later the pit boss came by to measure the partners' output. Although forty-five minutes had elapsed since he'd seen the fire blazing at the escape shaft, he hung around a bit to talk to the two miners and never said one word about it, most likely presuming the fire was under control.

Work went on as usual. A short time later their mule driver dropped off an empty coal car at their entry and Quartaroli shoveled in the coal they'd dug. About 2:45, when he'd filled the car, the partners were startled by a shotlike bang in the distance.

"Must mean it's quitting time," Quartaroli said.

"Okay," his friend answered. But he nodded toward where Quartaroli had left his jacket with his pocket watch inside. "Maybe you'd better go see what time it is."

Quartaroli set down his shovel and headed for the entry to the square where they were working. He pulled out the watch at exactly 2:55 and in that same instant smelled smoke. He turned around to see great bursts of it rolling toward him, and ran back to warn Zanarini. The two scooped up their jackets and lunch buckets and made a dash for the escape shaft, but the closer they got to the exit, the hotter and denser the smoke became.

Panting, they got to within one hundred and fifty meters of the shaft but were forced to stop to catch their breath there at the trap door. They shouted out and thought they heard a voice answer through the smoke. They shouted again, but there was only silence. The two friends pushed through the trap door, but after just a few steps they found themselves in smoke so hot that they couldn't breathe and so dense that they couldn't see more than one step ahead of them. Their eyes stung and watered and the smoke burned down their nasal passages into their throats. After only a few more steps, the men were completely disoriented and had no idea where they were. They turned first in one direction and then in the next, becoming so confused they lost all hope of finding their way out.

"Well, Frank, this is where we've come to catch our death and I am sure this is our last moment of our life," Quartaroli said.

But Zanarini was of stronger spirits. "Don't lose your heart, Quartaroli. *Coraggio!* We must have courage."

Quartaroli was struggling for each breath and his strength was ebbing away. He could feel himself falling and he struggled just to remain on his feet. Near them, they spotted a miner's lamp hanging from a timber, beckoning. They followed its feeble light to the man lying immobile on the ground beneath it. Quartaroli called to him, again and again, but he didn't answer and they couldn't find any sign of life.

Growing weaker by the second, Quartaroli drew back from the suffocated man with a single thought: *If I stay here in this smoke one more minute, I too will succumb.* He turned to find Zanarini gone. A minute later, his friend yelled to him.

"I don't know how, but I found the trap door again. Hurry, come quick. I've found the way to escape!"

Quartaroli could hear him but he couldn't see a thing. With great effort, he used Zanarini's voice for direction and followed the sound through the thick smoke directly to his friend.

"The best thing we can do is return to our entry," Zanarini said. The two started back. Inch by inch they crept along, the hot smoke sapping their strength with every step.

"How could this horrible thing have happened to us? Where is the fire, above ground or down here? How can we tell? All we've seen is the smoke. How did it even start, this terrible fire?" All the way back, the friends talked about their plight.

When they reached the second crossing, they discovered a gallon of petroleum belonging to their mule driver. Since the lamp they had with them was dying out for lack of oil, they refilled it and then took the gallon with them, just in case.

The closer they got to their entry, the better the air became and the easier they found it to breathe. Finally, the two reached their workplace and collapsed to the floor to rest. They sat on the ground for more than thirty minutes, sucking down the better air.

"The best we can do is to try to reach the air shaft," Quartaroli finally announced. "So if we can get there, we can go up the stairs. This is our only way to safety."

Still, neither of them moved. They sat in silence, each in his own thoughts. Finally, Zanarini got up off the ground and picked up the gallon of oil and his lamp, which was still burning. Without a word, Quartaroli got up to follow him through the dark. He could barely see where he was going because the light cast by his own lamp was too dim to do much good.

"We have no time to lose," Zanarini said, lengthening his stride. Quartaroli, never as strong as his friend nor able to match his pace in ordinary circumstances, struggled to keep up. Aside from the smoke doing him in, the road they followed was one that hadn't been in use for some time. Timbers, fallen rock and refuse were strewn the length of it, and Quartaroli never experienced such stress and fatigue in his life as he did trying to cover that stretch of road.

At last they reached the entry of one west, where the path was easier to travel. But by then, both were exhausted. With great effort, they made it one hundred feet farther and through the darkness spotted another lit lamp. They called out, but no one answered. Yet, they were cheered because the lamp was pointing in the direction of the air shaft. But their hope was short lived. In another few steps they reached the lamp and saw a young Italian boy, maybe seventeen or eighteen years old. He started to whine.

"Poor us. We are unlucky."

"Why do you say that?"

"What? You don't know that there is fire around the air shaft and one can't get near it? We cannot even go near the air shaft because the smoke is too thick and hot."

Farther on, they could hear more voices and Quartaroli started off toward the sounds. He discovered the men he'd heard were fellow Italian miners Federico Lenzi and Giacomo and Salvatore Pigati. Salvatore was sitting on the ground with one of his coat sleeves covering his mouth.

"What's the matter, Salvatore?"

"I can't stand this smoke anymore. It's nearly drowning me." Pigati pointed to smoke rolling thickly toward them, and together, the five Italian miners fled to try again for the exit.

Thomas White and his buddy John Lorimer were probably the most isolated men in the mine. Stationed deep into the second vein, they were digging about a mile south of the hoisting shaft. About 2:00 P.M. they also heard some shots being fired but figured the men were just quitting work a bit early. They hurried to fix their shots of dynamite too and fired them off before starting on the twenty minute walk back to the shaft. Working farther away from the hoisting shaft than anyone else, they had no inkling that anything was wrong until they finished packing up and quit for the day sometime after 3:00 P.M.

They filled their pipes and headed off to make the day's last runs up on the 3:30 cages, meeting up with an old Polish miner Henry Kroll, and his fifteen-year-old son, Alfred, on their way.

About half a mile toward the shaft, the four first noticed a faint odor of smoke. The closer they got to the shaft the more pronounced it became, increasing to the point where White said it was almost unendurable. They knew from the smell that the mine timbers were on fire and that greater danger lay ahead of them.

The path was dark and smoke-clogged and empty. Although they would learn later that bodies were found along this path, the four didn't see or hear anyone else and feared they were the last ones left in the mine. Weaker than the younger men, who were in their early thirties, the fifty-eight-year-old Kroll struggled to make headway through the smoke. His lungs strained to bursting and his legs were like lead. Even with Lorimer and White supporting him all the way, he nearly fell several times. They caught him and plodded on. Young Alfred kept right behind them, continuously begging Lorimer and White to save his father's life.

It seemed to take them forever to reach the bottom, the large open area around the main shaft. There, they were thwarted by intolerable heat and smoke spewing at them in such volume that the men couldn't even see one another. With their eyes smarting and tearing, the men braved the heat and staggered forward in search of the hoisting shaft. Just when they thought they'd be roasted alive, they found it. But there was no cage.

For certain we were forgotten down here when everyone fled, White thought. Everyone else has gone up, leaving us alone to die in the fire.

Lorimer grasped about in the smoke, trying to locate the lever on the pneumatic gong so he could signal up to Cowley in the engine room to lower a cage to them. The iron handle was glowing nearly red hot, but in desperation he grabbed it anyway, searing his fingers and palm as he pulled. The four listened, but there was no return signal. Frantic, the men looked up the smoky shaft, watching long minutes for a cage that never came. Lorimer took off his cap and used it like a potholder to cushion his burned hand. Despite the pain, he tried again and again to trigger the gong, but finally had to stop. His hand was too burned.

Unable to stand the heat, they paced around the shaft, dodging flames and praying for the cage to appear. Suddenly, they tripped over a man lying unconscious. They tried repeatedly and unsuccessfully to rouse him and finally were forced to leave him there, somewhere between alive and dead. In their weakened state, fighting the smoke, the heat and the poisonous gases, it took every ounce of strength they could harness just to keep themselves from losing consciousness.

"We'd better go back," Lorimer said to his buddy.

With no hope of rescue at the main shaft, the other three decided he was right. It was so hot they knew they would die if they stayed there another minute and they figured they could still make it the two hundred and fifty feet down the manway. They set off for the stairs at the escapement shaft, never guessing that conditions there were even worse. Less than halfway there, they were driven back by the searing intensity of the heat and the worsening smoke. They retreated to the area around the main shaft. Lorimer and White stumbled along the smoky passage, all the while using precious breath to call out to the Krolls so that they could follow.

They were answered with silence. The father and son were no longer with them when they reached the hoisting shaft and collapsed.

They found the smoke and heat had worsened. Again, it was impossible to stay. The buddies plunged down a turnaround, figuring to head back in a roundabout fashion toward the air shaft. Immediately, they found the air less smoky and as it began to clear the farther down the road they walked, their stamina slowly began to return. Suddenly they heard voices ahead of them, coming from somewhere down a road that branched off their own. For the first time since scenting smoke they realized they were not the only ones still alive in the mine.

A few minutes earlier, Walter Waite and George Eddy had met up on the main road, each leading a small band they'd gathered. These trembling men were the only ones they'd saved, though they'd shouted at others who rushed headlong into the flames like a drunken mob and wouldn't stop, even when the two bosses jumped in front of them to head them off. Helplessly, Eddy and Waite had watched the shrieking lot of them fall in bunches.

The group tried for the exits but found them impassible. With Eddy and Waite in the lead, and the air getting heavier and heavier with black damp as they walked, the fourteen miners hurried toward safety back in the mine. Suddenly, Waite and Eddy watched in horror as three mules dropped dead just ahead of them.

"We're caught like rats in a trap," Waite whispered to Eddy. "But there is no need to tell the boys about seeing the mules."

Instead he turned them back, directing the men into a corridor they'd just passed, where he told them the air was fresher. Waite lowered his slight frame to the ground, pulled out his pipe and lit up. Discerning no fear in the mine boss' deep hazel eyes, some of the other men sat down too, stretching out their legs and leaning back against the coal for a smoking break.

At the sound of those voices, Lorimer and White quickened their steps, turned onto the road and found the group. By now, some were sitting or lying down calmly as if they were taking a break, some were standing about agitated and discussing their predicament.

"Where are you going?" It was mine boss George Eddy who asked.

"We're trying to reach the escapement shaft."

"It's no use. Conditions are much worse there. It's where the fire started," he told them. "You're better off staying here with us until the fire dies down and they get the cages running again and get us out of here."

Cheered at finding human company, Lorimer and White accepted, and learned that Eddy had stopped a number of these men from a mad dash to the exits once he'd found that both of them were blocked by flames. He was a longtime miner and kept his composure as he talked of going deeper into the mine, where he knew it was safer to wait out the blaze.

Minutes later, still searching for the way out, Quartaroli, Zanarini, Lenzi and the Pigati brothers stumbled upon the group. Quartaroli recognized Eddy, Walter Waite, Frank Waite, Thomas White, John Lorimer, William Clelland, John Brown and other miners whose names he didn't know.

George Eddy, the night pit boss? What is he doing down here at this time of day? He should be home, Quartaroli thought. He approached Eddy and questioned him in halting English.

"How come you too are here?"

Eddy explained how he'd been home, asleep, when his wife woke him with news of a problem at the mine, that he'd come right over, seen the smoke and asked for a cage down to the second vein. He told him he'd grabbed the lamp he was still holding and headed for the west, and that when he reached the front of the entry leading to the air shaft and saw the fire advancing at full speed, all he could think of was saving as many men as he could.

Eddy said he'd wasted no time running down to second west. He'd heard that some of the men had been sent out, but didn't know how many got out or how many might have gotten lost along the way.

For a time the men stood there in a group talking. With the addition of the five Italian miners, there were now twenty-one men congregated in the passageway. Suddenly, about 3:30, a tremendous gust of smoke was thrown on them, sending the miners running back for all they were worth to escape asphyxiation. *Someone up top had reversed the fan, blasting superheated smoke right at us!*

A number of the men began to cry in desperation. *Someone really wants to kill us!*

They ran back until they reached an area they considered more secure. At least the air there was breathable. The men huddled in a circle and began asking each other how this calamity happened— where had the fire started—but none of the miners had a clue.

"I was told the fire started in a bale of hay," George Eddy told them. "That is, there were six bales of hay in a cart and one of them caught on fire. How, I don't know."

A murmur went up from the men. Suddenly, they were filled with hope. Not one of them was willing to accept that a single burning bale of hay could cause mass tragedy.

Still, the smoke kept advancing on them, and they retreated by degrees, moving deeper and deeper back into the mine.

The anxiety up top around the main shaft was palpable as the rescue party prepared for another descent. Bundy rang the pneumatic gong and Cowley lowered the cage for the third trip down. The initial plunge was through smoky blackness, but the temperature escalated with every foot the cage fell. The men knew they were only moments from the blinding flash of the fire. The fumes were overpowering, forcing them to work quickly this time. Within minutes they'd had enough and sent up the signal to raise the cage.

Cowley's armpits were sweat-soaked as he hurried again to pull the men out.

Thank God! Oh, thank God! They had saved still more! They were weak. They were injured. But they were all alive.

Before the cage could even jerk to its stop, able-bodied men ran forward to grab up this next group of injured miners and race them to the triage.

Spent from exertion, Bundy and most of his group fell wheezing from the cage. Two of the them lay unconscious on the cage floor, overcome by smoke and fumes. Unable to assist the onlookers who dashed to their aid, Bundy watched them roll the two men from the cage and rush them to the tracks for treatment.

Though taxed to their limits, the rescue party refused to rest and they refused to give up. They denied themselves even one extra second to recuperate from their ordeal. Adrenaline and desperate purpose spurred them on. Still struggling for breath, all fourteen assembled once again for their fourth trip down.

But this time, when the cage resurfaced with additional survivors, Dr. Howe and Rosenjack were in alarming condition. Near asphyxiation and in a semiconscious state, they fell to the dirt, writhing and groaning. Slowly, the restoratives administered to them began to take effect and Rosenjack leapt suddenly from the ground, sobbing and hollering so hysterically that he collapsed again and began clawing at the dirt like a man gone mad.

"Boys, we can't save them all." His words hiccoughed out, racked with sobs. "Some of them are too far back in the mine. Oh! If we could only help them! That is a living hell down there and my heart goes out to them."

As if drunk with despair, he struggled to his feet and staggered toward the hoisting cage, fighting off friends who tried to restrain him. Ignoring their pleas and attempts to reason with him, Rosenjack wiped blood from his face and kept on. Unsteady as he was on his feet, he still managed to climb onto the cage. He was going back down.

"We need some fresh ones," Norberg said. His light eyes scanned the crowd around the tower, seeking more volunteers. "I'll have to stay up for a trip."

Herbert Lewis grabbed one of the lanterns his brother had requested and jumped onto a cage with Dr. Howe and Stuart Johnston. The cage started down the tower, but stopped when it reached the ground. A train bringing doctors from Mendota had just arrived and Dr. Howe had to jump off to put the physicians to work.

Yet the cage stood there, until finally Lewis asked someone nearby what the problem was.

"They have no water in the boilers. They have no steam."

Lewis knew they were taking boiler water to fight the fire at the fan house. He jumped off the cage and ran to the boiler house to ask if it wouldn't be better to shut off the water, fill the boilers and run the cage. He got there just as they had the water back on. By the time he ran back to the tipple the cage had gone down.

Again, for a fifth trip and then a sixth, the injured heroes persevered, trying to save as many as they could.

Rosenjack, who'd watched the fire escalate from a small blaze in a hay bale to this monstrous inferno, charged into the flames as if fighting a personal enemy. He knew there was a fire hose in the second vein mule stable and was convinced he could conquer flames enough to save additional lives if only he could get to it.

Rosenjack prepared for battle. He outfitted himself like a dragon-slayer, draping his head in a water-soaked rag and clamping on goggles to protect his eyes from sizzling in their sockets. Hurrying, he tied a length of rope around his waist and handed the other end to his fellow rescuers.

"I'm going for the hose . . ." He didn't have to finish. As they watched him plunge fearlessly toward the fire-engulfed stables, they knew what he expected them to do.

The air wavered before them in a shimmering curtain of heat, making Rosenjack's fire walk all the more surreal. He headed down the blazing tunnel, ignoring the flames sizzling his damp dark hair and eating at his clothing. Deeper into danger he went, groping his way without hesitation. Tall and straight as always, he zeroed in on the hose just beyond his reach with singleminded focus.

Rosenjack is insane! In another second he'll be immolated and the rope will be a single thread. Damn the hose. It's useless.

Pull. Pull!

They yanked him from the flames just inches before he was able to grab the hose. Chests heaving from adrenaline and relief, they pounded out the flames devouring his clothing and dragged him to the cage. They brought him up, unconscious, together with the others who'd just been rescued.

The flames had burned Rosenjack from head to toe. After they'd finished with his shoes, they'd eaten into his feet. His flesh was bright red and blistered, his face and hands were swollen, distorted, burned raw. Yet the minute he came to, he struggled like a man possessed with those who tried to restrain him from going back down.

Bundy wiped the sweat from his eyes and surveyed his intrepid group. This sixth effort underground had exacted its toll not only on Rosenjack but on Dr. Howe as well. It was closing in on 3:30 and they'd been at this dangerous, difficult work for nearly two hours. Was it humanly possible for them to forge on?

Many in the crowd didn't think so. The fire had grown exponentially since the heroes' rescue efforts began. It was risky to go on. Wives urged their husbands to stop. Mine officials insisted they call off the work. It was futile.

When their husbands persisted against all reason, the wives clung, grabbed and threw themselves in their husbands' paths, but the men could not be budged from their mission. Not even warnings, and then threats, from mine officials could dissuade them.

Rosenjack began to hobble toward the cage. Dr. Howe took him gently by the arm.

"Al, you are too weak to go down there. You won't be of much use in your condition. Stay above."

As the men readied themselves to go down again, Alex Norberg turned on Rosenjack.

"Such a goddamned piece of business!" he shouted, his mustache flapping above his lip. "A boy wouldn't do it!"

Rosenjack didn't answer. The tall young man only stood there, shivering in the face of Norberg's anger about the hay cart catching fire. Then Norberg turned on his heel and headed over to the engine house to speak with John Cowley. He thought there was an outside chance he and some of the men could reach the newly built wooden emergency cage and attach its cable to the bottom of the main hoisting cage. Half the size of the regular cage, it lay hidden beneath metal sheets in the third vein bottom sump, but could only be attached from above, by men on the second vein.

The hoisting shaft was the third vein miners' only hope of escape now that the stairs in the air shaft had been incinerated. If they could hook on the emergency cage so Cowley could hoist it in tandem with the main cage, they could save the lives of an additional eight or more third vein miners on this next trip.

Norberg found McDonald and Cullen and W. H. Ferris on the top landing of the engine house and told them his game plan. He knew Cowley would never raise the cage without a signal. State law prohibited it and the engineer knew he could lose his license. But he didn't want Cowley responding if a few panicked miners sent up premature signals. Every second, every rescued life, counted now.

"Tell Cowley he's got to listen carefully for the gong," he told Cullen. "It's extremely important. I want him to pay strict attention to the signals and not make a move until he receives the proper sequence.

"Three bells to hoist, four bells to hoist slowly. Four bells followed by four more means to hoist even slower than that. One bell means to stop and two means to lower the cage. And to hoist on any signal for danger."

Norberg turned back for the tower and Cullen ran inside to deliver the assistant manager's orders. Norberg reached the cage just in time to see Bundy shove Dr. Howe aside.

"You stay here," the mine boss ordered, blocking the physician from the cage. "You will be needed to take care of the next load. It is getting pretty bad down there."

Reluctantly, Dr. Howe stepped away and began preparations to resuscitate the next load of smoke victims as Norberg apprised John Quimby of his plan.

"The third vein men are in more danger than those in the second vein. We're going to try to hook on the dummy cage and get them out first."

Pressing near to the hoisting shaft, the families and friends of the rescue party stared through tears at their loved ones up on the cage.

Across the yard in the engine house, John Cowley got the signal to lower them. Muscles knotted with tension, he threw the levers and let the cable unwind. Like a tiger ready to pounce he stood there, his hand on the throttle and all of his senses on alert, waiting for the next signal to clang out.

Immediately, he plummeted the cage to the second vein. The cable went fully slack.

"They're down there now. They're down in those flames," Cowley said to Ferris, the engineer who was standing next to him. Three minutes passed, an eternity.

"God! Why don't they signal to hoist the cage? What is the matter?"

In answer, the pneumatic gong pealed out three times to let Cowley know the men were boarding the cage. He signaled back with three bells to let them know he'd heard them, and then they rang again—Hoist us.

He threw the levers and sent the cables churning around the drum, but before the cage had come up even fifty feet, the gong suddenly belled again. Stop. He threw the steam brake and brought the cage shuddering to a halt.

"They must be putting on the emergency cage."

Within minutes four bells rang out, the signal to hoist slowly. Inches at a time, Cowley cranked the cage up. There was a different feel now to the machinery.

"It's running heavylike. The emergency cage is on."

The hoisting cage rose steadily. It had cleared the first crosstimber in the shaft, eight or nine feet up from the second vein, when suddenly two bells sounded.

Lower down? What's going on?

He had no clue what they might be up to, but Cowley reversed the cage, sending it creaking back into the pit. Almost immediately the signal to raise rang out, then six bells clanged.

Reverse the fan!!

Before one signal stopped reverberating through the engine house the next one sounded over it. With sweat sheeting down his face, Cowley rushed to comply. *How bad is it down there?* He had no time to guess before the signals continued their rapid-fire commands.

Stop.

Lower the cage.

Cowley stopped the cage, then lowered it clear to the bottom.

Almost immediately a confusion of signals rang insistently, clanging out a pattern that made no sense.

"My God, boys, those signals don't mean anything!" Cowley screamed.

"Pull up the cage!" his companions shouted. "Those men are right in that fire!"

Cowley's heart was nearly exploding in his chest.

Seconds ticked by. Then minutes. Five. Ten. There was only silence.

Outside, the crowd was near hysterics. Herb Lewis, Dr. Howe and others on the tipple asked the cager to pound on the pipe in hopes of getting an answer from the men below. Instead, Cowley replied to them from the engine room.

"I don't want you. I want them below." Again Quimby pounded on the pipe, but there was only silence from the men who'd gone down. Suddenly, Lewis, Dr. Howe, Charlie McDonald and several other onlookers saw the cage rope jerk wildly three or four times.

"They're too weak to sound the bell! They're trying to signal to come up! What is he waiting for?"

Convinced the men below were signaling, they asked Quimby to give Cowley a bell to raise the cage. But state law forbade a mine engineer from raising a cage without a signal from below. When Quimby hesitated without replying, the men didn't waste another second trying to persuade him.

Herb Lewis ran down the tower and over to the engine house

with Dr. Howe and check weighman Martin Powers on his heels. "What is going on down there?" Lewis shouted at Cowley. "Bring them up!"

"I don't have any signals to raise the cage."

"Raise the cage, Cowley, they are roasting alive!"

The engineer grasped the levers, his knuckles blanched as white as his face. His mind reeled with torment as the men challenged him. These three had no authority to force him. He was bound by his orders.

Wait for the proper sequence. Don't make a move until you hear the correct signal.

Please God, let them send the proper signal!

But there were no signals at all.

"Come to the window and look at that smoke," Martin Powers demanded. "Do you think a man could survive that?" Powers finally persuaded him to go to the window, but Cowley wouldn't look out.

The onlookers' voices carried to the engine house from the mine shaft where black smoke billowed, proof that the coal seam was burning now too. Cowley could hear them growing more frenzied by the minute. Still, he stood steadfast. What if he hoisted the cage prematurely, while the rescue party was in the middle of loading on men? Or he brought it up too suddenly, snapping the cable between the two cages and pitching the men in the emergency cage to their deaths? How could he risk either eventuality?

"Snap the rope!" Lewis urged. "If you hurt only one or two it will be better than killing them all."

No. He couldn't risk it. He'd wait. Like he was ordered to do.

The men surrounded him, all but pulling his hand from the levers, yelling at him to raise the cage. "For God's sake, John, bring up that cage!" Lewis screamed. "There is something wrong with the signals."

Cowley didn't budge.

The crowd outside had grown insane, despite the arrival of a spe-

cial engine and train car bearing Captain Jack Evans and the entire
Ladd Fire Department. They would have been on the scene earlier if
more than an hour hadn't passed before anyone realized the young
boy who'd been ordered to place the call for help had run off in a
panic instead of following through.

With no hard road between the two towns, the three-mile trip
across the prairie was arduous in good weather, impossible in bad.
And precious time had already evaporated. So when the call finally
came, Ladd yardmaster Joseph Yearmouth had pulled the engine
and car from service in order to dispatch the firefighters to Cherry
by the quickest means possible. They'd dragged their equipment the
few yards from the fire station to the railroad tracks and steamed
across the prairie in a matter of minutes.

The firemen jumped from the train already outfitted in their firefighting gear. They conferred quickly with mine officials and set immediately about their work, connecting hoses to water tanks and
dumping water down the air shaft even as angry men in the crowd
grabbed up lengths of pipe from the ground and rushed the engine
room. Flailing their makeshift weapons at the engineer, the men demanded he raise the cage. But even in the face of physical assault, he
was not cowed.

"Bring them up, John," Dr. Howe insisted, his voice firm and calm.
"Now, John. Bring them up."

Cowley turned to John Chedister, the mechanic. "What do you
think?"

Chedister looked at the engineer with an expression as grim as
his reply. "I don't believe there's anyone alive down there, John. I
think we could get the men off the cage."

Finally, Cowley caved. He threw the levers and the cables began
to creak.

CHAPTER ELEVEN

A s the cage began to rise from the mine, Dr. Howe and the other men ran from the engine house toward the shaft. The cage was taking forever to break the surface, and the smoke was blowing a deadly black. They gestured wildly toward the engine house. *Faster, hurry!*

The families and onlookers gathered around the shaft were nearly insane with fear, peering intently straight ahead, waiting for their loved ones to appear. Slowly, the cage came smoldering into view.

A tongue of flame leapt from the mine. There was silence for a heartbeat as people grappled to make sense of what they saw. Then they screamed—a collective, inhuman, howling scream. Near to fainting, Dr. Howe turned away and said the most fervent prayer of thanks of his life. He had beaten death by mere minutes.

Men moaned at the sheer horror of the sight and turned their backs, sobbing. Women went wild with grief. Scores fainted from shock. Others took leave of their senses and ran in circles, tearing at their hair and howling madly.

John Bundy, Alex Norberg and the other eleven men aboard the cage were human torches. Nine of them were on the floor, heaped together in a macabre mass of twisted smoldering limbs. The other four had crawled on top of the cage to shimmy up the cable in a last desperate bid to escape the fire eating them alive. One man was on his knees, his hands clasped heavenward in final prayer.

The heroes were burned nearly beyond recognition, some scorched black, others with skin bleached and peeling off their upper bodies. They looked like statues cast in ghastly postures. Some held charred arms across their heads in a futile attempt to shield their faces from the fire. Most stared out from gaping sockets where their eyeballs had been burned away or had ruptured. Flames still skitted across their skin and clothing and blood dripped down their faces, hissing as it hit the red-hot cage.

Most hideous of all was the sight of cager John Szabrinski dangling across the top of the hoist. His head, which had slipped between the sides of the cage and the buntings on the way up, was decapitated at the eyebrows, splattering his blood and brains onto the men below him.

Herbert Lewis and others rushed to the smoking hoist and began beating out the flames and pulling the burning men from the cage, praying that some of them were still alive. As merchant John Flood was lifted from the cage and lowered to the ground, he opened his eyes briefly and gasped for breath. "The flames got us," he managed to get out through blistered lips. And then he was dead.

The wives and children of the ill-fated rescue team ran to the tower, shrieking the names of their loved ones. A group of men quickly formed a human chain and fought hard to hold them back from the shaft. One young immigrant mother managed to break through. She hurled herself onto the smoldering bodies, screaming for her husband and struggling with all her might against those who finally managed to pull her away and take her home.

"Take that man off over there," someone shouted, "or he may fall into the shaft." Herb Lewis took the dangling victim from the cage and then worked feverishly to douse the flames still eating at the clothing of another of the victims. He grabbed the three full pails of water handed off to him and tossed them on the man before he was able to get the flames out. Immediately, he set to work on the next victim. He pulled the man from the cage by his leg, carried him a short distance and set him on the ground. Then he rolled him over.

He looked into the blackened, distorted face and screamed. The naturally full lips were blistered double in size. "Oh God! It's my brother!" Herbert threw himself across Isaac's burnt body, sobbing and screaming. "Oh, Ike, Ike, my brother." Friends tried to lift him from the body and comfort him but he refused to budge. He resisted them, screaming on and on until he was spent. Finally, he was led away, babbling incoherently for his beloved brother.

Eleven-year-old Charlie Galletti took off, his feet slamming into the earth as fast as his heart slammed in his chest. The boy had to tell his mother, Beatrice, what was happening. Charlie raced through the streets, screaming at the top of his lungs that the mine was all on fire.

In hopes of saving still more lives, mine officials decided to send the hoisting cage into the mine at intervals, unmanned. Over a period of time they had Cowley and Ferris raise and lower the hoisting cage five or six more times, but no one else came up.

With mine officials directing removal of the bodies, the thirteen heroes were transported quickly to the triage. Dr. Howe and Dr. Mason worked ceaselessly, trying for any more signs of life. They found none. Wrapped in white linen and canvas, the dead rescuers were laid in a row next to the engine house, piled like cordwood. A short time later, they were removed to a storehouse that was hurriedly emptied to create a makeshift morgue, and laid on little cots to await the arrival of coroner Dr. A. H. Malm. It took Malm several hours to travel the twenty miles from Princeton, Illinois, accompanied by deputy coroner W. I. Kendall and a representative of Cherry's local newspaper, the *Bureau County Tribune*.

*   *   *

Besides the phone calls to Ladd, pleas went out to Mendota and
other neighboring towns for water and manpower to fight the fire
since Cherry's supply of mine water was limited to a shallow reservoir retention pond. Water for the boilers or for firefighting pur-
poses had to be shipped in by railroad tank cars.

Spring Valley's drugstores were ransacked for medicines and sur-
gical supplies. They were heaped into automobiles and dispatched
across the prairie. Meanwhile, every doctor in Spring Valley sped to
Ladd by automobile, then took the train to Cherry, arriving ahead of
their supplies.

Telephone and telegraph wires within a twenty-mile radius of the
mine instantly sizzled with appeals for additional physicians, nurses
and clergymen. The St. Paul Coal Company dispatched the railroad's
chief surgeon, Dr. Boufler, and other doctors. Several prominent
Chicago physicians joined them. Since Dr. Howe knew most immigrant families would rather starve than come to authorities to ask
for help, he had nurses visit them to assess their needs for food,
clothing and medicine.

Help flooded into Cherry within hours, with hordes of morbid
curiosity seekers on its heels. While most of the out-of-town gawkers hampered the frenzied emergency efforts, one hapless young
man found himself called into grisly service. Joe Oberto had pulled
into Cherry early that afternoon with a wagon loaded with fresh
bread. It was a trip the sixteen year old made daily, surrounded by
the yeasty fragrance of the loaves he brought from his father's
Seatonville bakery. The teen had barely finished unloading the
wagon when the mine's first warning siren blared. Like many others, he rushed over to the mine where his empty wagon was soon
pressed into use. Young Joe spent the rest of the day hauling the
charred dead in place of his father's bread.

Meanwhile, at the St. Paul Coal Company's Granville mine, superintendent James Steele rushed from his office yelling for Robert

Maxwell. He barged into the office of the company's mining engineer and expert, holding the wire he'd just received.

"Bob, the mine up at Cherry is on fire! We've got to get there just as fast as we can."

They hitched the company's fastest horse to a buggy and took off at full speed toward Spring Valley. They covered the nine-mile distance in record time, jumped from the buggy into the interurban car line's first auto bound for Ladd, sped to the railway station and boarded a special engine which delivered them to Cherry.

Anxious faces looked to him for direction, but superintendent Steele needed more information before deciding on a course of action. Immediately, he and Maxwell went into conference with the men most familiar with the situation, those who'd been at the scene from the beginning. In minutes he knew what he had to do.

"Boys, there is no use fighting that fire with that shaft open and the air sweeping in currents to feed it. We've got to seal that mine shaft if we are to save more lives."

It was near 4:00 P.M. when a handpicked squad of men began the task of sealing the hoisting shaft. There was no announcement. Onlookers knew what was happening and why. The crowd surged forward in hysteria and disbelief, straining against the ropes and the human chain of volunteers keeping them from the shaft. There wasn't a dry eye among any of them. Trying to shut their ears to the wails of those grief-stricken relatives, the squad dragged rails to the shaft and placed them across the opening. Next, they laid down huge water-soaked planks and heavy iron sheets, clanging them into place in an alternating lengthwise-crosswise pattern.

Mrs. Timko broke through the restraints with the strength of a lioness. Undaunted, she tried time and again to fling herself down the shaft as the men worked to cover over the mine. Each time she was captured and dragged away until, finally, the metal covering was in place. To ensure a tight seal, the squad began hauling over yard after yard of sand to heap across the metal, shoveling it into every nook and cranny where air might sneak in. Each load thudded into place with the finality of earth hitting a coffin.

Mrs. Waite hugged herself and fought tears. *Oh, no one can know how terrible it is here, among these mothers and children. No one can know except these mothers and children here.*

Rumblings against John Cowley began to reverberate through Cherry long before Herb Lewis returned to the mine, burst into the engine house and charged at Cowley, shouting that the engineer had murdered his brother, Ike, and the other rescuers by refusing to raise the cage when he was begged to. Although a number of citizens refused to serve, by evening, the coroner's jury was impaneled and Dr. Malm began his preliminary inquest, calling only engineers Raisbeck and Cowley. Raisbeck reported how he managed to drop the burning cart down the air shaft into the sump and later helped reverse the fan. He also testified that third vein cager William A. Smith fled his post at the first sign of danger, abandoning men who might have been saved.

Cowley told the jury the rescue party used both of the counterweighted hoisting shaft cages in their attempts. He recounted his actions from the moment he first smelled smoke, and defended his refusal to raise the cage with his instructions from Norberg to wait for the proper signals.

"Dr. Howe and the men with him insisted that I jerk up the cage quick, but I was afraid that would break the cable, to which I thought a third car was attached, to bring men up from the third vein. I think the third cage may have been detached before I was ordered to raise, stop and lower twice." Grieving, he told the jury, "How was I to know that the last time was the last time?"

For several hours after the coroner's preliminary examination, the bodies lay unclaimed, until the families were ready to face the unbearable task of bringing them home for the last time. Fragments of clothing, watches, pocket knives and wedding rings were the only clues some of the grieving families had to identify their charred loved ones.

Liveryman Ike Lewis was a supremely popular resident of Cherry, and a crowd of weeping men and women followed as his body was taken home. Most of the heroes' bodies remained in the morgue overnight. Joseph Robeza's corpse would remain unclaimed for nearly a week. He had no family in Cherry.

Working tirelessly, the Ladd firefighters poured tank after tank of water down the air shaft. The fire crackled still louder, mocking their efforts. Steam and smoke spewed out as the flames gulped up the water. The water tumbled straight down the shaft and into the sump, never even touching the three hundred feet of thick, overhead pine timbers blazing between the two shafts. Undaunted, the firemen said they'd go down into the inferno if mine officials thought they could either save more lives or beat the fire by confronting it face-to-face. Their offer was refused.

Instead, blasted for hours by caustic steam and smoke, they fought heroically from the mouth of the mine, hoping some of the water they poured down would flow out into the passageways. One by one, as the fire's by-products felled them, they were dragged into fresh air and given smelling salts and restoratives by the doctors.

Daylight was waning and a fine mist began to fall as the stunned town milled about, staring at the sealed hoisting shaft through a blur of tears. Some of the women could take no more. Bowed with grief, they gathered their children and made their way to their homes. Others, like Mrs. Timko, Celina Howard and Sam's girl, Mamie Robinson, refused to budge. With no thought but their loved ones trapped below, they would rather die than leave. They huddled on the damp ground to watch and wait. The vigil began.

As darkness fell, women with babies wrapped them tighter inside their shawls and lay down on the ground, overcome by the events of the day. Defying sleep, they kept their eyes fixed on the air shaft, intent on the firefighters' every move.

Throughout the evening and into the night, the Ladd Fire Department plied water down the air shaft until it appeared the active flames were finally put out. Though he was nearly overcome several times by the steam and smoke, Captain Jack Evans never left his post. When flames were no longer visible, the rescuers lowered a light down into the air shaft, but its glow was swallowed up by the great clouds of smoke still clogging the shaft. Superintendent Steele considered sealing up the air shaft as well, but truly feared the people of Cherry would kill him if he did.

Hour after hour Mrs. Timko paced, watching, wringing her hands. Finally, unable to contain her anguish, she began attacking the sand, trying to tear the sealing from the mouth of the mine. "I must go to my man and the boys. They need me! I must go to them!" Repeatedly and gently, individuals took her away from the shaft and tried to lead her home, but each time she broke free and rushed back to the mine and her vigil. Finally, she fell to her knees, praying aloud for the safety of her husband and sons.

By morning, she had slipped over the fine line of sanity and was raging in her grief. Though they repeatedly tried, her neighbors were unable to take her home and care for her until she physically collapsed.

Martyr John Bundy's son, William, telephoned word of the disaster to the St. Paul Mine's main offices in Chicago. He reached W. W. Taylor, who prepared at once to leave for Cherry with railroad president Arthur J. Earling. In a train complete with diner, sleepers, kitchen and a chair car, Taylor, general superintendent of mines for the St. Paul Coal Company, and Earling, president of the Chicago, Milwaukee and St. Paul Railway Company, set off for Cherry accompanied by the general manager and several other company executives. Their train pulled in between 3:00 and 4:00 on Sunday morning.

After a quick assessment of the situation at the mine, Earling and Taylor realized that before anyone could reenter the mine, they needed oxygen helmets and additional assistance from experts throughout the country.

They first telegraphed Professor R. Y. Williams, mining engineer of the United States Geological Survey, stationed with the government rescue operation connected with the University of Illinois in Urbana. As soon as he received word of the disaster, Williams and his first assistant, James M. Webb, gathered oxygen carboys, oxygen helmets and other rescue apparatus from the State Mine Experiment and Mine Life Saving Station and secured a special train to take them to Mendota. There, they transferred to another special train already waiting to bring them to Cherry, where they and their lifesaving equipment were eagerly awaited.

CHAPTER TWELVE

Saturday, November 13, 1909
St. Paul Mine, Second Vein

About 7:00 P.M., the group of miners trapped with Eddy and Waite noticed that the smoke was diminishing. Full of joy, they told each other, "Now we can go out." But one of them was wary.

"My dear companions," Quartaroli heard from behind him, "my greatest consolation would be that we all get out safely, but I still don't believe it."

Indeed, after only a few steps through the dissipated smoke, they encountered the heavy gas miners call black damp. It was too strong for any man to last in it for five minutes. They began to turn back, but one of them proposed they try another route out.

"Let's try to go to the air shaft, and when we're there, we can decide what is the best thing to do."

Someone else disagreed. "No, my idea is to go down along the entry of seven north and then to the northwest entry, and maybe from there we can reach the exit well, because by going to the air shaft we will be walking through the area where the fire started and there is danger of being crushed by falling rock."

The group decided to try the second plan. They found the air good along the entry to seven north and traveled down the road quickly and easily, but the minute they got to the northwest entry, their strength began to fail. The passage was free of smoke, but the air was heavy with black damp.

Becoming weaker by the second, Antenore despaired. Yet he pressed on, with men in front and behind, fixated on the thought of seeing sunlight again. Five minutes along the northwest entry, one of the men in the lead called back, "There's black damp here too. It's impossible to continue."

The men came undone. Roars of terror bellowed from twenty-one mouths. Quartaroli's heart thudded with abject fear. *Anyone who could see us at this moment would not know us as human beings,* he thought.

With exits on both sides closed off by black damp, their only recourse was to retreat somewhere deeper into the mine where the air was better and pray that rescue from the outside came to them ahead of death.

They decided to retrace their steps and head back to where they'd started in the second west. With every fiber of his being, Antenore Quartaroli struggled to move his feet. Even though he was living it, he couldn't believe how weak, hungry, thirsty and tired he was. He could barely lift his legs, yet he forced himself to, feeling his strength ebb more with each step. He didn't even notice that he'd fallen to the very back of the line, just behind his friend, William Clelland. He took a few more steps and suddenly felt like he'd been jolted by electricity. The earth whirled, he closed his eyes and fell like a dead man. Clelland heard him fall and turned back.

"Friend Antenore, what is it? Are you ill? Is that why you fell?"

Quartaroli heard the words, but hadn't strength to form an answer. Clelland came to help him to his feet and repeated his questions. It took all Quartaroli's strength to get out the words.

"Nothing. I had a fit of dizziness. It's only weakness."

Everyone else had kept on walking, unaware that Quartaroli and

Clelland had fallen behind. Quartaroli sat for a while and then started walking again, finally joining up with the others at the second west entry. The minute he got there, he threw himself on the ground in total exhaustion. He closed his eyes and instantly slept, but his companions would not let him, fearing he'd never awaken. They asked him what happened and Clelland answered for him. They all began to encourage Quartaroli, telling him the fall was nothing. Courage he still had. What he desperately lacked was strength, and he had no hope of regaining it in these conditions.

For a time the men sat there. The air was better and their breathing was less labored. But at certain moments the heavier black damp drifted in, pushing up the lighter good air and making them struggle as if they'd just been punched in the stomach.

By 8:00 P.M., hunger pangs began to set in. One of the young Italian boys, Ruggeri Buonfiglio, suggested they kill a mule but Walter Waite urged them to wait a day, saying that everyone could hold off overnight and rescue might come in the interim. Most agreed, but the Lithuanians were strongly opposed to killing a mule for food. According to Slavic superstition, attempting to prolong their own lives by sacrificing even a dumb beast would bring them certain death. They would rather starve than take that chance.

Some of the miners had not finished their lunches and the bosses suggested they pool their resources, dividing the food among them and eating little bits at a time to make it last. Frank Zanarini had a sausage and some rye bread. George Stimez's pail contained four slices of bread, one piece of pie and a huge dill pickle. Salvatore Pigati contributed his bottle of beer.

Since Waite had seen a number of miners fleeing without their lunch pails, Francesco Zanarini, William Clelland and Ruggeri Buonfiglio began searching all the nearby workplaces for abandoned lunch pails, hoping to find some other leftovers and a bit of water. But their two hours of work netted only one slice of bread and a half bottle of water for the twenty-one hungry, languid men.

We shouldn't despair, they told one another. *Maybe this is our destiny?* But no one had the answer. *Even if they did,* Quartaroli thought, *who would say? Blame is so ugly, no one wants it at their door.*

They were a half mile from the air shaft, but the air was getting more difficult to breathe. They decided to search for fresher air. Happy to discover a place where breathing was much easier, they stopped for the night at seven north. The minute they arrived, night manager George Eddy spread his coat on the ground like a blanket, lay down, then took his head in his hands and cried like a baby. Walter Waite, who was near him, asked him why.

"Dear brothers, by now our last day has expired and we'll be lucky if we live until noon tomorrow. Ah, poor us! We've slaved all our lives and sacrificed to raise our families and God repays us with this kind of death."

But Waite encouraged him, saying it wasn't their time to die and that they had to find the courage to fight to the death.

"You did not see the fire like I did, and I am sure we can never come out of this tomb alive," Eddy said.

Again Waite tried to give him courage and hope, saying that the fire must be out because of all the water they had both inside and outside the mine.

"I would be really happy if all of us could see daylight once again and that those miners I glimpsed were all safe, but that fire was indomitable." It was the last coherent thing Eddy said before slipping over into delirium, frightening the others as he babbled on about his wife and eight children.

The men settled in for the night. Some slept, but with anxiety and fear running high, some only talked about sleep. Most, like Thomas White, believed the fire had not claimed many lives and that they were among the very few left trapped in the mine. They talked through the night, speculating about their odds of being rescued and the scenes they imagined were going on topside. Recovered from his delirium, Eddy ventured off twice during the night with Waite to see if the flames around the air shaft had died down. Both times they were driven back by dense volumes of smoke.

Quartaroli sat with a thousand thoughts running through his mind, one on top of the other. He didn't care about death. He only longed for the consolation of kissing his family one last time. *What have I done wrong to be condemned to die in a strange place like this?* he despaired. *I am down in an abyss three hundred and fifteen feet underground with no way out. Almost, almost all of my hopes are in vain.*

Sam Howard should have been with Mamie Robinson this night, planning a future bright as the light sparking off the engagement ring secreted in its box at the post office. Instead, separated by nearly three hundred feet of rock, shale, coal and fire, Sam and his brother huddled in the second vein waiting for rescue, while Mamie and their mother sat weeping and sleepless on the ground above them. To distract himself, Sam began to keep a journal, adding his entries one after the next:

> . . . *14–1909 Alive at 10:30 o'clock yet.*
>
> *10:45. 11:00 sharp. Big Sam D. Howard. Alfredo my brother is with me yet. A good many dead men and mules. I tried to save some, but came almost losing myself.*
>
> *If I am dead give my diamond ring to Mamie Robinson. The ring is at the post office. I had it sent there.*
>
> *Enry Comianti can have the ring I have home in my good clothes. The only thing I regret is my brother that could help mother out after I am dead and gone. I tried my best to get out, but could not. I saw Gim Giamieson and Steve Timko lying dead along the road and could not stand it any longer.*
>
> *So what 'tis a fellow going to do when he has done the best he can?*
>
> *It is five minutes past 11 o'clock and the air is fine, but sometimes it is so bad it almost puts a fellow's life out.*

It is something fierce to see men and mules lying down all over like that.

To keep from thinking I thought I would write these few lines. There is rock falling all over. We have our buckets full of water (sump water) and we drink it and bathe our heads with it.

Half past 11.

10 to 12:00 o'clock.

7 after 1 o'clock.

2 o'clock.

3 o'clock and poor air and black damp.

4:15 o'clock. Change of place.

No black damp but poor air. We lost a couple of our group. Two men tried to get out and could not get back . . .

CHAPTER THIRTEEN

Sunday, November 14, 1909

By daybreak, news of the disaster had traveled the world—and the immediate world had traveled to Cherry. By buggy, by foot, by train and by the thousands, people poured into the mine yard. Every train pulling in from Ladd was filled to capacity, bringing doctors, mine inspectors, curiosity seekers and the distraught families of those trapped or injured miners who made their homes in neighboring towns. Photographers captured the gawkers milling about the mine yard or perched atop boxcars for a better view. Dressed in large fancy hats and their Sunday finery, they stood in stark contrast to the poor families of the miners.

The morning had dawned cold and bleak, yet while news reporters and photographers from throughout Illinois ran about covering the story for their papers, photographers from several competing commercial photography studios set up their tripods to record the disaster. Even as a fine rain began to fall, they snapped the hundreds of photos they would print up and sell as postcards.

Sunday newspapers across the country carried reports of the catastrophe, with headlines "Mine on Fire, Entombs 391" and "Thrilling Heroism Is Witnessed at Ill-Fated Shaft in Illinois Town."

Most were verbatim stories filed by The Chicago Daily Tribune and local Illinois papers and sent clacking into newsrooms over teletype machines, a 1909 version of modern newswire services. The Tribune-sponsored nurses arrived to tend to the needs of the miners' families, and France, Italy and Russia dispatched their consuls to the scene. Smelling a profit, food vendors rushed in to set up shop, hawking their wares to the hungry spectators and completing the circuslike atmosphere suddenly superimposed on the tragedy. The influx of mine inspectors, rescue workers, physicians, nurses, relief workers and spectators overwhelmed a community still reeling from shock. With half the male population employed by the mine, nearly every home in the tiny hamlet was touched by the tragedy. All twelve men who lived in one of the boardinghouses were missing, and of the sixty miners who lived in the thirty identical houses lining Steele Street, all but two were either entombed in the mine or lying in the temporary morgue, wrapped in canvas shrouds.

The wait for Williams and Webb and their lifesaving apparatus was excruciating. Many of the women who kept vigil at the shafts were widows whose husbands had been cut down in previous mining mishaps. Now their sons, many just teenagers, were probably lost as well. Yet all they could do was pray and wait. No rescue attempts would begin without the oxygen carboys and helmets on their way from Urbana.

Mrs. James Leadacke had left two older daughters home to walk circles around the mine yard with her ten-year-old daughter, Annie. She asked everyone they encountered whether her husband and sons, Frank, twenty, and Joseph, sixteen, were still alive. Tears streaming, she kept worrying aloud that they'd either burned to death or were going to starve to death. From person to person the mother and daughter went, asking, crying, sobbing in each other's arms.

Eyes welling and red with tears, Clara Governor, seventeen, and her sister, Martha, fifteen, sought their father's fate while their mother and little brother Theodore waited in their soot-coated home. "Papa did not come up with the rest of the men. Maybe he is dead. Martha and I are trying to find out."

Andrew McFadden's mother also sat at home, weeping for the son who had stayed with his mule charges even when others running past him urged Andrew to flee. "His brother Michael escaped," she sobbed. "But the foreman told Andrew that it was only a little smoke and it would soon blow over. Now the poor boy is dead and all because he stuck to his post."

Miners who'd escaped on Saturday mourned Walter Waite, telling reporters he'd given his life in selfless heroism. Isaac Remulti, one of the men on the first cage out, said Waite refused to come up with him, insisting instead on staying down to help others.

"I know Mr. Flood tried to pull him into the cage, but he refused to come. 'Let me stay where I am,' he said. 'There are a lot of other fellows who ought to get out of here. Hurry up that cage and get them. I'll try to do what I can do down here. Maybe it ain't as bad as it seems.'

"When I asked about him after the second load had come up, nobody knew anything about him. It looks like he was overcome by smoke and died down in the shaft. He didn't have to, because he could have climbed on the cage the first time if he had wanted to."

By the time Duncan McDonald, District 12 president of the United Mine Workers Union, arrived early Sunday morning, not only was the hoisting shaft sealed, but the air shaft had been partially covered over under the direction of William Bundy.

Mine experts from across the country hurried to Cherry, several of them arriving during the morning hours. Governor Charles S. Deneen ordered Illinois Mining Commission president Richard Newsam and his state inspectors to the site to take charge of the rescue work. All ten inspectors—James Taylor, Walton Rutledge, John Dunlop, Thomas Weeks, Thomas Hudson, Thomas Moses, Hector McAllister, W. W. Williams, Thomas Little and W. S. Burris—were on the scene before noon. One, James Taylor, told reporters he felt the disaster would have a far-reaching legal implications.

"The Commission was appointed by the legislature to investigate the workings of [the] state's new mining laws," he said. "Primarily, that is why we are here, and of course, to do everything possible toward removing the living and the dead from the mine. But this disaster should be investigated thoroughly, for one thing, for the purpose of improving our mining laws."

The inspectors were joined by Lawrence M. Eckert, the state's attorney for Bureau County, who aborted a trip to conduct a deposition to rush to Cherry. Also on their way were experts from Iowa, Missouri, Indiana and Ohio, and J. W. Paul and George S. Rice, bringing rescue apparatus from the National Mine Experiment and Mine Life Saving Station in Pittsburgh. They wired the coal company to have someone meet their train in Chicago at 8:00 A.M. Monday to direct them to Cherry.

Sunday Mass was held as usual at Holy Trinity Catholic Church. In fact, throughout the day Father Ernest, Father Wencel's assistant, offered up masses for the departed souls of the dead miners and for the widows and orphans they'd left behind. But instead of leading services at the Congregational church, Reverend Thomas Gleason continued visiting with his congregants and ministering to their needs. The two local clergymen were joined in their ministry by Father Ernest, who had arrived in the morning from St. Bede's College in Peru, Illinois. Tirelessly, the three pastors devoted themselves to comforting the bereaved and to offering courage and hope to those who'd had no word about their loved ones.

But even as these families clung to hope, St. Paul Railroad president A. J. Earling directed that a house-by-house canvass be made to ascertain the number of men still missing. Canvassers encountered some men previously believed entombed, but who, for one reason or another, had not been at work the previous day. Pending any additions from families not found at home during their poll, they set the total unaccounted for at two hundred and fifty-six. Likewise, Illinois United

Mine Workers Union president Duncan McDonald issued a roll call of
the immediate family members of the entombed miners. In a town of
twenty-five hundred, canvassers tallied two hundred probable widows
and nearly one thousand probable orphans. Their work, however, was
hampered by the incoherent state of the grieving women. Whether
from the language barrier or from hysteria, many couldn't answer who
they were or for whom they were searching.

"Almost two-thirds of the missing men leave widows," McDonald
said. "Each of these widows has from one to three children. I saw
one woman who has nine children, all under twelve years old. She
has not enough money to pay for a week's provisions. In a month
from now, the distress of these people will be pitiable."

But Earling wasn't convinced all these women were widowed. He
hoped some of the old timers had led others deep into the mine
where pockets of good air might keep them from suffocation and asphyxiation. "If the men were alive yesterday, every man may be alive
now," he said. "This mine is too big and has too many ramifications
to be filled with smoke yet. Besides, the smoke is not being carried
downward by any air movement."

Later in the afternoon, Williams and Webb arrived from Urbana
with the rescue apparatus and immediately began assessing the conditions. State Mining Commission president Richard Newsam, called
out of bed at midnight by the governor, beat them there by minutes.

Unsealing the mine to determine if anyone below was still alive was
uppermost in the minds of the officials, inspectors and families
alike. Following a preliminary evaluation, Williams and Webb decided to attempt a descent as quickly as possible. Although no official or inspector had legal authority over their colleagues, the task of
supervising their efforts fell to mining engineer Richard Newsam,
named chairman of the inspectors' conferences.

However, with the exception of Thomas Hudson, whose second in-
spection district included Bureau County and the Cherry Mine, none

of these experts had any knowledge of the layout or conditions existing inside the mine. They were forced to rely on maps and blueprints to familiarize themselves with its roads, air passages and layout.

After Newsam directed the mine inspectors to examine both shafts, they concluded that the only chance of entry was through the air shaft. The inspectors cautiously removed some of the coverings placed over the entrance and explored whether the attempt should be made. For a long time they stared down the shaft, smelling for smoke and looking for any evidence that the fire still burned below. Convinced the fire was either extinguished or had diminished to the point where a rescue attempt was not only feasible but safe, they prepared for Williams's and Webb's descent.

With Newsam directing the flurry of activity, a dozen men with picks and sledgehammers started hacking away at the six-inch-thick concrete block capping the shaft. Another crew began constructing a framework of timbers on which to hang the descent bucket. Others worked at smashing in one side of the engine room so they could get the cables running again. Instead of holding back to allow the men to work unhindered, the crush of onlookers pressed closer. The ropes strung up to keep them at bay were useless as they tested the strength of volunteers doing their best to restrain them.

As rumors floated that coal company officials had ordered the mine sealed prematurely, putting property preservation over the trapped men's lives, and angry rumblings about engineer John Cowley swelled, Cherry mayor Charles L. Connelly deputized extra marshals to maintain order and quash any potential trouble. One of them was Alexander Rosenjack, who with Robert Deans was himself a target of threats from many who blamed the two for starting the fire.

Over at the small temporary morgue, state's attorney Lawrence M. Eckert stood by while coroner Dr. A. H. Malm, Dr. Howe and others were busy examining the bodies of the burned martyrs. Since the families were anxious to claim their dead for burial, Dr. Malm was pressed to quickly impanel his coroner's jury and begin taking testimony at city hall in order to determine exact causes of death, as juries always did when a miner was killed on the job.

At the shaft a short time earlier, Eckert had heard angry rumblings against Rosenjack, some men saying he ought to be beaten, even shot. When he spotted the cager with a sprag in hand, trying to keep the crowds back, he warned him to turn in his deputy's badge and leave the shaft. Rosenjack then headed to the morgue to tell the coroner what he knew about how the fire began, but Dr. Malm was too busy with the heroes' bodies to take any statement. A frightened Rosenjack told Malm he was going to lie low a while. Before leaving, he assured both the coroner and Eckert that he'd be available on short notice to give his account of what occurred.

Eckert and the sheriff were already talking about sending Cowley away for his own protection.

After Williams finished checking tests of the gases in the air shaft and decided they were favorable, he and Webb donned oxygen tanks and heavy steel-and-glass helmets and prepared to go down. As inspector James Taylor put on another set of gear and announced he was ready to go, a request for volunteers went out to the crowd. A dozen men vied for the chance, but only two who stepped over the ropes were selected—Spring Valley's James Hand and Peru's Henry Smith, both miners who'd come to the scene. While doctors examined them, rejected volunteers begged to be allowed into the mine too, even if they had to go without oxygen helmet protection.

After the two volunteers passed the quick physical they were outfitted with oxygen tanks and helmets at the mine offices. With their faces peering out of the mesh-covered circles of glass in the wieldy round helmets and with forty-five-pound oxygen tanks strapped to their backs, they resembled underwater divers or knights in coats of mail. The two volunteers were escorted about the mine yard for about forty-five minutes to acclimate themselves to the weight of the equipment and to breathing the bottled oxygen.

When word went into town that men were about to go down into the mine, still more people rushed to crowd the shaft. It took a force of special deputies to push them back and hold them two hundred feet away. Of the several thousand at the scene, only officials, workmen and working newspapermen were allowed in the vicinity of the shaft. Williams and Smith were chosen to descend. Taylor, Webb and Hand walked over to wait in readiness at the tipple.

The bucket was nothing more than half of a whiskey barrel attached to a pulley apparatus made from a combination of clothesline and insulated wire marked at intervals of five to ten feet. It was so small that the men would have to ride down one leg in, one leg out, tied in by a rope around their waists to prevent them falling out. Once again, a system of signals for hoisting and lowering was determined and rehearsed. One pull on the rope meant *Stop and stop quickly*. Two pulls meant to lower the bucket. And one pull immediately following the two pulls meant to hoist away. As a backup measure, Williams was also given an automobile horn to sound. Doctors Howe and Mason and several nurses stood at the air shaft, hovering nearby the emergency medical supplies they had readied. The sight of carefully arranged hypodermic needles, stimulants, restoratives, ointments and rolls of bandages reinforced to everyone the risk of this venture.

The crowd cheered and strained against the restraints as the men prepared to step into the bucket. Newsam rushed forward to restore order. In a calm, even voice, he warned the crowd of the peril looming directly beneath their feet.

"You people will have to get far back. We are all in the most imminent danger." He told them that if air leaked into the shaft, opening an air passage into the mine, Cherry would see one of the most disastrous explosions in the history of mines.

After one final check to make certain the oxygen helmets were working perfectly, an order for quiet was given about 1:20 P.M. So that every sound from within the shaft could be heard distinctly, everyone standing near the shaft was forbidden to speak above an undertone. The signals were reviewed one last time. All was ready. A hush still as church fell over the crowd.

The signal came from Newsam.

"Lower down."

With memories of John Cowley's dilemma fresh in his mind, third vein engineer John Raisbeck stood at the levers. Sentiment against Cowley kept him hiding in fear of his life, and Raisbeck didn't want to accidentally suffer a similar fate. The town held its breath as the bucket dropped slowly into the mine. Officials knelt at the surface, listening hard for any sound from Williams and Smith. Markings on the makeshift rope and wire cable indicated the bucket was ten feet down the shaft when officials heard one muffled toot of the auto horn. *Stop the bucket.* Immediately, they relayed the signal to Raisbeck. The bucket came to a halt.

Two muffled toots of the horn followed, and once more Raisbeck lowered the bucket. Almost immediately, the signal to hoist the bucket sounded. Everyone's nerves were stretched taut with suspense. Fearing the worst, the crowd leaned toward the shaft as one, willing the men to come up alive. As Raisbeck pulled, the medical team moved in closer, preparing to swing into action, if need be, the second the bucket broke the surface.

Finally, the bucket came into view with no evidence of either man except their legs straddled outside the bucket. With that, a gasp went up and the crowd surged forward once again. The special deputies struggled to push them back, using everything short of violence to control the anxious mass.

Hidden below the rim, Williams and Smith crouched in the center of the bucket. As those closest to them rushed to pull them from the bucket, Williams waved them off and lifted the heavy helmet from his head so that he could speak.

"Boys, that bucket isn't hung right. You'll have to fix it."

Improperly balanced, the bucket had clanged against the sides of the shaft. The men had spent the trip hunkered down in the bucket clinging to the sides, fearing each time it careened into the shaft buntings that it was about to overturn and pitch them head first down the shaft. While workmen made the necessary adjustments, Webb, Taylor and Hand readied for the second foray. At 2:00 P.M. the bucket was lowered again. This time the bucket made it three hundred and twenty feet down the shaft before the auto horn resounded with signals to stop and raise them. The bucket had hit an obstruction. The men peered out into the smoke and made out what they thought was a heavy piece of planking jutting across the shaft.

For its third trip, the bucket was lowered with weights instead of passengers in order to determine if it would clear the plank. Again the bucket hit the obstruction and was raised to the surface, where officials inspected it. When they found the sides scraped and splintered, damages consistent with hitting a wooden plank rather than a cave-in of rock or coal, they ran the cage up and down several more times to try to clear the obstruction.

At about 5:00 P.M. the men again prepared to go down, cautioning those above to pay close attention to their signals. This time Williams changed places with Webb and the men took axes with them to chop apart the planking. With the obstruction finally cut away, the men signaled to be lowered. This time the bucket made it down three hundred and eighty feet, to the top level of the second vein, before the men signaled for a hoist. Smoke ran along the roofing with considerable velocity, but beneath the smoke ceiling they were able to see ten feet in on either side. A rock fall on the northwest side tumbled nearly to the shaft. Air temperature at the vein registered 68 degrees Fahrenheit, eight degrees cooler than it was just twenty feet higher up the shaft.

With each successful foray into the mine shaft, the hopes of Cherry's residents rose. There was little evidence of smoke and the fire seemed to have been quelled. The missing men could have retreated into the far recesses of the mine and survived.

Intent on stepping off at the second vein to explore, Smith and Taylor took the fifth trip down, reaching that seam's bottom and exiting the bucket. Finding temperatures and conditions better than they'd expected, the two men walked one hundred and fifty feet from the shaft using the electric lanterns they'd brought to help them search for live men or bodies. They said they found neither.

While Smith and Taylor were in the second vein exploring, James Hand had removed his helmet and stood waiting at the main hoisting shaft. Suddenly, from below he heard a distinct, repetitive noise that sounded to him like rappings on a pipe. And then he heard it again. Then nothing more.

After ten or fifteen minutes, Smith and Taylor signaled for a hoist. They were encouraged by what they'd found and hopeful that with rapid rescue efforts they could find and save more of the men.

"We found, on investigation, no excessive temperature in the second vein," Taylor reported up top. "If the same temperature prevails throughout, away from the landing, there may be enough oxygen to keep those men down there alive for some time. We searched through the darkness around the landing and found no men or the bodies of dead men. Tomorrow we can make another descent and proceed further into the mine from the second vein landing."

With that, they covered over the shaft and waited for daybreak to resume the demanding work. Williams headed to the coal company offices to wire Urbana for more oxygen helmets and rescue apparatus. He was promised they would arrive by special train the next morning. Perhaps then they might be able to unseal the hoisting shaft as well and descend the five hundred feet to the third vein.

Although the coal company had thrown open its general stores to the families, before the day was out the invasion of gawkers had cleaned out all of Cherry's stores of foodstuff and other goods, leaving the destitute residents with nothing. Most mine families lived from pay period to pay period, buying with their company scrip only what they'd need for the coming two weeks. With only two days remaining until this next payday on the sixteenth, the families had no stores of food or coal in their tiny homes.

"We need aid and plenty of it, and it must be forthcoming quickly or there will be great suffering among the destitute families of the miners," said Cherry's Mayor Connelly. "If the weather becomes very cold, the suffering will be terrible.

"While we do not like to ask for outside assistance, this town is too small to handle the situation alone. Most of our citizens are miners and the majority of them are down in the mine or their bodies are. We are doing everything possible to handle the proposition, but it is too much for us."

At his home at Long Row and Cherry avenues, miner Andriano Muzzarelli hung between life and death. From his sickbed, the father of two small sons reluctantly told a *Chicago Daily Tribune* reporter of his escape from the third vein and railed that the company raised coal for two hours without ever notifying the men to escape. Only when a young French trapper boy whispered to John Pellegrini that the mine was on fire and Pellegrini whispered it in turn to his cousin Muzzarelli did he flee.

"All of us, at least one hundred and seventy-five men in the third vein, rushed to the elevator," he said. "John Brown, the cager, was surprised. 'What the hell are you fellows getting excited about?' said Brown. 'Ain't you got any nerve? Stick.'

"Brown was game. Finally I said, 'This is serious. For God's sake, Brown, take us up.' Brown rang and he rang and he rang, but he got no signal. Then he said that the Polish fellow on the second vein was not watching his job. While I was waiting for John Muzzarelli, my cousin, to come forward, I discovered that the cage was not working. Brown said, 'The Polish guy refuses the signals. He must have run.'

"My cousin and I and a number of other men who were down in the third vein scaled the interior of the wall. There was general confusion and when I reached near the top I was shocked to have other human bodies fall down on my head. The poor devils had scaled the interior, but were overcome."

Muzzarelli fought his way up the air shaft and made it to the main shaft by climbing over dead men and mules, stumbling and falling over the bodies, picks, shovels, torches and dinner buckets left behind.

"Brown, the cager at the third vein, was a hero. He died, good God, like the heroes of the Civil War." Overcome from the exertion of telling his story, Muzzarelli sank back onto his bed. "He was a brave boy."

Mine manager W. W. Taylor had not slept since he'd arrived. He still limped from a recently broken leg and needed a cane to get about, but despite his pain had stood vigil at the mine shaft the entire time, along with mine president A. J. Earling.

"This is an awful thing," he said, tears streaming down his face. "Some of the best men who ever lived lost their lives all through carelessness. Bundy and Norberg died like heroes. They were on the surface. They went down to save their fellows.

"I thought that every possible fire precaution had been taken in the mine. The stables themselves were lighted with electricity, and no one was allowed to enter them with a torch," he said. The men were also forbidden to smoke in the shafts and tunnels.

"There were two four-inch hoses running from a central point among the stalls and all that was necessary to flood the place with water was to open a valve," he said. "Of course, all of the mine timbers are always soaked with water and it seems they wouldn't catch fire readily. There is no gas in the mine, and the fire started in the afternoon at a time when there could have been no dust in the air. After the shots are fired at eleven-thirty in the morning the roads are all sprinkled, and all of the dust must have settled long before the time when the fire started. The buildings on top are all of steel and concrete and it seems impossible to me that they could have burned."

Construction engineer Warren R. Roberts, whose company had

built all of the mine above ground, concurred. "Without exception, it was the safest mine in the state," he said. "The long wall system of mining was in use. This requires no powder. The method is to undercut, or dig under, the coal and let the pressure of the earth break down the coal. It is regarded as the safest system. This is the first accident of any consequence since the mines were opened. Mr. Taylor has been mighty good to his men and is always ready to spend money for their protection."

Although mine inspector James Taylor had flatly denied locating any bodies in the mine, the rumor that dead men had been found spread like wildfire through Cherry, causing a flurry of consternation all afternoon. Newsmen cornered superintendent W. W. Taylor, who admitted that rescuers had seen a number of bodies charred beyond recognition huddled at the bottom of the air shaft.

"Bodies were found by inspector Taylor, but will not be brought out today," W. W. Taylor said to reporters. "They will not be taken out until a number have been brought to the shaft and until all arrangements for their disposition have been made."

Still, James Taylor denied the claim. "We found no bodies, although we penetrated the second vein one hundred and fifty to two hundred feet. We found a number of dinner pails, empty and melted apart, and a number of empty coal cars. I judge that the pails were thrown down by the men in their haste to get to the shaft and out by the lift."

Mine superintendent James Steele contradicted inspector Taylor, however. "The men who went down into the mine with helmets found many charred bodies at the bottom of the shaft," he said late in the day. "At a conference, we decided not to make the news public nor to remove the bodies for fear of exciting the people to rash acts. For another thing, it was plain that only a few of the bodies could be removed before the fire would sweep the whole shaft again and end all hope of rescuing any living or dead."

Officials also said once they reached the air shaft at the third vein, they expected to find many dead bodies clustered at the bottom of that shaft. Based on the reports of Muzzarelli and other escaped miners, a number of men had almost climbed out to the second vein before they were overcome by smoke and fatigue and fell back down the shaft to their deaths.

Throughout a second night, lights burned in the tiny homes and few slept. Women sat on their tiny wood porches, sobbing. Others could be seen through their open doors, kneeling in prayer with their faces turned toward the mine shaft. At the shaft, Reverend Gleason held night services for his congregation. Likewise, Father Wencel went from group to group leading them in prayers. One group began to sing "Nearer My God to Thee," but broke into tears after only a few words and collapsed sobbing to the mud. The two clergymen decided to return home for the time being.

"The women are braver without us just now," Father Wencel said. "They are grand in their grief, and I am not fit to talk to them. When their hopes or fears are realized, I may be able to comfort them."

After the air shaft was covered again for the night, mine officials placed men on night watch, hoping that they might hear some signal from the miners. Throughout the night they reported hearing noises echoing up from below. They sounded like detonations, sporadic signals from men frantic to let those topside know they were still alive. Farmers as far as a mile from the shaft also reported hearing sharp reports that sounded like pistol shots deep in the ground below their fields. While the farmers were sure the men were signaling for help, officials feared they might be committing suicide.

About midnight, Win Dochsteiner, whose farm sat just above a second vein gallery one quarter mile from the shaft, was awakened by such noises. He jumped from bed and ran to the mine offices.

"Boys, there are living men down in there! I heard a report just a few minutes ago. I think those fellows down there were trying to

An example of a mine tunnel. In attempting to make their escape,
the Cherry miners found tunnels jammed with coal cars,
terrified mules and fallen comrades.
*From the Henry W. Immke Photographic Collection
in the Archives of the Bureau County Historical Society, Princeton, Illinois*

Antenore Quartaroli, an Italian-born miner. His journal chronicling his experience inside the burning mine survived the disaster.

Walter Waite, mine boss. He helped lead a small band of miners trying to flee the blaze and kept the morale high while the twenty-one men waited and prayed to be rescued.

Alexander Norberg, assistant mine boss. He rallied volunteers to join in the cage rescue effort and, despite his own injuries, continued to go down to save his men.

Firefighters raced to Cherry with their equipment, bringing in tankers of
water from Chicago to fight the monstrous blaze.
From the private collection of Jack Rooney

Thousands of gawkers thronged to Cherry by foot, car and train. This
train, loaded with spectators, traveled three miles from Ladd to Cherry.
From the private collection of Jack Rooney

As horrified families watched, workers resealed the mineshaft to
deprive the fire of oxygen, entombing hundreds of miners
trapped below.

*From the U.S. Bureau of Mines photo collection at the National Mine Health & Safety
Academy, Beckley, West Virginia*

Found with Mine Victims, April 11th, 1910 Cherry, Illinois "All Alive 2 P. M., 14 Nov.," Copyrighted by Albert Ch

Miners tore support timbers from walls and tunnel roofing to craft crude
fans in futile attempts to keep poisonous black damp at bay.
From the private collection of Edward E. Caldwell

In many instances, the dead were so unrecognizable that their families
could identify them only through property found on the bodies.
From the private collection of Lester Corsini.

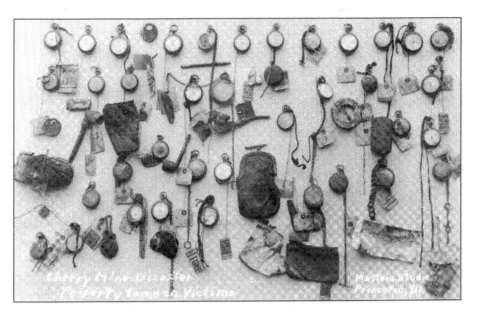

Cherry Mine Disaster
Property found on Victims

Masters Studio
Princeton, Ill.

The new head of a family leads his young sisters from the morgue tent.
Their grieving mother follows.
From the private collection of Edward E. Caldwell

Two of the author's family members attend this double funeral. Cousin
Attilio Corsini stands second from the left; grandfather John Tintori peers
from back row, right, directly beneath the hearse driver in top hat.
From the private collection of Lester Corsini

An Italian double funeral proceeds down Cherry's Main Street,
escorted by a brass band.
From the private collection of Lester Corsini

Identical drab houses lined only one street in Cherry,
later dubbed "Widows' Row." Just four miners from this block survived.
From the private collection of Edward E. Caldwell

Nearly five hundred children, four hundred and seventy of them under fourteen, lost their fathers in the disaster. Thirty-three were born in the months afterward.

From the private collection of Jack Rooney

signal to us to save them. Oh, can't we do something for them?"

CHAPTER FOURTEEN

Sunday, November 14, 1909
St. Paul Mine, Second Vein

About 3:00 A.M., tired as if he'd just walked one hundred miles, Quartaroli threw himself on a pile of timbers. Tonight he would not be sleeping with his wife in their comfortable bed. Instead, he'd roll from side to side until he could no longer feel his bones. At 5:00 A.M., Walter Waite asked him how he'd spent the night.

Quartaroli's large round eyes were ragged and rimmed red from lack of sleep. "A night like this could not happen even to those who want to purge their sins forever."

Then Waite addressed the group. "Friends, something has just come to my mind. I think we should all write a letter to our families, relatives or friends and then put it in our coat pockets. If by chance we die, then they will be found on our bodies."

Everyone agreed. But the only writing implements they had were in William Clelland's and Walter Waite's pockets. Each had a small notebook and a pencil, which the men took in turns to compose their letters. Without enough paper to go around, some of the men had to share a single page. Welcoming the diversion, John Lorimer took pencil in hand and began.

Dear Wife,

I am still living yet this is five o'clock Sunday morning, but we have poor hope as the black damp is getting the best of us there is twenty one of us all together here dear wife don't grieve we will meet again, God bless you and believe in him. He will take care of you, I gess we will meet in a better land, when you get over this let them know at home, that is all dear, God bless you.

Your loving husband,
John Lorimer

As they faced death, talking and even laughing in wild hilarity to pass the time before it was their turn to write their own letters, the miners' trust in God did not falter. Young Thomas White ran a hand through his short dark hair and put pencil to notebook to write his Maggie to keep her faith.

Dear wife and Children,

    I am now writing just before we all go.

    I know Maggie you will be in an awful state. I have been thinking of you Mag and the children. I loved my children and wife, But if it is God's wish for us to go, God knows what is best. It is five o'clock Sunday morning when I am writing. Maggie I am praying to God and my Saviour.

    Good-Bye wife and children, be good to the children Maggie.

    Please give all the all folks at home my best wishes.

Tom White

    Maggie I wish you and the children to attend church and live good christen lives, believe in God Maggie.

From your loving husband,
Tom White
XXXXXXX

It was now twenty-four hours since they'd eaten, drank or bathed and every man was feeling the effects of hunger and thirst. Again, one of them proposed killing a mule if they could find one, since that would be their only hope of nourishment. Quartaroli and several others set off for the stables but made it only one hundred me-

ters before the black damp drove them back. When they returned to
the group with the sorry news, the others complained and twisted
their mouths in resignation.

Though gripped with fear, these men were determined to face
death bravely, and struggled to show faces of courage to one another. Walter Waite's blistered hand stung as he penned his last missive.

November 14, 1909
Dear Wife and Family,

 I write these few lines to let you know that we was alive at this
time and if we are found dead, try and keep the family together and
use your best judgement about what you can do for them for I may
not see any of you again so good-bye and God Bless you all.

From your loving Husband and Father
Walter Waite

George Eddy, who shouldn't have been in the mine at all that day,
explained his predicament to his family.

November 14, 1909 Cherry, Ill
Dear wife and children,

 I wright these few lines to you and I think it will be fore the last
time. I have tried to get out twice but was driven back, thier seams to
be no hope for us, I come down this shaft yesterday to help save the
mens lives. I hoped the men I got out was saved. Well Elizabeth if I
am found dead take me to Streator to bury and move back. Keep Es-
ther and Florence and Jennie together as much as you can, I hope they
will not forget thier father so I will bid you all good bye and God bless
you all

George Eddy

Elsewhere in the second vein, exhausted from lack of sleep, Sam Howard sat and wrote as well.

> . . . 7:50 o'clock—Tired, hungry and sleepy, but I could stand quite a bit of this if I could get out of this hole. So what is the use of knocking when a man is down.
>
> 7:50 o'clock in the morning. This is Sunday.
>
> 12 after 8 o'clock on Sunday morning. There is no air. We fanned ourselves with the lids of our buckets.
>
> 25 after 9 and black damp coming both ways.
>
> 25 after 10. We were past the parting and could not get any farther. We gave up all hope. We have done all we could. The fan better start above soon.
>
> 25 after 10 A M .Sunday.
>
> Still alive. That is, you will find me with the bunch. It is 11 A M .That is five of us, Alfredo Howard, Legshorn Miller, Sam D. Howard, Steele. Gus Francisco.

The handwriting changed as Sam's life-long friend, Gus Francisco, added his own name.

> We are still alive. The only hope is the fan.
>
> I think I won't have enough strength to write pretty soon.

Desperate to keep the black damp from encroaching on them, the men tore away planks and timbers and built themselves large makeshift paddle fans.

> 15 after 12 P M .Sunday. We are having a swell time making fans. If they can't give us air, we will make some ourselves. That is the best we can do. We take our turn at the fan. We have three going. Joe Rapsel was the man who invented the fan.
>
> 27 minutes to 3:00 P M .and the black damp is coming in on us.

Only for the fans we would be dead.

11 minutes to 4 P M . Dying for the want of air.

20 after 6 P M . Now we are trying to make the bottom with the fans. We have six of them moving. One fan after the other, about 15 feet apart.

15 after 9 P M . Sunday. Still alive. We had to come back with our fans.

25 after 10 P M . Sunday. We all had to come back. We can't move forward or backward. We can stand it with our fans until Monday morning . . .

It took hours for the men walled deep in the mine to finish writing those painful letters in turn. Finally, the last man took up the book and pencil—a somber-faced Quartaroli. He didn't have much to say, but began to print in Italian, capitalizing every letter.

In Mine of Cherry, Ill on Sunday, 14, Nov 1909

Dear Erminia and Son:

Now being half past one P M . I am very hungry but suffering much more from thirst. Dear Erminia, am very sure that my last hour has struck and never will leave this grave, I beg of you not to think no longer of my death for I feel I will have an easy death. You will write to my unfortuned mother and brothers and tell them of my sad death. I have nothing more to say, only that to educate my dear child the best you can, and when he grows you may tell him that he had an honest father. Would like to say hoping to see you again but must say good bye forever, last kisses from your Antenore.

Shortly after he finished his letter, bad air found the men and chased them away once again. Hunger gnawed at their stomachs but thirst was the worst of their sufferings, surpassing even their exhaustion. They spent the next three hours half a mile from the air shaft between six and seven south in the second west entry. Suddenly, while preparing to accept their own deaths, the miners' thoughts shifted—not with jealousy, but with compassion—to co-workers who had probably survived. They discussed the overwhelming responsibility the cagers and bottom men must be feeling toward them, prompting Waite to pen a message absolving those men on the back of George Eddy's letter to his wife.

"*We, the undersigned, do not blame anyone for the accident that has happened to pen us in here, and we believe that everybody has done all in their power to relieve us. With best wishes to all concerned, we are . . .*" and then he signed the twenty-one names.

By five in the afternoon the chest-crushing sensation of black damp's presence forced them to retreat a quarter mile more to just past the doorway in front of eight south. The air was good and seemed to flow much stronger, raising hopes of eventual return to open air. Those hopes were soon killed. Black damp was coming at them from the other side. Heavier than pure air, it buffeted the good air first in one direction and then in another.

Some of the men sat, some lay down. All at once, Paolo, the Frenchman, jumped to his feet with his lunch pail under his arm. Grabbing up lantern and carbide, he started off for the air shaft.

"Where do you intend to go?" someone asked.

"I'm hungry and thirsty and so tired. I plan to reach the air shaft and go out."

The men tried to change his mind, insisting it was foolish to go alone. He would not be dissuaded. Half an hour later he came reeling back, dizzy and unable to speak. He collapsed to the ground and fell immediately into deep sleep. The men quickly dragged him to fresher air and began fanning him with the lid of his lunch pail and with his cap. Within a few minutes he regained consciousness. Waite asked him how far he had gotten, but Paolo had come from France only a few months ago and didn't understand much English. Giacomo Pigati, who knew a little French, acted as interpreter. Paolo told them he had made it to two hundred and seventy-five meters from the air shaft but that the bad air had blown his light out twice.

Walter Waite was encouraged and his confidence was contagious. "Companions, hope for the best, because if he reached that far alone, I hope that, all together, we can make it a little farther."

Some said they wanted to leave at once. Others wanted to wait a couple of hours until the air got a little better. They decided to wait, hoping the later they waited, the easier it would be to reach their destination. The next two hours passed in a flash and soon the group was edging its way to the air shaft. But after walking only one hundred and fifty meters they smelled black damp. Among them the men had three lamps still lit, two carbide and one petroleum. Clelland turned to Paolo.

"You're tired and weak. Give me your lamp and let me go ahead of you."

The Frenchman refused, declaring he would go first. Quartaroli tried to restrain him but Paolo insisted on going on. He took a few steps and began to wobble. Overcome once again by the black damp, he dropped like a felled tree. Those closest, brothers Giacomo and Salvatore Pigati, tried to help him to his feet, but he showed no signs of life. They hoisted him on their shoulders and brought him back thirty-five meters to the passageway between five and six south where the air was somewhat better. With the little water they still had, they moistened his mouth, then fanned him with their caps to give him more fresh air. But nothing helped. In less than three minutes Paolo lay dead.

Instantly Quartaroli realized that the black damp was even stronger than before and that in a short time he and everyone else would suffer Paolo's fate. His heart began to beat so irregularly, he thought he was fainting. A million thoughts beat in his brain, mainly the notion that he too had to end this same sad way. *I am going to die without any comfort, with no one to moisten my lips with fresh water and no loved one looking down at me.*

Quartaroli stared at his dead companion. While he was not afraid of dead people he was loathe to touch them. Still he didn't feel it was proper to leave Paolo lying in the middle of the road and he said so. When no one came forward to move him to one side, Quartaroli screwed up his courage and asked another man for assistance. Together they lifted Paolo and placed him behind the wall. And then a faint voice broke the silence.

"Dear companions, every hope has vanished for us too. The black damp is stronger than before. It is best we retreat to where we were before and wait for death."

Quartaroli recognized the voice as Walter Waite's and his heart suddenly filled with such weight that he could hardly draw breath. He had no idea what was keeping him from falling to the floor. The men began walking back to where they'd been. When they reached eight south, Waite spoke up again.

"Dear brothers, at this point there is nothing for us to hope for as far as leaving this tomb alive. We might as well resign ourselves to die as men. Hold dear those few lines you wrote. Before we die, however, my idea is to pray to God not to give us such a cruel death," he said.

Waite, born in England and a Presbyterian, suggested they begin with a memorial service for Paolo, with the Protestants and Catholics each offering their own prayers.

They did. Waite began to pray in English and they all followed him, every one in his own language. The Catholics said the Pater Noster and the Protestants sang "Rock of Ages," though no one knew more than the first verse. William Clelland, a staunch churchman, led the men in singing "Abide With Me" and gave a short sermon. Together, they sang "Nearer My God to Thee" and bits and pieces of other hymns. None of them knew anything all the way through, and some took comfort in just trying to hum along.

As the men finished their prayers, they exchanged a few words and prepared themselves to die. At about 9:00 P.M. they all stretched out on the floor in a row, brother next to brother, friend next to friend. Antenore Quartaroli and Francesco Zanarini embraced and found comfort in telling each other that their friends and relatives who knew they were friends in life would also know that they had remained friends even to their deaths.

"Brothers, if you can try to sleep, do so," William Clelland told them. "That way the black damp will send you to the other world sooner and without suffering."

Sleep was impossible. Quartaroli's large round eyes refused to shut. *Not even the fiercest beast would be able to close its eyes,* he thought. None of the men did.

After a while, Waite got up and embraced each man, and all they could do was say good-bye forever before delirium overtook them. For an ungodly hour they lay there, all in a line, waiting for eternal sleep. At about 10:00 P.M. Waite called out in a trembling voice.

"Companions, I've got another idea and it's this. Do you all believe that if we make two walls, one at the entry or the road, we can hold back the black damp from us for a couple of days? And if you believe it's opportune to do this job, it's better to start working at once."

Not everyone agreed. Though each of them had the courage, they lacked the strength for the work. Yet there was no time to waste. They had to fight and either win or die. The men struggled up from their death vigil. I *will never forget this past hour,* Quartaroli told himself, *not even if I live for another thousand years.* He and Waite got up to begin building the first wall.

Francesco Zanarini and some others set off to search for piles of picks and shovels left behind in workplaces. Their desperate search produced only one of each.

"Take whichever you want," Zanarini told his friend.

Quartaroli reached for the shovel but was so weak he could barely grasp it with both hands. The shovel proved too wide for the work and hard to use, but he persevered. Two or three others stood up to help, and with their bare hands began stacking the coal and rock hacked from the seam and floor to build a wall in second west, filling in any cracks with clay. Others began to do the same at one west, but by now they doubted the walls would save them. With every shovelful, Zanarini felt he was hammering nails into his own coffin.

Still, the men mustered every ounce of energy to fight off the viselike suffocation and overwhelming weakness caused by black damp. They sweated away precious fluids with the exertion, but with fire raging three-quarters of a mile away at the air shaft, the men worked feverishly to wall themselves in.

Within just half an hour the air became so bad that they could barely breathe and exhausted men fell fainting. Their lamp confirmed the presence of black damp as their slightest movement kept extinguishing the flame. To preserve some light, they hung it high on a timber where the purer air floated. Finally, parched and unable to work another minute, Quartaroli gave up his place to one of the others and sat to rest. After a short time he got to his feet and resumed working, but he didn't last for long. Gratefully, he watched the others continue to work. *Thank God for others stronger than me, or we would all have to die.*

Eventually each wall stood two meters high, one meter thick and three meters long, with only a crack remaining to be blocked up across each top. The second west wall was finished first. Though they worked doggedly, the strength of the men building at one west was ebbing quickly. Quartaroli was glad to see Zanarini and the Pigati brothers of the first crew rush to help the others finish.

The room in which they'd buried themselves alive was twelve feet wide by about three hundred feet long and five feet high, and they'd worked with such zeal that the air hadn't had time to become too contaminated. By the time they finally sealed themselves in they could tell the air was purer. With a solid wall of rock and coal between them and the black damp, it was much easier to breathe.

The strenuous work had exacerbated their thirst and the men suffered greatly. Though they had nothing to eat or drink, at least they didn't have to fear darkness. They had several lamps and enough oil to last a few days.

"Boys, let's put out all the lamps but one," Eddy instructed, "so that we don't use up the small amount of air we have here."

John Lorimer was a man of abiding faith. He stood up and told the men that God was with them.

"We'll live to tell this if we trust in Him. Let us join together in the Lord's Prayer."

Lorimer began in his rich voice and nineteen other fervent voices joined his in offering this universal Christian prayer. Some of the men tried to settle in then, but it was so cold and damp in their tomb that none of them could rest on the ground for very long without being chilled to the bone. Still, some had no energy to stand. So cold they couldn't feel their limbs, they succumbed to sleep.

But Thomas White could not sleep. Even though he was exhausted, starving and thirsty, he walked and walked to keep his blood circulating. Certain he had not yet closed his eyes, all he knew is that he suffered without relief, sometimes sitting, sometimes standing, mostly moving about to keep himself warm.

CHAPTER FIFTEEN

Monday, November 15, 1909

As Cherry's mining families grew agitated over the nightlong delay in the rescue attempts, and rumors of retaliation against Cowley, Rosenjack, Deans and mine officials continued to circulate, Cherry officials feared that keeping the saloons open would only fuel a fury just beginning to simmer. Mayor Connelly ordered every one of Cherry's seventeen saloons closed. Accompanied by two aldermen, Frank P. Buck and Joseph Neidetcher, he advised each saloonkeeper in town, one by one. Without exception, the saloonkeepers promised to keep their establishments closed until the mayor decreed the crisis had passed.

Although Connelly was offered peacekeeping assistance from his counterparts in neighboring towns, he was confident that by deputizing extra marshals in Cherry he could maintain order. He accepted help only from Mendota and from Princeton sheriff Alfred Skoglund, who sent some of his deputies.

With the hotels and boardinghouses bursting to capacity with rescuers and the curious, housing for the additional rescue workers and relief aides was critical. In addition to the nurses and doctors and Roman Catholic sisters who had rushed to Cherry, three Salvation Army officers, two deaconesses of the Methodist Episcopal Church, a deaconess and a nurse from the Congregational church, one Methodist minister and three employees from the United Charities of Chicago had come to minister to the stricken families. Railroad president A. J. Earling ordered special trains to bring dining and sleeping cars to Cherry to house this additional help.

An early morning train brought Professor George S. Rice and his assistant, J. W. Paul, with their Draeger oxygen helmets and other rescue equipment from the Pittsburgh mine rescue operation. Like
thirty-two-year-old R. Y. Williams, Rice, forty-five, and Paul, forty,
both fathers of small children, graduated from the School of Mines
of Columbia College in New York. Paul served previously as chief of
the West Virginia Department of Mines, and all three were considered prominent in their field.

Workers had begun unsealing the main shaft at 5:30 A.M. and officials decided to try sending the rescue team down on the cage.
Shortly before 9:00 A.M., as workers removed the last of the coverings and started a steam jet in the air shaft to circulate air, the crowd
now reassembled around the shaft saw a burst of smoke belch from
the mine. Then the air was clear. Officials took this as proof that the
fire was smothered and that the initial smoke that belched out was
just two-day-old residue that had been trapped right beneath the
sealings. They decided to go in to begin pulling out bodies and any
living men, and prepared for the hysteria they were certain would
come.

As Sheriff Skoglund swore in dozens more deputies to help maintain order, R. Y. Williams and Thomas Moses donned their oxygen
tanks. Once more, the rescue team reviewed the hoisting signals
while the restraining rope strung around the shaft area was moved
back five hundred feet and reinforced with deputies. They stationed
themselves both at the shaft and along the ropeline to hold back the
crowd now estimated at more than two thousand. This wall of hu-
manity stood silent—at the ropes and all along the railroad tracks
and in the cornfields to the east and west. State's attorney Lawrence
M. Eckert turned to the one hundred special deputies, many of
them newspapermen, and instructed them.

"Just as soon as these bodies are brought to the surface there will surely be a rush of relatives and friends from outside the ropes, and they must be kept back, peaceably if possible. I want every one of you to appreciate the gravity of the situation and to comprehend the feelings of these people. Explain to them the necessity of maintaining order. Tell them that the lives of their dear ones depend on their conduct during these vital hours. Should anyone attempt to break through the ropes, explain and argue in a gentlemanly way, but on no account resort to violence. Do all you can to dissuade them, but do not lose your temper. Should the occasion require, then call for assistance."

Finally, the men boarded the charred, ill-fated hoisting cage for their descent. They reached the second vein and walked about twenty-five feet into the southwest side of the shaft but it was too smoky to see and too hot to endure. They signaled to come up.

Webb, Taylor and Moses geared up for the second descent about 10:30 A.M., giving their auto horns a final test. The tension was palpable as Newsam gave the order to lower them and the cables began to creak. Families held their collective breath and prayed, their hearts hammering with unanswered questions of life and death.

Officials leaned over the shaft as the cage reached bottom and immediately heard the men's signal to return. Everyone in the crowd stared at the shaft, fervently praying to see their loved ones on that first cage up. The cage broke surface. The crowd groaned in unison. No one except the three rescuers was aboard.

The rescuers held a short conference with officials. There was still some fire below in the area of the mule stables but they wanted to go back down to explore. Again they descended, using their auto horns to order the cage's movement, alternately traveling up and down the shaft until their signal sounded to stop at the second vein bottom. Rumors quickly circulated through the crowd that the rescuers had found men alive but had not brought them up immediately because the trapped miners were too exhausted from smoke inhalation and hunger.

Such false hopes were buoyed above ground for fifteen minutes while the three men explored in the second vein. Although they ventured some one hundred and fifty feet from the shaft, calling as they went—"Are you there? Are you there?"—they found no one, living or dead. They signaled to ascend.

At the surface they reported their findings. While they had been able to see clearly with their lanterns in the area immediately adjacent to the charred shaft, dense smoke hindered their vision the farther they traveled into the passageways reticulating deeper into the vein. Taylor asked officials to start up the fan, running it in reverse as an exhaust.

"I believe that the fan will clear the entries of smoke and that before the end of the day we will know more about the fate of those entombed miners and may be able to rescue some of them who may still be living, despite the terrible experience they have gone through."

Although some experts worried that sucking smoke from the mine might rekindle the flames, most believed the fire was sufficiently smothered and that ventilation would simply dissipate trapped smoke to let the rescue party see. The mechanics went to the ruined fan house to repair the giant fan as best they could, building a temporary casing to replace the one destroyed in the fire. Afraid to run it at full power with the babbit metal melted from the fan's bearings, Chedister started it up at less than half speed, allowing the fan only sixty revolutions per minute. It ran for thirty minutes, upcasting fumes and smoke through the air shaft until the air flowed clear. Newsam shouted when heavy smoke began pouring from the mouth of the hoisting shaft.

"Boys, stop that fan as quick as you can!" he yelled.

They stopped the fan but the smoke kept billowing out, nearly obscuring the cage sitting at the shaft. Something was terribly wrong. Protected only by their oxygen helmets, the three men boarded the cage to investigate. Taylor announced they were ready.

Following his lead, Webb and Moses pulled down their oxygen helmets. Anxieties ran high as the cage was lowered with excruciating slowness, with everyone listening intently for the slightest signal from the horns. Suddenly an insistent series of toots resounded and Newsam began shouting at the top of his lungs—even as a second round of frantic toots began echoing from below.

"Raise, raise and raise that cage fast!"

The cage was zoomed up the hoist.

Fresh fire had broken out and the three men had been lowered almost directly into it. The mine was burning out rapidly and the fire had to be extinguished as soon as possible to prevent the entire mine from caving in, Taylor reported. The three saw walls and ceilings already starting to crumble, a great danger to any rescue party attempting to penetrate the depths. "We've got to fight it," Taylor said, "or, boys, there won't be a chance in the world of saving those poor unfortunate men. Give us a fire hose."

Williams and Moses went back down, carrying a hose connected to a railroad water tank car. They spotted three separate fires, one in the pump room, one in a corner of the cribbing in the south compartment of the hoisting shaft and one in timbers about fifteen feet from the shaft on the northeast bottom. Although they encountered smoke, it was thin and clear enough that they were able to see fairly well. They opened the nozzle of the hose but couldn't force out a strong enough stream of water, so they left it spitting water in the vein and returned up top to confer with the Ladd firefighters. Deciding there must be a problem with the nozzle, they went back down to try again, but signaled to come up even before they reached the bottom. In the ten to fifteen minutes they'd been up top, the fire had intensified and new rock falls were crashing in the tunnels near the bottom.

"If we had a barrel of water, we could have extinguished the fire when we discovered it," Taylor said. "Whether the fan was responsible for the second outbreak or not, it is certain that the original fire was never extinguished."

Professor Williams from the Urbana rescue station described the heat and conditions they'd found below.

"The interior was hot and I could feel the heat waves beating against my body. I left the cage and started to walk away from the shaft. I hadn't proceeded very far when I felt some objects at my feet. I leaned over and trained my electric light on them and discovered they were dinner pails which had evidently been dropped by their owners when they fled back in terror from the trouble."

He said he stumbled against a heavy object a short distance farther and began to tremble, afraid to shine his electric light on it and look into the burned, distorted face of some man who'd fallen down and died. Gathering courage and realizing it was his duty, he trained his light on the object and was relieved to find it was a discarded hose—the one Rosenjack and the others had tried to attach to the fire pump to kill the fire on Saturday.

"As far as I went I did not see any bodies. I feel confident that nearly everyone of the men, led by an overwhelming instinct, rushed away from the flames and sought protection in the galleries and entries where they may be dead or where some of them, using the proper means, may still fight for the oxygen that was very scarce," he said. "When we realized how futile any attempt to get through the flames was, we decided to come to the surface again on the cage."

Taylor, however, doubted it was possible for any of the miners to have lived through the catastrophe. He said they'd gone down less than fifty feet before the smoke became so dense they couldn't see more than a few feet in front of their faces. The fan had driven air currents through the tunnel, amplifying the fire and increasing the terrible volumes of smoke. "If we hadn't been equipped with the oxygen apparatuses, we would have all been suffocated," Taylor said.

By midafternoon, it was clear the firefighters were no match for the blaze, and most of the inspectors on the scene now doubted the wisdom of leaving the main shaft unsealed. Officials once again moved to seal up the mine. President Earling, who'd been on the scene directing firemen and rescue workers, nearly broke down.

"My God," he cried. "Can nothing be done? Let's put out this fire and get these poor miners."

"There is nothing to be done," Newsam said, ordering the mine resealed. "We have tried everything and now it remains for us to get more firefighting apparatus in order to extinguish the fire as soon as possible, but we need chemicals and longer hoses."

It was a hideous conclusion, but the only conclusion. The officials knew resealing the mine meant certain death for any who might still be alive, and yet it was impossible to bring out even one man with the fire still raging.

"The mines are on fire again," one woman shouted into the crowd. She turned to leave, sobbing. "John will be dead now, even if he was alive before."

A woman flung herself at the feet of a mine official, both shrieking and begging.

"Don't seal that mine. You must not. My husband is there and if I can't have him alive, oh, at least give me his dead body." Overwrought, she fainted and was carried home by nurses.

Again the women had to stand helpless as their men were buried over, but this time their hysteria was multiplied. They watched workmen collapse before their eyes, suffocating topside as they struggled to replace the wet boards and steel sheets.

At about 4:00 P.M. workers threw on the last shovel of sand. The brigade of Sisters of Mary of the Presentation, who'd hurried from St. Margaret's Hospital in Spring Valley to minister to the families, helped some of the women home. Pressing them to eat for the sake of their children, nurses and the nuns finally convinced some of the grieving women to force down the first food or drink they'd had since Saturday afternoon.

As hope drifted away, the crowd around the shaft began to thin.

Finally the only ones left were a few shawl-draped women and those men who could not abandon the mine for the warmth of home.

The afternoon brought with it payday and the first three funerals. John Tuhy, a young boy who had managed to escape on a rescue cage but later died, was buried in Cherry, as was Dominick Formento, the grocer who was among the first aboard the rescue cage on which he lost his life. John Szabrinski (Smith), the second vein cager and Cherry alderman who also died on the rescue cage, was buried in nearby Spring Valley. Szabrinski was a popular leader among his fellow Lithuanians, and every one of them who was able joined the funeral cortege to help bury the man they regarded as a martyr.

The scene at the mine's cashier's office was a piteous one. Although they couldn't cash their husbands' or sons' wages at the bank until the following day, the sixteenth, the women lined up throughout the day to collect the last scrip vouchers from the cashier. With babies in their arms or on their hips and little ones clinging to their long skirts, they wept and waited for the desperately needed funds. One young newlywed was nearly insane with grief. "Give me back my husband," she sobbed in Italian as she was handed the voucher. "I don't want this money. Give me back my husband." Her relatives, who were collecting vouchers for their own lost men, sobbed with her as they took her home.

After reading the dailies' news reports that Sunday's influx of gawkers made nearly a clean sweep of the town, leaving miners' families in sore need of food, clothing and money, Americans from across the nation began sending contributions. Governor Deneen, head of the Illinois division of the Red Cross Society, wired off urgent appeals for food and necessities to the Red Cross and other charities, and asked for assistance from citizens in every state. Immediately, the Red Cross dispatched its national director, Ernest P. Bicknell, to Cherry to assess the community's needs. In Chicago, a twenty-member detachment of its military branch, the Illinois Red Cross Legion, readied themselves for service in Cherry.

In addition to providing nurses and medical supplies, The Chicago Daily Tribune instituted a relief fund and began publishing a daily list of contributors' donations. Montgomery Ward & Co. not only gave $500 in cash, but sold The Tribune's relief fund managers $1,800 worth of supplies at a discount, waiving any profit.

While a large shipment of food and clothing was being readied, The Tribune purchased and shipped off an emergency consignment that included two hundred fifty loaves of bread and a hundred pounds of sausage. Within an hour, this smaller interim shipment was loaded onto the 1:25 Rock Island Railroad's passenger train and rushed to Cherry so that it could arrive by evening.

A representative of The Tribune accompanied the huge shipment sent to Cherry by freight car. When the loaded horse-drawn wagons arrived at the train station just as a train was ready to depart, United States Express employees dropped everything in order to get the goods quickly loaded on. With warm clothing a major concern, the shipment included shoes and garments for one hundred women, fifty youth, fifty children and twenty-five infants, all piled high at one end of a freight car. In addition, the car contained five barrels of flour, five hundred pounds of flour in small sacks, twenty sacks each of corn meal and beans, twenty cases each of tomatoes, corn, pork and beans and salmon, two barrels of sugar, one chest of tea, five hundred cans of soup, bacon, salt, fifteen boxes of crackers, one thousand loaves of bread, three barrels of sausage and one barrel of provisions donated by J. R. Beiers Bros. The freight car left on an all-night journey that would put it in Cherry by 6:00 A.M. Tuesday.

*   *   *

In Chicago, the North Avenue Business Men's Association went into action to help swell the relief fund and Congregational ministers attending their weekly conference at the Masonic Temple passed resolutions of assistance, sending their sympathies to the victims' families. Meanwhile, at The Tribune, discussions got underway for turning over administration of the newspaper's relief fund to the Red Cross.

Also in Chicago, women unionists unanimously passed a resolution extolling the thirteen heroes and sent it to the United Mine Workers Union of Cherry, with sympathies to the bereaved families.

> Resolved: That in the opinion of the Women's Trade Union League of Chicago, these heroes of peace are greater than the heroes of war, notwithstanding that the idle praise of the thoughtless multitude goes out to the gaily caprisoned man whose only tools were murderous weapons rather than to this sacrifice on the part of the plain miner, who lives daily in serving his fellowman, and who dies for them as simply as he lives.

Later in the afternoon, Orson Smith, president of the Merchants' Loan and Trust Company and treasurer of the Illinois Red Cross, announced that he would accept any and all donations, and Dr. Gustavus M. Blech, director of the Illinois First Aid Corps of the Red Cross, departed for Cherry.

Even with the seals in place, smoke and 110-degree steam leaked ominously from the shafts. Officials considered flooding carbonic gas into the mine during the night to choke the flames, but feared the swiftly traveling chemical would kill anyone holed up in the farthest recesses of the mine within just fifteen minutes. Instead, hoping for a more systematic plan of attack, they looked to Tuesday to renew the battle of water against fire. From Chicago they ordered two special fire engines with four thousand feet of hose and two chemical wagons, plus more chemical wagons from LaSalle, Spring Valley and a number of other neighboring cities. The two large fire engines arrived that evening by special train and quantities of small chemical extinguishers kept arriving throughout the night.

Newsam was marshaling all the firefighting power at his disposal. He saw no hope of entering the mine until the fire was extinguished.

"Had it not been for the insistence of the bereaved families, we would never have opened the mine in the first place," he told reporters. "The fire should have been allowed to die down before any attempt was made to enter the tunnels. Now the work is delayed and it will be several days before any bodies can be brought out. But we couldn't withstand the pleas of the women and the cries of the children and we simply had to make an attempt at rescue. It was a mistake.

"I never did believe any of the men were alive, and I'm positive of it now."

With hopes for survivors so slim, The St. Paul Coal Company decided to arrange for the miners' burials and to donate a five-acre plot at the north end of the town for a cemetery. Carefully guarding this information from the miners' families, they ordered three hundred pine coffins from Chicago, expecting half to arrive Tuesday and the other half by Wednesday.

CHAPTER SIXTEEN

Monday, November 15, 1909
Cherry Mine, Second Vein

Sam Howard's pencil scratched across the paper.

> . . . 15 after 2 A.M. Monday. Am still alive. We are cold, hungry, weak, sick and everything else. Alfredo Howard is still alive.
> 9:15 A.M. Monday morning. Still breathing. Something better turn up or we will soon be gone.
> 11:15 A.M. Monday. Still alive at this time . . .

Midday, he began his final entry.

> . . . 10 to 1 P.M. Monday. The lives are going out. I think this is our last. We are getting weak, Alfredo Howard as well as all of us . . .

There was a soft buzzing in his head, cottony, distant. Suddenly, Sam was aware only of a great fatigue. He couldn't feel his fingers. The buzzing grew quieter, farther away. The pencil fell from his hand.

*   *   *

Morning found the twenty men huddled together, hungry and weak. Few had slept. Thirst throbbed in their throats. Finding water somewhere became paramount.

"I believe now that we can live for at least two or three days," William Clelland told them, "We have nothing to eat, but we must find some water to moisten our lips once in a while."

Though damp spots are common in mine floors, the area where the men had sealed themselves was quite dry. Three of them took the carbide lamp and set off to search for any humid spots in the floor. They discovered only three. Using the pick and shovel, they had to work hard just to dig out little cuplike crevices where water might pool. But precious few drops accumulated—so few they had to be rationed. The men returned to tell the rest.

Throughout the day they went in shifts to wet their lips with the putrid liquid, then had to endure six to seven torturous hours before they could do it again.

Since Salvatore Pigati's watch was still running, periodically he would run his fingers down the chain, pull it from his pocket and announce the time.

"Now it is seven A.M.," he called out. Then, "It's time for breakfast." At 11:00 A.M., he told his companions it was time for lunch. Their mouths watered, giving some relief from the sour slime building up inside their cheeks and on the roofs of their mouths.

While they had camped just beyond the second west entry Sunday night, they spent most of Monday in one west. The air there was not bad, but the roof was. Fearing falling rock or a cave-in, they changed position slightly, moving to nine north. While they weren't cold unless they were on the ground, they shivered constantly with goosebumps of fear. To warm themselves, they took down the canvas curtains that hung across some of the entries to route air circulation.

Walter Waite made a small opening in the wall and periodically stuck his nose inside it to test for black damp. Usually he fell staggering backward from its effects and the others would hurriedly plug up the hole again with a pick handle, but several times he smelled swift cool air. *The fan is running, outside air is flowing down!*

Throughout the day, the thought of escaping this hell and returning home kept dancing through Quartaroli's mind, even though he didn't believe any of them would ever get out, fan or no fan.

But these thoughts were something to occupy the interminable hours. Yesterday they'd had hard work—finishing the walls—to keep their hands and heads busy. Today, their only jobs were to turn themselves from one side to the other and to search for water. One of the men griped that none of them had a deck of cards to help pass the time. The day's silent, weary monotony was punctuated only by the intermittent sobs escaping first from one throat, then another.

As night approached, the men removed themselves to nine north and lined up in a row to preserve body heat. The six Italians grouped themselves together, Quartaroli and Zanarini, the two Pigati brothers, young Ruggeri Buonfiglio and Federico Lenzi.

Struggling with his emotions, Salvatore sat down to compose a letter to his sister-in-law.

15 November 1909 Monday
Dear Sister-in-law,

It is 7 P.M. Monday. There is no hope that I will come out, up until now we are like rats in a trap. Many times we have searched for a way to save ourselves. It was useless, the smoke was too hot, we were obliged to retreat always.

Write to my bereaved parents, and tell them about our end. When they will find my corpse, I pray you have me buried beside my brother, as we unfortunately will have the same death. If you have the band at my funeral, pay for it at my expense. You know my business, do as if it were yours, so that my parents will have a memento of me.

I send my best regards to you and your children. Send regards to my dear parents, brother and sisters. Regards to the members of the lodge to which I belong.

With tears in my eyes, I tell you for a short time.

Your affectionate brother-in-law,

As he had that morning, William Clelland again conducted the men's prayer service and with his rich voice led the hymns. He did his best to impart his faith to the others, ending the twice-daily services with sermons of hope.

"Lads, keep up your hearts," Clelland urged. "God is with us. Don't despair. Others have been shut off from the light of day, but in God's own good time they have come out alive. So shall we. The Lord is with us, even here, and great is His Mercy."

Some of the men settled in then to try for sleep. But Quartaroli knew he faced another sleepless night. *Who can sleep in such a bed of naked earth, and with steel rail tracks beneath their back?* For the third straight night he sat up awake.

Tuesday, November 16, 1909

G ray skies shrouded Cherry as lashing winds swooped down
on those who came to bury the remaining eight heroes. The
funerals were conducted under the auspices of the Knights
of Pythias, whose membership in this town had been slashed from
seventy-five men to six by the catastrophe. Knights from the
Seatonville and Spring Valley lodges arrived to flank their bereaved
brothers. Nearly the entire town turned out, gathering in the freez-
ing muddy streets before 10:00 A.M. to walk as one to Ike Lewis's
home, where the bodies of brothers-in-law Ike Lewis and Alex Norberg lay in state.

Inside the tiny wooden home, only the two widowed sisters and
their immediate families were able to crowd beside the flower-
adorned coffins for the service. Outside, men dressed in their Sunday best shifted from foot to foot and women drew their shawls
tighter around their heads. Children shivered in cloth coats while
their little hands turned blue from the cold.

Reverend Killburn, a Congregational minister from Woodstock,
conducted the service for the dead, telling the mourners " . . . in
times like these, words are feeble things. Nothing we can say can
heal the wounds that this catastrophe has caused. We know not why
the Almighty in His wisdom has visited us in this affliction. Some
of us perhaps may turn in the delirium of our sorrow and revile
Him. But in the end we must all turn to Him for that comfort in our
anguish that none but He can give."

As pallbearers carried the coffins down the front stairs, Mrs. Norberg followed with her six-year-old daughter and small son, with Mrs. Lewis, her two daughters and seven-year-old son. The crowd stood back, respectfully baring their heads to the slashing wind. The two widowed sisters were hysterical with grief as the coffins were loaded into carriages headed to Peru for interment. Women in the crowd began to weep with them and Mrs. Lewis's knees buckled. Several men rushed to catch her as she pitched toward the ground.

Before the afternoon funerals of the four miners, Cherry's children gathered in the Congregational church basement for a special lunch. It was hosted by village barber John A. Stenstrum, a big-hearted, baby blue-eyed Swedish immigrant who'd earlier established a boys' club in Cherry. Aided by women volunteers from Arlington, he prepared the first substantial meal the little ones had eaten in more than three days. Several mine officials and rescue workers attended, but Stenstrum was shocked to see fewer little guests at the banquet tables than he'd anticipated.

He soon realized the inclement weather had superseded their hunger—it was too cold to walk over barefooted. Immediately, he sent word to the Red Cross and shoes were quickly dispatched to the homebound children. Newly shod, they came in such droves there weren't enough chairs to go around and they had to eat standing up. The barber, who paid for the entire banquet from his own pocket, charged officials fifty cents each for their meals, then deposited that money in the Cherry Relief Fund. He sloughed off expressions of gratitude, saying the event made him feel good inside.

Just as the third course, a thick beef stew, was served, the footsteps of pallbearers bringing the four caskets into church thudded overhead. Sobs and moans rang through the church as W. W. Newell, Reverend J. G. Brooks, Reverend Thomas Gleason and Dr. J. T. McCollum conducted the service. Graham Taylor delivered the funeral oration, calling the men "glorious martyrs."

"Greater love hath no man for his friend than this that a man lay down his life for his friend. My friends," he said, "the four heroes whom you mourn here died in your cause, in the cause of friendship and in the cause of better mining legislation. These heroes, dying, have left a heritage that will live forever in your town. In years to come your children and your children's children will be as proud of them for the deed they did and for the new mining laws their deaths evoke as they would have been had they died in the field of battle."

The men were buried behind the Catholic church in the plot the coal company had donated as a cemetery. One of the widows fainted repeatedly as her husband's coffin was lowered into its grave.

Cherry residents passed the rest of Tuesday dazed. The shafts remained sealed the entire day as mine inspectors debated their next move. Using physicians' thermometers dangled on string, they took frequent temperature readings of the steam and smoke hissing from the covered shafts. The only reading taken at the air shaft sent the mercury to 93 degrees, but whether inspectors lowered thermometers down to the second vein or took readings directly under the wood coverings at the surface, hoisting shaft temperatures varied by only five degrees, hovering between 110 and 115. This steady, extreme heat precluded any rescue attempts.

Throughout the night workmen assembled a lengthy hose. Sometime after 12:30 P.M., the Ladd Fire Department threaded onto it a perforated nozzle made of two-and-a-half-inch pipe to complete the sprinkler apparatus suggested by the Geological Survey's J. W. Paul and George S. Rice. They suspended it down the middle of the shaft and began shooting water into the mine at a rate of eighty gallons per minute, but the weight of the water and the nozzle kept pulling on the canvas hose, flattening it and reducing the rate of flow. As the smoke continued to billow, choking the firefighters and the volunteers assisting them, mine officials were terrified the fire could burn indefinitely, feeding off the vast, rich stores of coal.

James Steele, mine superintendent for the St. Paul Coal Company, told reporters he abandoned hope for survivors. He believed any man who'd been alive when the shafts were resealed the previous night could not have lived longer than two hours.

"What would kill them so quickly?" reporters asked.

"Black damp," said Steele, who had served as the superintendent of several other mines and worked in mines since he was nine years old. He told them from thirty-three years of experience that within two hours' time, the deadly gas could expand to fill even the farthest recesses of the mine. Reporters then demanded to know why it had been necessary to seal the shafts, since the deadly black damp proliferates when a fire is starved of oxygen.

"Had we left the shafts open, both shafts would have burned out within a few hours and then caved in. That would have sealed the mine for good and we could not have reached the bodies of the dead miners without excavating several hundred feet of earth."

A box containing $19,000 in currency arrived by express during the night. It was guarded by deputies until morning, when bank clerks began disbursing it to miners and to the women presenting the final pay vouchers they'd collected the day before. Despite opposition from many who feared the mix of liquor and emotions, authorities surrendered to the saloonkeepers' persistent requests to open for a few hours on payday. Though state's attorney Lawrence M. Eckert vowed to put them out of business if intoxicated miners caused any disruptions, saloonkeepers poured freely and pocketed a good chunk of the miners' pay. In no time, inebriated men were wandering the streets, shouting curses and threats against mine officials.

Bitterness and grief ran high, with miners and townspeople increasingly restless over the lack of progress. Even Coroner Malm said he was convinced there had been criminal negligence and promised "to put somebody back of the bars." The state's attorney agreed, vowing prompt action if evidence warranted prosecution.

But inspector James Taylor said it was too early to place blame, especially against hoisting engineer John Cowley.

"The engineer in charge of the hoisting apparatus, could not, in view of his license, disobey the signals he got from those on the cage, but that is not the question now. We are here now for the purpose of getting down into the mine, and, if by any chance there are any yet living down there, to aid them. The investigation and placing of the responsibility will have to come later, so therefore I cannot hint at placing the blame."

Early in the day, however, rumors were rampant that Herb Lewis had attacked and injured Cowley. Though these proved untrue, Lewis was warned and Cowley was placed under guard by Sheriff Skoglund and state's attorney Lawrence M. Eckert. They ordered his counterpart, engineer John Raisbeck, to get out of town. Later in the day, when a murder plot against Cowley was discovered, Skoglund and Eckert quietly made arrangements for him to leave Cherry as well.

Vociferously, miners accused the mine company of sealing the shafts to preserve property instead of human life. Penn, a miner for twenty-eight years, was particularly scathing in his criticism not only of the decision to seal the shaft but of the men in charge of the operation, Taylor and Newsam. He was certain the action killed men, since during the first hours of the fire experienced miners would not have rushed to their deaths through smoke and fire to reach the shafts, but instead would have retreated deep into the mine to wait it out. He groused to reporters that men who hadn't worked in a mine for at least twenty-five years had been entrusted with extinguishing the fire and rescuing the men.

Meanwhile, as union official James Powers called for a mass meeting of Cherry miners the following morning to demand state mine inspectors rescue the bodies of the entombed men, authorities feared the miners might vote instead to take matters into their own hands. Rumors already flew that a crowd of men from outside Cherry planned to take over the rescue work and that local men were conspiring to dynamite railroad president A. J. Earling's private sleeping car. Though mine and railroad officials scoffed at these rumors, the sheriff sent deputies to guard the string of sleeping cars and immediately ordered every bit of dynamite and mine powder pulled from the mine storehouses and removed from the county.

When reports of additional threats against the mine company officers, rescue officials and inspectors reached Sheriff Skoglund, he telephoned Governor Deneen in Springfield to insist he summon the militia to help preserve order. Two companies of the Illinois National Guard's Sixth Regiment left in secret for Cherry—Company K of Kewanee, under the command of Captain W. F. Hall, and Company C of Galesburg, under the command of Captain W. F. Latimer.

In vain, Mayor Connelly and local police tried to close up the saloons. With the prevailing mood so volatile, Coroner Malm postponed scheduled testimony before the coroner's jury until the next day. Journalists questioned him about the growing number of reports from survivors who said no one had warned them of the magnitude of the fire and that they watched coal being hoisted out long after the fire began.

"I have reliable information that coal was hauled for nearly two hours after the fire was discovered, but I have no affidavits to this effect," Dr. Malm said. "Because of the feeling against certain employees I deem it advisable to go slow. I want everybody to have a fair show."

By late afternoon, Chief James Horan and the Chicago Fire Department arrived with a fire engine and supplies. It was a record-breaking train trip to Mendota and then on to Cherry, covering eighty-three miles in sixty-two minutes. Horan brought with him Captain Thomas P. Kenny, Lieutenant Patrick E. Smith, engineer George M. McGhie, assistant engineer Bert J. Hester and seven hand-selected pipemen, William D. Shea, Martin A. Loftis, Henry E. Beckstrom, Frank J. O'Connor, Thomas J. Redmond, Michel J. Mc-

Govern and John J. Keegan, plus equipment that included five thousand feet of two-inch hose, five hundred feet of three-inch pipe and thirty-six Babcock extinguishers. A special engine and car from Milwaukee delivered two thousand additional feet of a special type of hose not available in Chicago, bringing hose sent to Cherry to a total of seven thousand feet. Five tank cars waited on the railroad tracks, each holding ten thousand gallons of water.

Earling and W. W. Taylor, exhausted from lack of sleep since their arrival, prevailed on Horan to lead the firefighting efforts. During their preparations, James M. Webb, one of the helmet men, fell under the weight of a heavy pipe he'd tried to lift. For a time doctors thought he'd broken his back, but he'd only sprained it.

The Chicago firefighters decided to withdraw the sprinkler and flood the hoisting shaft with water from the engine's four-inch hose. The fire engine and larger hose enabled them to throw down six hundred gallons per minute, a volume more than seven times the sprinkler's capability. From 4:30 P.M. until 11:30 P.M., when the water was about to give out, they washed ton after ton of water down the shaft. Horan believed this heavy water pressure would have the flames out by the following evening.

"That's all that has been the matter with the fight against the fire so far," Horan said. "The shaft will not be unsealed until I am assured that the fire in the mine is practically extinguished. There is no use sending men into the tunnels until this is done. They would only lose their lives if they attempted to enter the mine under the present circumstances."

Horan refuted reports that the mine company was delaying rescue efforts in order to save the main shaft.

"There is nothing in the stories. As I stated before, no man can enter the mine and live today. The company is not anxious to sacrifice more human lives in this mine."

At 8:30 P.M., J. W. Paul wired the Pennsylvania Geological Survey office: *Express to Cherry Draeger Telephone helmet and attachments.*

Mine afire and temporarily closed, 256 entombed.

During the evening, Pinkerton secret service agents hired by the mine company ran four men out of town. They were suspected to be professional bank robbers plotting to rob the Cherry Bank.

Just after midnight, the first troops arrived and set up their military camp along the railroad tracks. Armed with loaded rifles, they circled the string of sleeping cars with orders to keep all suspicious characters at a distance. Under their protection and the cover of darkness, more than five hundred pounds of explosives removed from mine property earlier in the day were secreted out of Cherry.

Late into the night, nurse Maude McGinnis and two grieving young widows hovered at the bedside of a Lithuanian woman in labor, offering encouragement and caring for her until it was time to call for the doctor. Toward midnight, in a house numb with grief, the first of Cherry's fatherless newborns let out a thin wail.

CHAPTER EIGHTEEN

Tuesday, November 16, 1909
Cherry Mine, Second Vein

The carbide lamp burned throughout the night, but it clearly wouldn't last much longer. The men replaced the charge, which made little difference—the problem was with the air. Terrible thoughts plagued Quartaroli, depriving him of rest.

Morning brought prayer and small sips of putrid water. It was slimy and so vile that the men retched violently the moment it touched their tongues, yet they screwed up the courage to drink those few drops rather than die of thirst. Many times Quartaroli made the rounds in search of water only to discover someone else had already beaten him to it.

Hunger drove the men to gnaw on the leather of their belts, gloves, hatbands and shoes and to chew "sunshine," the wax they burned in their head lamps. After a while it formed into a gum and cleansed the slime from inside their mouths. Some turned to chewing tobacco to alleviate both hunger and thirst but the idea backfired, ratcheting up their thirst once the tobacco was masticated. One of them remembered seeing a young boy chewing on bark and the men peeled it from the pine timbers, then masticated it to a pulp.

By noon the light in the carbide lamp had nearly disappeared. Giacomo Pigati sat near it, writing a few lines to his wife on paper meant to roll the powder cartridges the miners used in the mine. The men stared at the lamp, mesmerized by its flare and flutter and measuring its waning existence against their own. It sputtered and spit and finally leapt into the air with one last gasp, burning out at 1:00 P.M., while Pigati was still writing his Last Will.

> . . . This is the fourth day that we have been down here. That's what I think but our watches have stopped. I am writing in the dark because we have been eating wax from our safety lamps. I also have eaten a plug of tobacco, some bark and some of my shoe. I could only chew it. I hope you can read this. I am not afraid to die. Oh, Holy Virgin, have mercy on me. I think my time has come.
>
> You know what my property is. We worked for it together and it is all yours. This is my will and you must keep it. You have been a good wife. May the Holy Virgin guard you. I hope this reaches you sometime and you can read it.
>
> It has been very quiet down here and I wonder what has become of my comrades. Goodbye until heaven shall bring us together.

The darkness was absolute. One of the men struck a match to relight the wick, but bad air ate the flame before it had a chance to even singe the end of the matchstick. Now their supply of oil and matches was useless. The men took this last defeat as a symbol that death, and freedom from their living hell, was near. They collected all their matches and gave them to one man, delegating him to keep time. Buonfiglio, the youngest, began to crack, sobbing that they had run out of hope. Older voices reached through the dark to encourage him, to encourage them all, but even as Quartaroli echoed the conviction that somebody would have to come to rescue them, his heart did not believe it. It raced in his chest with the terror that he was never getting out of this tomb alive.

The sudden blanket of blindness was a worse torment than the death they were certain was near. Very soon they expected that black damp would smother them. The loss of even the basics—the ability to see one another's faces, to move around safely or even know the time—brought a profound sense of isolation and despair.

They listened to the frantic gasps of their fifty-year-old asthmatic comrade with pity for him and terror for themselves. Their fear that the air-starved Slav wasn't going to make it just barely exceeded their fear that they would soon die the same way.

We would be better off losing our lives than to suffer like this, Quartaroli thought. At that moment he would have given all the gold in the world to fall asleep and never awaken. When at last everyone was quiet, he threw himself to the ground and prayed for sleep to overtake him.

CHAPTER NINETEEN

Wednesday, November 17, 1909

The residents of Cherry awoke under siege. Armed troops were everywhere. Khaki-garbed National Guardsmen ringed the immediate vicinity of the shafts, keeping families a distance from the officials and volunteer rescuers. They guarded the train cars. They patrolled the main streets and business district and even the road leading out of town.

Shock and disbelief was followed by an alarm that quickly turned to anger. As protests grew more vocal, officials began to fear that words would quickly be followed by direct action.

While the state mining officials debated the wisdom of unsealing the mine and sending men down to retrieve bodies, Coroner Malm engaged several hundred men to help him erect the large, white canvas circus tent he would use as the morgue. With the tent roped into place, he began outfitting it with stretchers, canvasses, coffins and anything else he would need.

Though not one of them had ever set foot inside a coal mine, the Chicago firefighters were antsy to get down into the fire to tackle it head on. Chief Horan took their pleas to be allowed into the mine to the officials. Superintendent Taylor told him he admired the firemen's bravery but felt nothing could be accomplished except the useless sacrifice of their lives.

At 9:45 A.M., Professor Williams took a temperature reading in the hoisting shaft—115 degrees, still too dangerously high. Next he and three other officials tested for gases escaping from the second vein by holding a Wolff safety lamp to the engine room speaking tube. Gas came whistling out under pressure and extinguished the lamp. Two of the men detected a minuscule indication of inflammable gas, lower than 1 percent, but the other two could not substantiate these findings. Knowing all of this, Williams concluded that no one could enter the mine and live.

The coal company called a conference of all the mine officials and inspectors to determine the next course of action. The group elected Glen W. Traer of the Illinois Mining Investigation Commission to chair the proceedings and elected two secretaries to record the participants' opinions. Traer began by recapping events from 1:00 P.M. Saturday to the present, then asked mining engineer Robert Maxwell to produce plats of the mine so that everyone present was familiar with its configuration.

"Gentlemen," he said, "there must be a prompt decision made for some definite action and the situation is so serious that it requires the combined judgment of all of these men present."

The first question put to a vote was whether to send men with helmets into the hoisting shaft without starting the fan. Owing to the high temperatures recorded earlier that morning, it was quickly and unanimously opposed. The next question, however, spurred intense debate. George S. Rice, mining engineer with the U.S. Geological Survey, suggested starting the fan as slowly as it could run without removing the cover on the hoisting shaft, and to then observe the temperatures in both shafts.

When some voiced concern that this would not only intensify the fire, but might even trigger a mine explosion, the coal company officials went on record saying that they didn't care what happened to the mine property so long as the efforts led to the recovery of the miners' bodies. The company officials said they did not want the question of damage to property to color or control any member's vote.

Rice pushed his proposal for cooling the hoisting shaft. At present, he said, fresh air was leaking into the air shaft, passing over the fire and coming up through the hoisting shaft, creating pressure there. The resulting column of heated air in the hoisting shaft made it impossible to send men down. He advised the men that turning on the fan would change the air current and suck any air leaking from the hoisting shaft back in to cool it. If his plan caused the air shaft to heat up or catch fire, he believed water flooded down the air shaft would remedy the situation.

He acknowledged that starting the fan would pull any gases in the mine back over the fire and that if these were combustible gases an explosion might ensue.

"In this case, I would see no alternative but to cover up the shafts permanently and wait until the fires are cooled enough to open same."

If his plan did reduce hoisting shaft temperatures, Rice proposed building an air lock over the shaft so helmeted men could take hoses down to fight the fire without admitting much oxygen.

"If this plan is not followed, under conditions which now pertain, I see no possible way but to seal the shafts for some months until they have cooled off. I think the present stoppings cannot be made tight and we would have to concrete and very carefully puddle down below the frame."

Illinois mine inspector John Dunlop was the first to voice opposition, citing a similar case in which the mine exploded. "The bodies have never been got out," he said. "I would vote no."

Although some of them did so reluctantly, nearly half the men agreed with Rice, saying that every reasonable effort should be made to get out the bodies. A number of them even discounted fears of the mine exploding. J. W. Paul of the U.S. Geological Survey felt Rice's idea was their sole hope for saving the only shaft through which they'd be able to accomplish anything.

Many pressed for sealing the mine permanently. A number of the group agreed with Dunlop, citing several mine explosions that occurred recently under similar circumstances. In one where the bodies were never recovered, flames shot up one hundred and fifty feet above the eighty-five-foot tower and scorched an adjacent meadow. In another, where an assay showed only 1 percent explosive gas, the mine blew after the fan had turned just a few revolutions.

Hector McAllister, an Illinois mine inspector, was afraid that reversing the fan would cause more of the mine to catch fire. "We don't know how far the fire is in the main shaft, but if it is reversed it will go over the timbers again and set more of them on fire. We know that will occur when you reverse the current and probably destroy the escapement shaft," he said. "Then, if this is destroyed, we might as well seal it up. Therefore, I vote no."

George Harrison, chief mine inspector of Ohio, asked to refrain from voting. He'd been sent by his state's governor as an observer to gain knowledge that might help prevent similar occurrences in Ohio. He did say he felt the proposition was too risky and that an explosion would not only destroy the mine property, but cremate the bodies they were trying to secure.

Illinois mine inspector James Taylor, who'd gone down with oxygen and helmet, made an impassioned speech against starting the fan. He suggested they could just as easily cool the hoisting shaft by taking a hose down the air shaft and fighting the fire without using the fan. He also said he'd seen no case yet in Illinois where a fire had been smothered by permanently sealing up the shafts.

"We have one shaft that is not on fire, now don't let us set that shaft on fire again," he said. "Let's get down the shaft that is not on fire and fight the fire. That would obviate the possibility of an explosion by not passing the gases over the flame, and I am ready to risk my life and I feel we ought to do something and do it now. We have the fire department here, we have the water here, and it seems to me that by concentrated effort at this time we can put that fire out inside of two days.

"If we are going to make this mine the grave of these fellows, we might as well erect a monument over it now, then seal it up, but I think at this time, with the temperature showing as it does, the escapement shaft is our only salvation—and for God's sake, don't reverse the fan, for you will blow up that mine and you will undoubtedly kill men on the surface, and we don't want to do that."

J. M. Webb said he didn't feel much like expressing his opinion. He made only a brief comment: "I am very much opposed to trying to go down that air shaft as I have been making attempts before. If you go down that air shaft now, my opinion is that the smoke would be so dense that a man could not see anything whatever, and after twenty-four hours, I believe we can go down as we went down before and extinguish that fire. I am quite sure that if Tom Moses and I and another man can go down, we can put out that fire. We put out a similar fire at Moweka a short time ago. I am not afraid to go down, but on this proposition I vote no."

Richard Newsam, in charge of the rescue operation, opposed Rice's idea. With 94-degree readings in the air shaft and 115 in the hoisting shaft, he was certain the coal itself had caught fire. "If the temperature in the main shaft is 115 degrees and the bottom of the shaft is on fire, what is there to prevent it from exploding if you put oxygen in there? What is there to stop it?

"And at 95 degrees I am advised that it is even too much for the helmets—85 degrees is all a man can go down on, and then he can do no work. I want to say here that the helmet men I have talked with will prove my statement, and I don't think I have said a word that hasn't been said to me. It is very nice for us to say that we will go down that shaft and we will put out that fire. We have said that several times and we have failed, and we are up against a condition now and we must be firm in it.

"I want to put out that fire. Don't say you are going to go down and put it out and not do it. Stay with it."

He talked about the smoke coming up the escape shaft, proof that something was burning. Would rescuers burn up there too? He talked about opening up the hoisting shaft and starting the fan. Would that more than likely cause an explosion? Before he finished, Newsam adamantly relinquished all responsibility for further loss of life if Rice's plan was adopted.

"That is the question you must consider. I will stay with you and I will go with you," he said. "But I want to say right here that I will vote no on that question. I want to be relieved of all responsibility after I have voted no. If there are any more lives lost at this mine, I want to be relieved of that responsibility and if the men that have brought this up, if a life is lost, I want him to assume that responsibility."

Their debate lasted the entire morning. Before the conference recessed at noon, the members moved that Traer appoint a committee to take temperature readings at the tops and bottoms of both shafts and report back with their findings at 3:30 P.M.

During the morning hours consuls from Austria, France, Germany, Italy and Russia arrived in Cherry to visit with their nationals and assess their situations. Busiest among the diplomats was the Italian consul, Guido Sabetta. He was overwhelmed by the suffering of the numerous Italian widows and orphans, and said that many were dying of grief and loneliness. Most, dependent on their husbands' wages, despaired of the future.

"They are just beginning to realize what this means to them," he said, offering several remedies. "The Italian government has decided to pay the railroad and steamship fare of all those unfortunate widows back to their native country if they desire to go. If not, I shall see that these poor women are given employment in the near future and are placed in such a position that they can properly raise their children." Only one decided to return home.

National Red Cross director Ernest P. Bicknell, whose first association with the Red Cross came during the 1906 San Francisco earthquake, found the relief problem at Cherry much bigger than he'd anticipated. The immediate aid they were dispensing was only short term. Permanent relief would also have to be assessed and provided. To expedite distribution of relief items and reduce the confusion and complaints fielded during the first days of the disaster, he and Sherman C. Kingsley of the United Charities of Chicago adopted an index card system to collect and file information on the needs of each family.

The nearly one hundred women crowded into the relief commission offices seeking help grew increasingly impatient and balked at the questions put to them. Some made unreasonable demands for aid. Others mistakenly feared that because they'd collected their spouse's final pay, they would be given nothing. Although the most urgent cases were handled with minimum red tape, it took time for the distressed families to understand they would not be denied food and clothing, but that rules and procedures were necessary.

As funds poured into relief coffers, Chicago entertainers scheduled benefit performances and opera houses, theaters and actors' unions across the country followed suit. Spurred on by *The Tribune*, Chicagoans found countless ways to donate to the relief efforts—from the dollar sent to the newspaper by "a widow," to five dollars from the Saratoga Hotel, to the $41.25 the Cook County Teachers Association collected, to the one hundred contribution boxes placed in its principal stores by the North Avenue Businessmen's Association.

In the meantime, after spending much of the day with deputy coroner W. I. Kendall and state's attorney Lawrence M. Eckert, interviewing rescued miners and others familiar with the mine's inner workings, Coroner Malm decided not to proceed until public sentiment had calmed.

"There will be no dearth of witnesses once the inquest is resumed," he said, "and I don't expect difficulty in arriving at the truth. There

will be censure, and in all likelihood something else for those responsible. The public mind is too inflamed to think of resuming the inquest now, and furthermore, it would be impossible to secure a hall
large enough for all the witnesses who would insist on attending."

Realizing that a lengthy inquest on three hundred bodies would
be cost prohibitive, Bureau County taxpayers appealed to Eckert to
try to keep expenses down. Though state law allowed each of the six
jurors one dollar in pay per body, per session, Eckert did not believe
the jurors would be so unreasonable as to demand three hundred
dollars for each of the twenty anticipated sessions.

Two representatives of the Carnegie Hero Fund Commission also arrived in Cherry during the day. F. M. Wilmot and W. R. Harris came
to investigate the rescuers' acts of bravery and assist with the relief
work.

Later in the day, the Illinois State Mining Commission determined it would not conduct an investigation to place blame for the
catastrophe. The commission, comprised of three miners, three
mine operators and three qualified but impartial men, had existed
only since July 1909. Telegrams flew between commission members
and Governor Deneen, with Professor Graham Taylor calling for a
rigid investigation to allocate responsibility and Richard Newsam
charging that such a legal investigation was not within the commission's realm. In his dispatch, Glen W. Traer agreed.

"I do not think we have the power to do that," he wrote. "We were
appointed by the legislature to investigate mine accidents with the
idea of recommending changes in the law which will cut down the
number of such accidents and render mining safer."

                    *   *   *

Outside temperatures hovered between 35 and 39 degrees during the
afternoon. When the officials reconvened, the report on shaft temperatures was the first item on their agenda. Readings at the bottom of
the air shaft were 58 and 60 degrees, while the hoisting shaft regis-

tered 107 at the bottom and 114 at the top. The discrepancy in the temperatures of two shafts just several hundred feet apart led officials to speculate that a cave-in had occurred somewhere between them, blocking fire and heat from reaching the air shaft. Chairman Traer asked if this information induced conferees to alter their morning votes, which had yet to be tallied and announced. They said it did not.

Then Traer suggested they suspend announcing the vote on Rice's original proposition to start the fan slowly and send helmet men down the hoisting shaft and consider instead a vote on sending helmet men down the air shaft. Rice asked for another statement from the men who'd already been down the air shaft, since he'd made his proposal under the general assumption that the air shaft was burned out and in dangerous condition.

Williams told officials that he and the others who'd gone down had been unable to see anything in that shaft due to smoke: "The only examination we could make there was by sense of feeling. The timbers seemed pretty well burned. And strangely, the timbers at the bottom did not seem to be burned, but when we started toward the top they seemed in pretty bad shape.

"I think there is enough air in there now so that we might not need helmets at all," he added. "It might be feasible, if safe to enter the shaft at all, to send first the helmets and subsequently act without helmets."

The final motion—"that the air shaft be opened and an attempt be made by men to go down with helmets"—was put to vote. Agreement was nearly unanimous, with two no votes and one abstention by Ohio Mining Commission member Percy Tetlow, who said, "I don't like to say that men could go down when I would not perhaps be one of the men that go down. I think that question should be left to the men who use the buckets."

By 9:00 P.M. they'd decided to send two helmet men down the air shaft in a bucket in the first descent since Sunday. The geologists were willing, but all five Geological Survey members were opposed to using a bucket. They urged mine officials to build a float or temporary elevator cage, arguing that a bucket was small, they'd have to be tied in, precluding them from exploring, and their helmets were too restrictive for bucket work. Unwieldy and fixed in place, helmets limited their line of vision to about 45 degrees vertically and horizontally, forcing the men to swing their entire bodies from side to side in order to inspect their surroundings. The geologists feared risking their lives just to glean scant more information than they'd already obtained lowering a thermometer down the shaft.

But the mine officials dispensed with the float idea. It was a bucket or nothing.

A great crowd gathered to watch by torch and lantern light as J. W. Paul supervised the operation. He still held hope of finding survivors. In 1906, he'd visited a mine in Courrieres, France, shortly after twenty-five of the twelve hundred men entombed there came out alive after three weeks.

Paul stood at the mouth of the shaft as George S. Rice and R. Y. Williams were tied into the thirty-six-inch-diameter bucket and lowered just below the mouth of the shaft to complete the tying-in process. But Rice outweighed Williams by seventy pounds, causing the bucket to tip markedly. Coupled with the added bulk of their oxygen apparatus, it became impossible for them to guide the bucket clear of the obstructions the helmet men had previously encountered. Geological inspector Thomas Morris, whose weight was nearer to Williams's, volunteered to take Rice's place.

Before dropping three hundred feet into the abyss, Morris and Williams composed final letters to their loved ones and asked that they be delivered in the event of their deaths.

Rice took charge, making sure that the two men were able to handle the precarious bucket. The crowd waited, their tense faces bathed in torchlight, until the men were hauled up again. Though neither left the bucket, they were nearly exhausted and had to be revived with stimulants.

"There is a great deal of gas down there, and it appears there has been a cave-in," Williams reported. "Whether it is between the air shaft and the main bore, I do not know. However, conditions are good for a genuine attempt at rescue tomorrow. We saw no bodies, and I don't believe there are any near the entrance of the tunnels."

Following this successful descent, conference members reconvened to plan a rescue attempt for the following day. This time Rice convinced mine officials to build them a float. Shortly before midnight, A. J. Earling called all carpenters, mechanics and other employees from their beds to begin building both a float in the air shaft and a small tower or head frame over it. Plans were for the crew to complete these by 4:00 A.M. so that helmet men could go down with picks and shovels to dig through any cave-ins blocking the tunnels leading to the hoisting shaft. Working through the night, they were to clear the tunnels by morning so that rescue teams could go in to retrieve the bodies and bring them up via the hoisting shaft.

As the men set to work on the float, Sheriff Skoglund again asked Captain Hall to station sentries around the mine and around the railroad cars where officials, nurses and newspapermen slept. And although the saloons had already closed for the night, he wanted Hall's soldiers standing outside them in the morning to make certain they didn't reopen.

"I realize that conditions here in Cherry are precarious at present," Hall told reporters. "Probably the worst will be when they begin taking the bodies of the entombed miners from the shaft. Then we will come in handy in keeping the crowd back and preventing any riot."

CHAPTER TWENTY

Wednesday, November 17, 1909
Cherry Mine, Second Vein

The men spent a cold and fitful night huddled together, several of them writhing in a delirious sleep. Moaning from head and stomach pain, they called out for food, for water, for escape.

Quartaroli teetered at the threshold of sleep, jolting back the second one of the others moved, jostling the rest. So weak he could barely walk, he was on needles and pins, convinced he was near death.

By morning, he and two others stumbled off seeking a humid spot to dig more holes for water. Though hope of ever seeing sunlight again had long faded, their new plan was to win or die in the attempt. Going this way and that, they finally found a small humid spot and made a small hole. Hindered by the dark, they dug too deeply and the water that collected was scarce. The men could barely touch it with the tips of their tongues and often couldn't reach it at all, driving them mad to be so thirsty and so close.

When he could reach the mositure, Quartaroli was grateful just to wet his lips. He drank it down, coal and all, then threw it up again.

Clelland continued to reassure the men with encouragement and prayer. Even in these dire straits he drew on his sense of humor, sneaking around in the dark to steal a sleeping comrade's shoes and carry them off to some distant corner. For brief stretches, his practical jokes kept them too busy feeling around for their shoes to feel the depth of their own sufferings.

Thomas White stared into an inky darkness he hoped never to know again. The only thing to penetrate it was Walter Waite's voice, periodically calling each man by name, making sure all of them were still together and asking how they were doing. But gloom and despair reigned supreme. They'd already eaten the sunshine from their lamps, gnawed the leather from their belts and shoes, licked the floors and walls for water and even torn their clothing to chew at the threads. Some of them answered it was better to die at once than to continue this unbearable life.

"Be patient and withstand this suffering. We will return to hug our loved ones again," Waite replied.

Quartaroli listened to Waite's words with skepticism.

He says this with his mouth, but if I were able to go into his mind, I am sure that he too thinks like all of us, he thought.

CHAPTER TWENTY-ONE

Thursday, November 18, 1909

Word of a new attempt to breach the mine via the air shaft shot through town, sending families streaming to the shaft before dawn. They huddled, watching as the men completed work on the float by torchlight. As the morning progressed, National Guard soldiers had their hands full, repelling the crowds that repeatedly broke through the rope restraints to get nearer to the shafts.

After a lengthy conference, officials and Chief Horan decided to partially unseal the main shaft and flood it with water to snuff out the flames encroaching at the second vein. From late morning until early afternoon, the Chicago firefighters poured ton after ton of water into the mine. Horan, in the lead position, told his men they'd soon get their chance to meet that fire face-to-face.

Construction on the float and air lock took all night and the entire morning. By noon, workers had cut away the air shaft's reinforced concrete roof and set the float in position, but the head frame was still not completed. Rather than delay their descent, geological inspectors Rice, Paul and Williams used a canvas to cover the top of the shaft while they went down in oxygen tanks and helmets. Using an automobile horn to signal, they descended into a slight haze at 1:20 P.M. The air cleared as they went lower and the men were able to inspect the shaft lining for damage. Responding to signals from the auto horns, engineers stopped the cage at the second vein and the inspectors were able to get off to investigate.

A heavy roof fall blocked the northwest side of the shaft, leaving an opening only two feet high by three feet wide, so Paul headed off to explore the southwest bottom. He stumbled on a charred body just a few feet from the shaft. The men spotted others about seventy feet away.

After about thirty-five minutes they rang to ascend. On the way up, they again inspected the shaft lining. It was in better condition than they'd expected. The water ring in the upper shaft was overflowing and keeping the lining timbers soaked. While the uppermost thirty feet were deeply fire-scarred and a narrower band of deeply scorched timber rimmed the shaft directly above the second vein, the upper shaft's middle section had suffered only superficial damage.

The rescuers emerged pale and shaken, saying that the bodies they'd seen were swollen and scorched.

"The sight of the men huddled about the shaft almost made me sick," Williams said. "I hate to think of what we'll find back in the mine and on the third vein."

The team reported that damage in the shaft wasn't serious enough to weaken the timbers or to prevent work from the float. They also suggested inserting a hose and spray nozzle through the hole in the rubble from the roof fall to prevent flames from reentering the air shaft.

State mine inspectors Moses, Taylor and McAllister donned helmets and went down to retrieve the single body, taking the hose and sprinkler with them. When they came up, their safety lamps were still burning, proof that fresh air was going down the main shaft.

The first body they brought up was kept concealed under the canvas for more than an hour until word leaked out and the body was released to the undertaker. As the ambulance made its way to the tent, the news raced through Cherry. Soldiers could barely hold back the rush of women running alongside the ambulance, fighting to get a glimpse of the corpse. They charged the tent and the coroner had to call for guards to haul back these anxious relatives who peered intently into the victim's twisted features, looking for something recognizable.

"He must have exerted every ounce of strength he possessed to reach the air shaft," inspector Paul said of the unidentified miner. "The position of the body indicated he'd put forth a supreme effort to reach air. His trousers were threadbare about the knees and his hands had been blistered, showing he'd crawled some distance."

The prevailing hysteria persuaded officials to wait for cover of darkness to remove the other bodies. Coroner Malm requested they be brought to the morgue twenty-five at a time and placed in caskets to await identification. Then he'd summon back the jury he'd impaneled to view the bodies, a task they would have to repeat countless times. After releasing each group to relatives for burial, he'd request another twenty-five bodies raised.

Relatives anxious to reclaim their dead surged about the shaft long after officials told them it might take eighteen hours to dig through the roof fall to reach the huddle of bodies they expected to find there. Officials had a hard time convincing the impatient populace that no additional bodies would be brought out that night.

A newsman from the *Bureau County Tribune* scribbled some notes for his report: *Fear that widows will be uncontrollable when they begin to raise dead in large numbers. Hardy characters. Behave not like most women. Desire to see their dead cannot be controlled.*

Despite the National Guard presence, rumblings against mine bosses persisted. As one of the foremen, Thomas Davis, walked down Main Street after supper a man sprang at him from an alley with a stiletto raised to strike. In that split second Sheriff Skoglund passed by. Instantly he was on the attacker and wrested the weapon from his hand. He hauled the brooding man, an Italian miner, to city hall for interrogation. Attributing the assassination attempt to grief, Skoglund extracted the miner's promise to leave town immediately, then released him.

Shaken, Davis asked Mayor Connelly for protection, fearing other miners would make good on their threats against his life.

As darkness settled over Cherry, ending the fifth day since the accident occurred, officials again took hoisting shaft temperatures and tested for any deadly gases. To cheers, Newsam told firefighters they could finally enter the main shaft.

"Boys, we can make a descent into that mine and see what the condition is and bring some of the bodies, perhaps, to the surface, and rescue the living if there are any down there."

Workers immediately began unsealing the main shaft and soon it was belching gas and smoke. To reduce temperatures further, firemen plied water down the shaft while engineers started the fan in reverse to suck in cold air. Since the fan could be run at just one third its regular speed, they knew it would take time to push black damp from the mine.

Before allowing any of them to step onto the ill-fated hoisting cage, doctors quickly examined the Ladd and Chicago firemen who rushed forward to volunteer. After signals were rehearsed to prevent fatal misunderstandings, the unhelmeted firemen were slowly lowered into the shaft. Carrying three hundred feet of hose, they attacked the fire at the second vein.

Working in shifts of five and returning frequently to the surface for fresh air, the firemen took turns battling the blaze. They were overcome time and again by smoke and flame, keeping doctors and nurses busy. Throughout the night they fought from the north side of the cage, unable to step off onto the second vein bottom because of fire still raging on the south and east sides of the shaft.

It appeared the blaze had been concentrated in the pump room and stables area and in the east bottom overhead timbers, which collapsed. West of this area there was no evidence of fire. An attempt to tunnel through the east fall failed. Tumbling rock made it dangerous, especially since it was so close to the shaft.

As flames smoldering beneath the roof fall grew active, firemen hit them with powerful streams. They fought flames in the tunnel leading to the air shaft. Eventually they won, beating back the red fury.

Before the evening was out, the first victim raised from the second vein was identified. It was Ole Freiburg, the thirty-three-year-old unmarried third vein cager who'd helped William A. Smith and John Brown douse the fire on the burning hay cart.

Back in the Long Row that night, Robert Deans opened the door of his grieving sister's home and let in a man Jessie Love had never seen before. Of the six family members Jessie had seen off to the mine last Saturday, only her two brothers, Bobby and Alex, had escaped the fire. Her husband, John, and his brothers, Morrison, James and David, were still trapped in the mine.

Afraid for his life since the first night of the fire, Bobby hadn't stepped foot from her house in nearly a week. Now she watched him pace, talking with a stranger who abruptly ended the conversation every time she entered the room. A short time later, when Bobby got in the stranger's automobile and sped out of Cherry, she was convinced the mine company had spirited him out of town.

CHAPTER TWENTY-TWO

Thursday, November 18, 1909
Cherry Mine, Second Vein

A ntenore Quartaroli lived through a night more horrible than he ever could have imagined. Salvatore Pigati grew increasingly disturbed as one or another of the men asked him the time. The matches were long gone, so he'd removed the glass from his pocket watch and approximated the time by running his fingers across the hands.

Quartaroli was growing increasingly disturbed with George Stimez, who worked in the same entry with him. Quartaroli noticed Stimez returning often to that area, staying there for ten minutes at a time. Nearly insane with thirst, he asked Stimez if he'd found water there. Stimez denied it. At first Quartaroli accepted it, since his own forays with Giacomo Pigati had never turned up water. But finally, he decided to investigate for himself.

Next to the coal face he found a shallow hole holding nearly half a glass of water. He put his mouth to it and swallowed it down in a single gulp. It was filthy and it stunk, but to Quartaroli it tasted like marsala wine.

With renewed hope of finding more water, he returned to the group and entreated the Pigati brothers to help him search. They walked from one area to another until Quartaroli discovered a hole containing nearly a glass of water in the entry where brothers Ruggeri and Gaetano Buonfiglio worked. He called Giacomo to drink. Giacomo was so confused, he couldn't make it on his own, so Quartaroli led him to the water to help revive him.

"In all my time searching by myself, I have never drunk so much water," Pigati told him. He'd barely finished half. It was the only new source of water the men found all day.

The strain finally became too much for one of the foreign-born miners. Periodically he'd start chattering on and on in his native tongue, keeping the babble going for hours on end. Finally Thomas White asked one of the man's countrymen what he was saying. The man had no idea.

"His mind snapped. Not a word of it makes sense to me either."

Throughout, Walter Waite worked to keep the miners' courage up, even when his own was failing him.

"We are better off than those on top, for we know we are alive and they don't know it," he'd say one time. Another, he'd urge them not to give up. "We are going to give those people up there the very biggest surprise they ever had yet."

With hopes that a rescue team might be searching for them, the men divided themselves into groups of two to five and took turns standing watch at second west. Quartaroli took his shift with Salvatore Pigati and Francesco Zanarini. Fiercely thirsty, he left the others to search for water, stumbled down a new road and became lost. He had to call to his friends to find him and lead him back.

They returned from their shift to find George Stimez arguing with the others. He was ready to tear down the wall and go out. Loudly, they fought with him for more than an hour, nearly strangling Stimez before convincing him of the folly of his plan.

Still believing a hand from heaven would reach down into hell to give them a ray of hope, the men joined together in their evening prayer. To Quartaroli, that moment, that ray seemed so far away. Unsure it would ever arrive, he fought for hope.

CHAPTER TWENTY-THREE

Friday, November 19, 1909

At 2:00 A.M., with firemen still in the hoisting shaft fighting the fire, an alarm rang out that the air shaft had ignited again. An official ordered the fan stopped, forcing the firemen to flee the shaft as fumes and smoke overtook them. The alarm proved false.

Sunrise brought missing miners' families back from neighboring towns, bracing themselves to view the first bodies removed. The curious soon followed by special trains, autos, carriages and on foot. Throughout the day firemen, U.S. Geological Survey inspectors and state mine inspectors risked their lives to roam the entries, dodging rock falls and picking their way over bloated, decaying bodies of mules and men. The temperatures were cool, but black damp still hung heavy as the air current slowly pushed it out.

They discovered four badly burned bodies in one entry and brought them up, triggering another scene of pandemonium. Upon seeing the charred corpses and realizing what horrors these men must have suffered as they died, women shrieked and fainted and men sobbed openly. The children in the crowd recoiled in terror and dogs ran alongside yapping, barking and howling as the relatives rushed to the morgue.

Once the coroner examined and tagged each body, relatives began the unbearably ghastly task of identification. Pitifully, one holding up another, they faltered from one gruesome cadaver to another, peering closely into faces eaten away by fire.

Suddenly, a woman's screams ended abruptly as she fainted across a body charred beyond recognition. Minutes later Mrs. Patrick Dobbins regained consciousness. She leaned on the arm of a friend, trembling and pointing.

"Oh, my God!" she cried in anguish. "It is Charlie, my brother, my dear, good brother, dead, dead forever."

It was night examiner Charles Waite, who'd gone down to the second vein just minutes before the fire exploded there. His sister knew him by the peculiar button she had sewn on his shirt just a week earlier. With tears streaming down her face, she looked at the other corpses, wondering if she'd find her brother, Walter, and brother-in-law next. Overwhelmed, she fainted again. With a physician and nurses on their heels, soldiers hurried her to the ambulance and sent her home.

Mrs. Kroll and her young daughter yielded to grief as they identified two of the bodies as Henry and Alfred Kroll, the father and son John Lorimer and Walter Waite fought to save. Just the day before the fatal fire, Mrs. Kroll had begged her husband yet again not to take their son with him into the mine. Young Alfred had sacrificed his own life to remain with his stricken father. The pair were found in the passage to the air shaft, clasped in each other's arms.

Mule driver George McMullen, whose young wife got to the morgue just as his body was carried in, was the other victim. The twenty-three-year-old father of two had escaped with his brother, Hugh, but had gone back down to try to save his wife's father and brother. Shrieking, Mary McMullen flailed her arms above her head.

"Oh, George, my George, speak to me, speak to me! This is killing me!"

She fainted into the arms of his brother, but instantly recovered and began battling her way into the morgue, throwing off two soldiers who tried to restrain her. Only the combined strength of her brother-in-law and two other determined men was able to drag her howling and thrashing from the morgue.

After the bodies were removed from their canvasses and placed in rough coffins, the families took them home. Dr. Malm said he anticipated many of the victims would be impossible to identify. Those he would hold for only twenty-four hours, and he expected a representative from the state board of health to arrive the next day to supervise disposal of all the bodies taken from the mine. (For a detailed list of victims and survivors, see Appendix A, Article 2.)

J.W. Paul, who'd returned to his wife and children in Pittsburgh, wired Rice: *Endeavor to secure blood samples of bodies in different parts of the mine.*

With the fire out and retrieval work well underway, most of the state mine inspectors also decided it was safe to return to their respective districts, where they were urgently needed. Likewise, geological inspector Thomas Morris headed back to Pittsburgh.

Clearing one pair of entries at a time, rescue teams shoveled through death and debris under the direction of state inspectors Harrison and Taylor, who left the mine only for meals. It was grisly work. Many bodies were swollen and unscorched. Fire had not touched them. Water that had poured in to squelch the flames had boiled, cooking them instead.

Groups of bodies, about eighty men in total, were found behind a number of the trap doors and along the entries. Deeper in the mine teams spotted a huge heap of bodies, men, boys and mules tangled together.

Although chloride solutions were used liberally as a disinfectant, the stench of rotting animals nearly felled rescue workers. The stretcher bearers had to wear nose pieces stuffed with wet sponges. As a group of them lugged four bodies to the hoist, the roof above them suddenly cracked loudly and began to crumble. They were about two hundred and fifty feet from the shaft when the lead man shouted.

"Drop the bodies and run for your lives! Get out or we'll all be buried alive!"

Seconds after the four of them dashed to safety the roof gave way, crashing several tons of rock and timber onto the bodies.

Although they'd seen many more dead deep in the entries, rescuers abandoned retrieval efforts for the day. The fire had finally been extinguished, but continuing rock falls, water-filled entries and blocked tunnels made the work dangerous.

"The bringing out of the bodies necessarily will be slow," Taylor said to reporters. "In fact, I do not expect it to be completed before Sunday or Monday."

First, officials planned to bring up the sixty dead mules whose carcasses were blocking the passageways, impeding the recovery work. They ordered construction of a special car to hoist them out the following morning.

As relief workers cared for the families' immediate needs, the Red Cross's Bicknell worried about their future. Complete figures were not yet in, but he put the estimate of orphans under twelve at thirteen hundred. Several families had ten little ones, none able to help support themselves or their widowed mothers. Since the disaster, eight newborns had arrived, nearly all of them to widowed mothers.

"The problem of taking care of all these children will be a big one," Bicknell said. "The relief work is now being done systematically. No one is allowed to go hungry if we know about it. The future, however, is staring us in the face. How are the widows and orphans going to get through the winter? It will take every cent that is contributed to prevent the suffering and want that may come."

Relief funds had swelled beyond $33,000, and letters containing from fifty cents to five dollars arrived daily at Mayor Connelly's office. Five-year-old Ladon Gallie of Chicago robbed her piggy bank of every cent and donated the 239 pennies to help the Cherry orphans. Her gift received so much attention, the little girl decided to organize a relief society among her playmates.

Still more entertainment benefits were held, including plays, minstrel shows, a performance by the Chicago Philharmonic Orchestra and an illustrated lecture on Italian earthquakes.

Mayor Connelly received numerous letters offering to adopt orphans from families outside Cherry. One Kansas farmer wrote him:

> I have a big farm, 320 acres, and no family. This terrible mine disaster has touched my heart and I feel as if I should do something for the women and children who are left. If it is possible, I would like to give a home to some poor woman and her children here on the farm. She could superintend the housework and I would raise the children just as if they were my own. If you know any that would like this proposition, please let me know.

Another Kansas farmer, H. Sanford, was more blunt:

> If you will pick out a widow with two or three children that are good looking and smart children and their mother is an American and she can sing so as her children can learn to sing and play, I would take them if she will do the work, as I haven't any family and I love children. I have a good house and 160 acres farm, and if she will do what is right I'll send the children to school and clothe her and the children, treat them all just like they were my own and love her too. I want her for companionship and to help me do the work. We own our farm, and would give a deserving woman a good home. I am not particular about the ages of the children, only would like for one to be ten to twelve years old, so they could milk two or three cows. We only milk one now, but with that much family we would have to have more milk and butter. So give one of them a chance for a good home. We have an eight room house; the dining room is fourteen by twenty. So we would get along fine. I hope to get a favorable reply.

Connelly also received the following letter from a Missouri woman:

> I am 45 years old and unmarried. I live at home, in the country, and I would like to get two small boys to come and live with me. I will be a mother to them and will see that they get every advantage in education and in youthful training. I write this letter because I think maybe there are some bereaved families in Cherry who can afford to give up two of their children. The mothers can see them whenever they wish.

Duncan McDonald, District 12 president of the United Mine Workers Union, received a letter from an eastern man. The machinist enclosed photographs of his machine shop and machines and asked McDonald to select a wife for him. In an era when more than a thousand European women a year sailed to the U.S. looking for husbands, this variation on a "mail-order bride" would not have been viewed as unusual or insensitive.

At nightfall, miners began replacing the shaft's burned timbers while debris removal continued. Following a conference in which they determined the situation was in sufficiently capable hands, seven of the state mining inspectors returned to their homes.

Since order prevailed throughout the day, Chief Hall felt comfortable reducing the soldiers' armament. He commanded them to report for duty the following morning without their guns but wearing sheathed bayonets.

CHAPTER TWENTY-FOUR

Friday, November 19, 1909
Cherry Mine, Second Vein

Quartaroli dragged his way slowly to nine north, number one, where two small holes had been yielding a meager amount of water. His good friend, Thomas White, was already there waiting for some to bubble up. The two wished each other a good morning and then Quartaroli asked his friend what he thought of their imprisonment. White was silent a while before he answered.

"Today, I think, is Friday. In England they say that Friday is a day that brings good luck. In my condition, I think that we are at the extreme and can't resist much longer, but I hope that today something new and good will happen and this thought gives me the strength to keep on fighting until death."

Quartaroli sighed. "The Italians consider Friday a day that brings misfortune, and I would be very content if I had died a long time ago."

"You must keep hope, Antenore, because you are still alive."

Quartaroli didn't think he could suffer one moment longer, yet the two remained at the dry holes for more than a half hour, unable even to wet their lips. Finally Quartaroli left and returned to the group. Soon after, he heard footsteps and called out. No one answered. He called again, and recognized George Stimez from his gruff reply. By this time thirst had rendered him nearly senseless. Quartaroli gathered his courage.

"Is there water in your place, George?" he croaked out.

Stimez denied it and walked away. Of all the men, he exhibited the most stamina.

Quartaroli listened to the departing footsteps and determined that Stimez had gone to his workplace two rooms away, same as he often did. *There must be water there*, he thought. *Why else would he go there so frequently, and stay for a half hour?*

Not long after Stimez returned, Quartaroli marshaled every ounce of strength to pull himself to his feet. He was so enormously fatigued and dizzy, he doubted he would make it to Stimez's workplace. Finally, he arrived and felt his way around with his hands and feet until he found a small hole containing about half a glass of water. At that moment, he could have drunk a potful. Overjoyed, he let loose a laugh, but his euphoria quickly turned to hate. *How could Stimez be so cruel?*

Quartaroli finished his drink and continued exploring the room. He found another small hole, but it contained only a few drops, so he sat for a half hour waiting for more water to collect. Just then he heard footsteps approaching and called out, again without an answer. He called again and recognized Stimez's voice.

"What are you doing in my place?" Stimez shouted. "Have you come to drink my water?"

Quartaroli kept his voice calm. "This water belongs to the both of us."

Stimez became furious, screaming in his face. "That water is mine! Get out of my place, Quartaroli, or I can arrange for a fight."

Quartaroli neither blanched nor rose to the bait.

"It's better if *you* go back," he replied. He couldn't believe that someone of this ilk was among them, to cause such trouble over so few drops of water. He'd known Stimez for some time, but had only thought him odd, never cruel.

Quartaroli made his way back to the group and told them that Stimez was a man without a heart. Then he told them all exactly where to find the water.

Others had gone to that spot to wet their lips and found it dry. Some figured the water had stopped flowing, but a few suspected one of them was stealing the precious drops for himself. George Eddy and Walter Waite stole silently to the spot to see what would happen next. When Stimez slithered to the hole and sank his mouth into the shallow puddle, their anger bubbled over. They accused him, they denounced him and when they'd finished with him, some of the men wanted to tear an opening in the wall and shove him through. They vowed none of them would lift a finger to help him if he ever again took so much as one drop more than his share.

"If I had a knife, I'd have stuck it in you," Eddy told him.

From that point on, Eddy posted men to guard the water holes to make certain every man had his rightful turn.

When Quartaroli crawled back from his encounter with Stimez, he'd overheard Giacomo Pigati telling Walter Waite that their hope was gone—they would never again inhale free air. He had the same thoughts. The black damp so weakened him, he had to get around on his hands and knees and, despite his small drink, his mouth and throat were parched and fetid. By now, their nasal passages were so dry and swollen the men could only breathe through their mouths. Everyone's breath was so rank, no one could stand being close, even to himself.

Sleep was worthless. Whenever he closed his eyes, Quartaroli saw fantasies. Some teased him, some horrified him. If he did succumb to sleep, within five minutes someone would brush against him and his bones would scream out in protest. Every so often someone would say the air was fresher, that it was possible the mine exit was opened. Quartaroli thought so too, then decided the air only felt fresher because their blood was so starved of oxygen.

Giacomo Pigati began to talk to them about his idea and his quest. "Comrades, we have already known for a couple of days that we must die in this tomb. I say 'for a couple of days' because before that we all hoped for some kind of help, but by now we know it will all be over for us in the next few days," he said. "I suggest we break one of these walls and go out to look for some water, because if we had some I'm sure we could hold out for three to four more days. If we can't and the black damp sends us to the next world sooner, it's better for us. We can stop suffering because we know how difficult it is to get out of this trap."

William Clelland reflected for a while, then suggested they determine how strong the black damp was before breaking down the wall. All the men agreed, so Clelland went to the wall at the other end of the crypt to test for the invisible killer. With no matches left, he couldn't see if the gas snuffed out a flame. If it was heavy, he would either smell it or be struck with dizziness, a rapid pulse or a violent headache throbbing at his temples.

During the half hour Clelland was gone, the men muttered their fervent wishes that the black damp was gone forever so they could return to their loved ones. Finally, his footsteps resounded and their hearts swelled in anticipation. The news was bad.

"Dear comrades, I am sorry to tell you that the black damp is still too strong and I don't believe any of us can resist it enough to get to water."

Giacomo Pigati persisted, insisting that a quick death from black damp was preferable to suffering on like this, but Walter Waite calmed him a bit, saying it would be better to wait a day to break out. In the meantime they could search the holes they'd dug and collect water so they could dampen their lips while they tried to make their way out. The men decided on this plan, but had no idea which of them could muster the strength to search, nor how they'd transfer water to a pail from such shallow holes, especially since they had nothing with which to dip.

Most of the men could no longer navigate in the dark and Quartaroli was too weak to lift even his finger. Though George Stimez was the most vigorous of the group, he made no move to go.

If not for the Pigati brothers, no one would have gone. They took a lunch pail and began an arduous room-to-room search. After a very long time they returned more discouraged and thirsty than they'd left. For Thomas White and some of the others who had no expectations of living out the day, the sorry news had no effect. To Quartaroli, all hope was lost. It was time to bid the world good-bye and sleep the eternal sleep.

Once more Walter Waite infected the men with his courage, telling them there was no time to waste—they had to find water somehow, because without it they wouldn't last much longer. Still, Stimez refused to speak up, even though Waite said he would go, weak as he was, to find water.

Again the Pigati brothers picked up the lunch pail and started their ordeal anew. As Quartaroli sat numbly to wait, his thoughts turned to the men who shared his tomb. Of all his comrades, Quartaroli felt sorriest for forty-year-old Federico Lenzi, who by this time was so distraught he hardly knew what he was doing. He wandered off at times and Quartaroli would have to bring Lenzi back because he could no longer find his way to rejoin the group.

Ruggeri Buonfiglio was the other one who evoked sympathy. The young boy's muffled sobs punctuated the dark and he talked incessantly of the verdant, sun-dappled Italian hillsides where he'd grown up, or the wine he had waiting at home or the various foods he liked to eat, until the men had to stop him because he was only making their mouths water. Every now and then Walter Waite would start talking about the bananas he'd bought once from a Chicago vendor. He was a slim man and was suffering great torments of hunger because, unlike the others, he hadn't had time to eat his lunch before the fire began.

"I wish I had those bananas right now," he said, beginning the story again with that Italian street vendor's call.

" . . . 'Bananas, ten cents a dozen . . .'"

The men knew what was coming next and groaned. " . . . So I gave him the ten cents and he counted the fruit into a bag. 'Two, four, six, ten, twelve," he continued with a wry smile. "But when I opened the bag, there were only ten—and I ate them all." They begged him to stop, shushing him before he finished that part of his story.

By late Friday, young Ruggeri had slipped over the edge. His mutterings no longer made sense. Throughout the night and on into morning, he repeatedly burst out of a half-dazed stupor with some raving, incoherent babble, then sank silent once more. Now two of their number had lost hold of reality, and their eerie chorus of nonsensical gibberish cast a frightening depression on the rest.

From the moment the Pigatis left to search for water, the men talked about nothing but how different things would have been had they found an abundant source of water—that even if the black damp was a bit strong, with ample water they might have been able to reach a section in the mine where they knew water flowed freely.

The brothers had not yet returned when the men bid an end to Friday with their nightly prayers. Another day had come and gone, Quartaroli thought, and they were still captives without hope of regaining the liberty God had bestowed on them.

Abide with me, fast falls the eventide. The darkness deepens; Lord, with me abide . . .

Echoes of the men's favorite hymn played softly in their heads, lulling many of them toward sleep. Quartaroli sat awake, certain that in all the seven days he'd been locked up here, he hadn't slept more than two hours.

CHAPTER TWENTY-FIVE

Saturday, November 20, 1909
Cherry, Illinois, Topside
Cherry Mine, Second Vein

Saturday dawned unseasonably warm. The combination of bright sunshine, balmy temperatures and National Guard troops without their guns at the ready, was a change Cherry welcomed. The populace appreciated the militia's relaxed attitude, taking it as a sign of respect for their grief. As bodies came up on stretchers throughout the morning, the townspeople followed the soldiers' instructions more compliantly than before. Though many still strained against the ropes trying for a better look at each scorched and swollen corpse, Captain Hall was relieved that under such difficult circumstances the soldiers never had to unsheathe their bayonets. At the shaft and the temporary morgue, chaos subsided but the grief did not.

Across the country, Cherry continued to dominate headlines as the major story of the day, garnering national coverage as extensive as modern day reports of devastating earthquakes or hurricanes. Blow-by-blow accounts of rescue attempts, relief work, funerals and speculations as to blame completely filled multiple pages, relegating to sidebar status such stories as Portuguese King Manuel's first visit to England, a Pennsylvania train wreck, a Singapore steamship sinking, various automobile accidents and local scandals. The mine tragedy shared front-page prominence with accounts of President Taft's approval of corporate income tax collection and the U.S. invasion of Nicaragua after it executed two American sympathizers caught fighting there alongside its insurgent army.

It was Saturday morning but those trapped men who still had the energy to think believed it was already Sunday. The night had been infinite, with unimaginable gasping and pain. So weak they could get about only by crawling, the men lay in their tomb and used their remaining energy to long for death.

It was incomprehensible to Quartaroli that he was still alive. It had been seven days since he'd tasted food and twenty-four hours since water had passed his lips. His mouth and tongue were hot as a broiling oven.

He was anxious as well. Not only were the Pigatis still missing, Walter Waite had also strayed off to look for water and had not returned. Had they found any? Were they still alive?

Quartaroli listened to Daniel Holofzak's asthmatic wheezing in disbelief. Holofzak had grown weaker, but he was still alive. How could such a sick man of fifty have survived so much suffering for so long?

It must have been 6:00 A.M. when a voice pierced the blackness. "Come on, comrades. It is time to gather our courage and try one last time."

Quartaroli and his friend Francesco Zanarini made the penultimate effort. Joined by Ruggeri Buonfiglio, they made their way toward wall number two of one west. They met up with others there, men Quartaroli determined were Walter Waite, Frank Waite, John Brown, two German miners and three or four others. Five or six of the men, too weak to walk, remained at nine north, where the men had spent the night.

After just a few minutes, the Pigati brothers stumbled up, exhausted beyond measure. The brothers had walked the entire night, but the only water they'd found was so filthy it was impossible to drink or suck up. They'd only wet their lips by tearing scraps of their clothing to soak up the liquid, then shaking off the filth before swiping the fabric across their mouths.

Waite hadn't fared much better. He reported finding just a tiny bit of water and handed the small glassful he had to Giacomo Pigati to dole out as the men walked back. It was torment—a few precious ounces to last the journey and twenty men with raging thirsts.

After a bit of discussion when they'd returned to the others, Giacomo Pigati repeated his quest for one last stab at freedom.

"For us there is no more hope. We must die and I'm not waiting even five minutes. I'm breaking this wall and I'm going to try to walk. If I can have enough water, I don't even care if I die from black damp. Rather than suffering this way, I prefer to die. It's better."

Waite agreed and proposed that the four strongest among them should be the ones to start out.

"I think if we can get to the south entry we'll find plenty of water there," he said. "The four should take two or three lunch pails with them. The rest of us must go back, because there are five or six who will be dead in a short time if they don't get water."

How can we take two or three pails, Quartaroli thought, when we've got only one, and the rest were left behind in eight south?

Without a word, Frank Waite got up and singlehandedly began to break down the wall at two west. He was one of the strongest among them, but the task was so arduous he finished with barely enough stamina left to walk two steps, let alone the fifty meters still ahead of him. Walter Waite confirmed that there was more black damp in the air at two west than where the group huddled, yet Frank Waite was determined to retrieve the pails.

It took immense courage for him to step over the threshold of their crypt and stumble out into the unknown, where black damp skulked like something human waiting to suck out his breath. It took every ounce of his strength to head for eight south, blindly feeling his way through absolute and overwhelming darkness to ferret out the hidden lunch pails.

Midmorning, inspectors on the second vein reported that the area around the main shaft was free of fire. A number of rock falls had been cleared and the flames smoldering beneath them were squelched. Heavy rock and roof falls still piled, one after the other, thirty-five to fifty feet deep to the east of the shaft. With rock continuously dropping from the falls, it was dangerous to exit the cage on the east side and impossible to explore those galleries. To the west of the shaft, black damp was so bad in so many entries it was impossible to enter them without oxygen helmets.

At 10:30 A.M., the last three inspectors assigned to mines elsewhere in Illinois left to handle their own districts' pressing business—one to investigate a mine explosion in which two shot firers had been killed in the past week.

By the time they departed Cherry, no one yet had been able to get down into the third vein.

———

For more than an hour, Frank Waite stumbled back and forth along the road. His legs turned to jelly and he crashed to the ground three times, nearly losing consciousness on the last fall. John Brown ventured out after him. Both men were felled by the black damp, but finally made it back. For all his efforts, Waite returned with the only bucket he could find.

A few minutes later Walter Waite told the men the only thing left was to try to get to the south entry. He asked those who felt strong enough to make this last attempt. For five minutes no one spoke. Finally a voice broke the silence.

"Do you want to go with me, Salvatore?" Giacomo Pigati asked his brother. Salvatore agreed.

Quartaroli found his voice next.

"Francesco, will you go with them?" he asked his friend. Zanarini said he was too weak, but Quartaroli encouraged him to venture out with the Pigatis, and Zanarini found the strength to go. Still, they needed a fourth.

Who? Me?, Quartaroli thought. I have the courage but I lack the strength, and if I go along I'll only be a nuisance.

Stimez was still among the strongest they had, but he wouldn't say a word. Time and again the others told him he had to go until finally they badgered him into helping hunt for water.

Giacomo was the first to tear an opening in the wall at one west. Finally, when the hole was large enough and the four were about to leave, Walter Waite stopped them a moment to issue orders he wanted followed to the letter.

"If you reach seven north of one west and the air is better, whistle twice. If it is the same or worse, whistle once."

With that, the sixteen remaining captives shook hands with the brave expedition team and everyone uttered what he believed were their last good-byes. Taking a pail holding about a half cup of emergency water, the four set off.

At 2:00 P.M., David Powell, superintendent of the Braceville Mine, boarded the cage. Powell, who was now in charge of the underground exploration at Cherry, was on his way down with several from his rescue team to bring out another load of bodies. Fifty of the victims had been raised and identified so far, one of them by the gnawed bone of the pork chop his wife had packed in his lunch pail. The bodies were found singly and in groups. The man in the center of one group of ten died kneeling in prayer.

Quartaroli stood at the hole Pigati had made, tears streaming down his face and his heart beating in his ears. Even as darkness swallowed his companions, he swore he could see them crawling away on all fours, now over a pile of rocks, now across a pile of timbers. Like every other man in that chamber, he listened intently for some signal.

For more than an hour no one made an unnecessary sound. Everyone strained to hear, anxious about the explorers' fate. Someone whispered that all four were already dead. Someone else said, no, they'd just forgotten to signal. The sixteen uneasy prisoners had no way of knowing who was right.

After long reflection, Quartaroli, William Clelland and Frank Waite decided to set out after the four. Clelland promised not to abandon those they left behind.

"Well, boys, I am going to try to reach a place of safety, and if I am successful, I give you my word that I will either return for you myself or I will send others to bring you out."

"Brothers, be brave. Do the best you can," Walter Waite told them. "I only wish you luck."

With these words of encouragement ringing in his ears, Quartaroli was the first to step through the hole in the wall. He immediately crashed to the ground, dashing his head. He lost consciousness for a moment and came to his senses much weaker. It took several minutes before he was able to crawl along with Clelland in the lead and Frank Waite behind him.

The road they took had been out of use for some time. It was littered with timbers and rock piles, huge impediments in the dark. The men could crawl only two or three paces at a time before bad air and their own debility forced them to stop for breath. Thirty minutes passed and they'd found no trace of the first group, despite calling out for them frequently. Although the three exhausted men were convinced their companions were dead, they trudged on, even at the price of their own lives as well.

Nurses watched with pity as Mrs. Patrick Dobbins thrashed through Friday night in a state of delirium. Semiconscious, she moaned and cried in her bed the entire night, calling for her brother, Charlie Waite. Nurses sponged her face and tried to calm her, but by afternoon she was beyond their assistance. Helplessly, they watched her die of grief.

The men forced to stay behind lost track of time. The explorers searching for water could have been gone hours, they could have been gone days. The men who still could moved about to stay warm. Those who couldn't moaned. Some stared into the velvet darkness stretching across the opening as if this would summon Clelland and the others back with water.

Thomas White lay immobile on the floor, too weak even to lift his hand. His tongue clogged his mouth, so caked and swollen he scarcely cared which came first to end his misery—water or death.

But their comrades were no closer to water than they were. Halfway to seven north, as the explorers tried to circumvent a pile of rocks in their path, they realized they'd gotten turned around on the road. Terror ran like ice through their veins. They were barely able to move, they were out of air, and they were lost. With enormous effort, Quartaroli was finally able to sort out the right road and suddenly thought he heard distant voices. He called out and thought he heard Zanarini reply. He called again, asking if they'd found anything new. The voices came back feebly.

"We think this air ahead is worse."

The words stabbed Quartaroli like a stiletto to the heart. He tried to answer, but he could not find his voice. Again his comrades called, but he could not reply. He couldn't even move. After a few minutes, the three men began to crawl toward their comrades' voices. The louder the voices came, the more the second group realized that the first explorers were nowhere near the south entry. They were on their way back to the crypt, lost. Quartaroli found his voice and yelled ahead for them to wait.

A few more steps and the seven were all together near eight north, arguing about which of the groups had taken the wrong road. Finally, they set off together but somehow took a bad turn and ended up in the wrong entry. Almost immediately, they recognized their mistake and got themselves on track.

The air was so heavy they could hardly breathe and their legs dragged like they were plowing through hip-deep water. It took well over thirty minutes to cover the ten meters between seven and eight north. Quartaroli remembered the group leaving a lunch pail with a small amount of water in this area that first night and groped futilely for it in the dark. Suddenly his nostrils curled at the cloying smell of burning wood. His companions inhaled it too, crying that there was fire nearby.

"Then we'll never make it to the south entry," Quartaroli exclaimed.

But it wasn't burning timber, they soon discovered, it was the high stench of decaying mule carcasses. They pressed on, the air improved and breathing came easier. Suddenly, they realized that instead of growing weaker, they were regaining strength, bit by bit. Overjoyed, they whistled twice to alert those they'd left behind, then stopped at seven north for more than an hour to build themselves up.

The sweet strains of those dry whistles carried back to the crypt, where the infirm they'd left behind had managed to drag themselves through the opening in the wall to sit silently outside their tomb, listening for a signal. The men, whose wait had seemed interminable, went wild with joy, shouting back like banshees. Buoyed, some of them drew upon strength they didn't know was left in them and began to inch along the passage to reach the good air.

When the group of explorers set out again, they found roads blocked and became confused, going in circles until some thought they were heading back again to where they'd started. Others argued that they were on the right path. Then Giacomo Pigati stumbled into a full coal car and, from the position of the mule hitch, ascertained the direction leading out. Buoyed, the men continued on and in just a few steps reached the door between five and six south. The second they opened it, the odor of putrefaction assaulted them so strongly it was unbearable. But dying here was even more unbearable. The will to survive forced them forward, into a passageway clogged by dead mules. Their bodies were so bloated and decayed, it was nearly impossible to crawl over them. Some were still hitched to coal cars, loaded and empty, and traversing the passageway was a grueling ordeal.

Quartaroli knew the road well—he'd worked in the second west, six south, six months earlier. He headed straight for the barrel kept filled with water near the six south entry. It was overturned, bone dry. *The mules must have gotten to it, desperate for a drink*, Quartaroli thought. His tongue was so swollen with thirst, he asked if Giacomo still had the lunch pail with the emergency ration of water. Pigati handed over a damp scrap of rag, which Quartaroli grabbed up and pressed to his lips. It barely moistened them.

Quartaroli assumed the lead, grateful his legs were bearing him up despite their occasional crash into coal or timber. Clelland was right behind him, followed by the other six. He thought of the other twelve—especially Ruggeri Buonfiglio, Thomas White, George Eddy and Daniel Holofzak—too debilitated to leave the crypt.

The men walked forever. Still, they hadn't reached the south entry. From the rear, Giacomo Pigati called to them to stop. His brother was ill. The men doubled back to gather around Salvatore, encouraging him and wetting his lips. After a while, he revived enough to continue on.

As they forged slowly ahead, Quartaroli could almost smell the water they would guzzle when they reached the south entry. The happy anticipation swelling in his chest died in an instant. Just one hundred and fifty meters from their destination, the road that moments before had been pitch black was suddenly radiating orange. Fire. The men were struck dumb. Paralyzed. Quartaroli, still at the head of the line, was the first to speak.

"We aren't going to make it."

Several of the men said their destiny was to die here in this abyss. Then Zanarini, who could whistle loudly, pursed his parched lips and gave it all he had. His signal was met with silence from ahead. Suddenly, the angry glow of fire filled the corridor again.

"Help! Help us!" the men shouted. But a sudden curtain of total darkness was the only reply.

Giulio Castelli, Antenore Quartaroli's brother-in-law, was among the small group doing cleanup work around the south side of the air shaft. Wearing a miner's cap and flame, Father James Haney of St. Mary's Church in Mendota was also in the area, helping superintendent Powell and several other men search for victims.

Sometime just after 2:00 P.M., Powell walked into the second west entry. He stopped in his tracks. His breath caught in his throat. He heard voices.

Quartaroli and his group screwed up their nerve and inched ahead, quickly finding their path barred by ten to twelve coal cars, each with its three mules still attached. All of the animals were dead.

Fighting down revulsion and horror, the men cringed against the walls on either side of the mules, making themselves as small as they could as they tried to avoid brushing against the rotting carcasses.

They stood at the south entry. They had made it. They were in absolute darkness but they knew one thing—air was flowing around them, fresh and pure. Heady with the joy of breathing sweet strong air, they stood and sucked it down, filling and refilling their starved lungs. Suddenly, instead of heading for the water barrel, they turned to feel their way toward the air shaft they guessed was only two hundred feet away.

It had taken them nearly six hours to travel just three quarters of a mile.

CHAPTER TWENTY-SIX

Saturday, November 20, 1909
Cherry Mine, Second Vein

They were fifty meters from the exit well where fierce flames had forced them back just a week earlier. Suddenly, they recoiled again from the sudden brilliant flare of flames. Pain seared into eyes that had not seen light in more than four days. Despair conquered them—after all this time, fire still blocked their escape.

Quartaroli blinked back the pain and opened his eyes to a squint. The orange fire was still there. It took him moments to realize that it danced alone, unaccompanied by the embrace of furnace-blast heat or a musical angry roar.

No, that wasn't fire he heard. *Voices. He heard voices.*

Quartaroli squinted into the bright orange flare. It seemed to separate itself into individual tongues of flame . . . moving . . . dancing, slightly less intense now, coming toward him . . . closer, closer, until suddenly he was staring into the astounded face of his wife's brother, Giulio Castelli, the astounded faces of other men with flame dancing in their miner's helmets.

The rescuers gave a shout of joy. The next instant twelve men fell upon one another and prayers of thanksgiving burst from the lips of the eight starved miners and the four rescuers who'd been certain no one had survived this death-ravaged pit.

The soot-covered, unshaven survivors didn't have voice enough to cheer, and little left to talk. Clelland was the first to address their rescuers.

"Is it Sunday or Monday?" he asked.

In time, Quartaroli stepped back from his brother-in-law's clutches.

"Erminia and the baby?"

His heart swelled with relief at Castelli's words. "They are well, Antenore. They are truly well. And your brother, Paradiso, came right away from Iowa."

On hearing the commotion, other workers came hurrying from the shaft and in an instant the room glowed brighter from their helmet flames and lanterns. The trapped miners shielded their faces. It was more light than their dilated pupils could bear.

"Are there others still alive?" Powell asked them.

"We left them back in nine north. Most of them are too weak to walk, and one is nearly dead."

Immediately, several of the rescue volunteers set off with their lamps and tools to find them, while others led the eight weary miners the last few steps to the hoisting shaft.

There, Quartaroli found another relative at work among the volunteer crew. With their hearts bursting with emotion, he and his other elated brother-in-law, Domenico Cresto, threw their arms around each other.

"Living men down here!" the workers shouted up the shaft. "We have just found them. Get ready to care for them!"

Sheriff Skoglund, who was crouching over the shaft, leapt up suddenly, waving his arms overhead. He shouted at the top of his voice to young Fred H. Buck, the mine's assistant chief clerk.

"Buck, there are living men in the mine! Telephone for the physicians and nurses—we will need them and all they can do for those men!"

The men closest to the shaft erupted in shouts of joy as Buck ran to the telephone in the mine's offices. Like wildfire, the news sizzled through Cherry. Although the number of living men below hadn't been revealed, the total multiplied as the report went from mouth to mouth—thirty-seven, fifty, one hundred.

Screaming children tore for the mine, well ahead of the bedridden mothers who dragged themselves up, reeling from illness and the dizzying news. Every woman ran to the mine—not only those whose kin were not accounted for, but even those who'd already identified their dead and now hoped they'd been wrong. Shopkeepers threw closed signs on their doors and business ground to a halt as the entire town rushed to the mine.

The soldiers were unprepared for the teeming mass of people, hysterical in their joy, crazed with the hope their loved one was among the saved. They broke through the restraints about the shaft and threw themselves to the ground, sobbing, screaming, praying with all their hearts. One young mother, frail and pale and clutching an infant, tore aside a soldier's arm with adrenaline strength and charged the shaft, sobbing the prayer of every bereaved woman.

"Oh God, give my husband and my boy back to me. Grant that they are among those still alive in the mine."

Adrenaline also pumped in the veins of David Powell, newly appointed mine manager Archie Frew, Father Haney and Captain Kenny of the Chicago firefighting team as they made their way back into the bowels of the mine, climbing over dead men and mules to find the crypt where the sick and dying miners waited for rescue. Numerous times they stumbled and fell, cutting their hands and faces in the rush to reach the men. Though the fan was pushing fresh air into the entry, the onset of headaches told them black damp hung in the air. A call went back for helmets and oxygen tanks.

Rice and Williams came down with a volunteer team, portable electric lights and six sets of rescue gear. Since each tank lasted only two hours, they decided to lug them in as far as possible to a base camp before donning them. Williams, the man most experienced in oxygen use, waited in reserve at the shaft, breathing fresh air while

Rice's group headed back toward the survivors.

They encountered black damp in varying degrees, but when they reached patches so thick it snuffed out their lamps, Rice and his four volunteers suited up.

Finally, the group neared nine north and heard the sounds of pounding. They quickened their pace, hurrying to the crypt where crazed and desperate men were trying to coerce the walls to sweat out some drops of water. They found several men lying outside, then ran to the opening Clelland had torn from the wall and shined their lights through a hole too small for them to breach in their gear.

"Are there any of you alive in there?"

The rescuers had barely made out the feeble yes when they were on the wall, hacking it apart with picks and axes and hands, yelling to the men to keep up their courage. Their lamps bobbed as they worked, playing an eerie mix of light and shadows across the area.

"How many of you are alive in there, boys? We will save you in a minute."

"Yes, we are alive and you bet we are hungry," a faint, husky voice replied. "Have you got any food out there?"

Father Haney crouched near the enlarging opening, calling into the dark cave. "God bless you, men. We will get you out in a minute and get you all the lunch you can eat. Be patient, if you can." He couldn't hear anything else from the men, so he retreated to pray while the rescuers worked. *Dear God, let there be as many living men as possible in that grave.*

"Hang on," the rescuers urged. "You'll soon be safe. The cage is down and ready to take you out."

A voice came back through the darkness.

"Most of us are all right and feeling fine, but there is one poor fellow in here who is almost dead, and I'm afraid he will be dead in a few minutes if he doesn't get some fresh air."

Inside, Daniel Holofzak struggled for each breath and White and Eddy lay on the ground, too weak to turn their heads from the blinding light pouring through the rapidly widening opening. A few moments later the wall was down and the rescuers crashed through with a shout. The miners gasped, overcome by the dizzying rush of fresh air and the painful bombardment of light blazing from the rescuers' torches.

Suddenly, they found themselves surrounded, pulled to their feet and slapped on their backs by men laughing, shouting, hugging them about the neck and nearly lifting them into the air, delirious with the joy of saving them. The stunned miners began to laugh with them, then to cry aloud, and the crypt where prayers and sobs had echoed now reverberated with the cheers of men who had cheated death.

Thomas White shook off his stupor to drink down the small sip of water a fireman held to his mouth. He asked for more.

"Not yet. Too much after so long a fast will do you more harm than good."

Yet that small swallow of water was so invigorating, White was able to get to his feet and walk unassisted. Others too insisted they were strong enough to walk out on their own, but some of them were too weak to make even an attempt. Father Haney took a torch and knelt beside Holofzak, still flat on his back, laboring to breathe. He stared into Holofzak's soot-covered face, but the miner's eyes stayed clenched against the light.

"Do you give your soul to God?" the priest asked, tracing a cross on the man's forehead as he administered the last sacrament.

"Yes," Holofzak gasped. "I am afraid I will never get up alive."

*   *   *

It was hot in the mine and stifling inside the unwieldy helmets. The volunteers, overexerted and unaccustomed to the apparatus, used them incorrectly and collapsed. Numerous times, Rice had to stop administering oxygen to the survivors so he could resuscitate the rescuers and refit their helmets.

Powell and Kenny sent two of the firemen back to summon

Williams and to call up for medical assistance and stretchers. By this time the air was better and rescuers could breathe without their helmets. Brattice cloth—canvas immersed in creosote—was brought down and hung across every entry in which they'd found no bodies, closing these off to aid ventilation.

Doctors Howe and Mason and the entire staff of nurses in Cherry hurried to ready three sleeping cars as a hospital, stocking it with beds, medicine, bandages, restoratives, soup and food.

Then Dr. Howe entered the mine, accompanied by inspector Crawford of the State Board of Health. They spent half an hour examining the miners.

"Some of the men are so weak they can hardly gasp," Crawford said when he came up, reporting that six or seven of the men were in such critical condition he didn't think they could withstand the exertion of being moved. "They were unable to take any solid food and artificial stimulants were administered."

The miners sipped small amounts of water and began to adjust to the fresher air as they waited to ride up. Someone brought down a pot of coffee and Quartaroli drank it down, even though it had no sugar. Excruciating hours passed before rescuers decided they could safely bring the survivors from the mine. A queue of volunteers led all the way back to the shaft, standing ready to assist the evacuation at every step. Some survivors were still unconscious and difficult to carry. As Williams and another man struggled to drag out Holofzak, they had to be resuscitated along with the asthmatic miner.

When all the survivors had been accounted for, the team hung a brattice cloth over the entry and retreated. Then they went to bring out the dead Frenchman called Paolo—Leopold Dumont.

By now daylight had evaporated, but doctors feared even moonlight and the torches would prove too painful to the survivors' eyes. To prevent permanent damage to their eyesight, rescuers threw protective blankets over the miners' heads. Francesco Zanarini was the first on the cage. His friend, Antenore Quartaroli, followed him. But Walter Waite refused to get on. Overhearing speculation that others were holed up in another part of the mine, he ripped off his blanket.

"Well, then, by God, I am *not* going out of this mine until I get the others!"

The rescuers insisted he had to leave, that remaining in the mine any longer could kill him. He wouldn't be budged.

"We will take you up to the fresh air and give you some nice warm food and then maybe we will let you help us do the rest of the work."

It didn't work. Finally, they had to forcibly drag him onto the cage. All the way up he kept shouting, "Let me go down and help get up the others!"

Outside, suspense had driven the populace to a frenzy and the throng at the shaft had swelled to a surging, screaming, shouting swarm. Fearing a riot, Captain Hall ordered the National Guard to draw their bayonets, circle the mouth of the hoisting shaft and drive the multitude back. The soldiers fortified the shaft and stood shoulder to shoulder, forming a gangway along the one hundred and fifty feet between the shaft and the railroad car hospital. They were nearly as excited as the crowd.

Finally, the words everyone had waited for came from below.

"Hoist her up."

"Hoist her up," the topside engineer replied and pulled on the lever.

"Everybody be quiet," the soldiers whispered. "Please do not cheer."

Murmurs went through the crowd. Mothers hoisted little ones above their heads, telling them to look for their papas when the rescued men passed by.

"Look sharp now. Here they come."

The crowd surged against the soldiers as the hoisting cage began to creak upward. It came up like a shot.

Rescuers wearing shiny rubber coats and white caps stood on the cage, supporting some of the blanket-covered men and carrying others. The crowd burst into applause but were quickly silenced by the raised hands of the soldiers.

The women's agony was palpable as the procession rushed to the train cars with the bundled men. *Who was saved?* Unable to contain themselves, women stretched their arms toward them, calling, "Billy," or "Frank," or "Oh, Andy, are you there? Speak to me. I am here." Some of them fainted. Others entreated the rescuers to identify the men they'd brought out. Taking pity, one of them called out.

"George Eddy. We've got George Eddy here."

"Oh, George!" The scream pierced the night. "Is it you? Is it you? Come here, George, I am waiting for you."

Eddy was too weak to answer his wife.

One of the men carrying the miners up was Robert Clelland, William's brother. At first word of the disaster, the miner from South Wilmington, Illinois, had rushed to Cherry and been told that all the entombed men were dead.

"I'll stay to help," he said to officials. "I'll stay until the last body is brought up."

He helped rush the first cageload of men to the hospital and hurried back to assist with the second load. A friend tapped him on the shoulder.

"Bob, don't you know that Will is up?"

Clelland went white as moonlight and staggered backward. "You don't mean . . . ?"

"Yes. Alive. He's up, alive. Why, Bob, you brought him up yourself, wrapped in blankets."

Clelland began shaking and collapsed in sobs. He was so overcome with emotion, rescuers had to help him to the hospital for treatment.

Women, children and reporters rushed to the train cars, fighting to follow the rescued miners. The wife of one of the first men to come up tore through the two lines of soldiers to reach him. She punched, pulled, kicked and bit her way to the train, tossing aside a deputy sheriff and yanking the guard from the train door. Then she crumpled in her husband's arms, limp and weeping.

Another young Italian mother recognized her husband as he walked, and was half carried, to the train. She let out a shriek of joy and threw herself on him. She hugged him and held his face in her hands. Then she kissed him and lifted their two children up to do the same.

Finally, she fell prostrate at the feet of the man holding up her husband. She took first one rough, grimy boot in her hands and then the other, and kissed his feet. Then she pulled her children down to the ground and motioned them to do the same.

Deeply moved, the rescuer extracted himself from their embrace and hurried back to the shaft. The reunited family called a chorus of Italian blessings after him and then turned to go home.

The men were suffering from their ordeal to varying degrees. One of them came to the surface bleeding profusely from his nose and mouth. Others' lips were cracked and bleeding, parched to a pasty white. Ironically, fresh air sickened them—they'd gradually become accustomed to breathing the black damp.

In addition to Doctors Howe and Mason, twelve other doctors worked to resuscitate the miners. First they injected them with strychnine to revive their hearts, then they gave them warm milk and rubbed their bodies down with alcohol. The doctors feared the men would eat too much if they released them. For several hours, George Semich was the only other man allowed to go home. He was so agitated about being kept away from his wife and children, the doctors relented, figuring it best to let him have his own way.

Later a reporter ran to his home with a Lithuanian translator in tow. They found Mrs. Semich humming in her backyard as she shoveled out their tiny coal bin. Semich was in the tiny bedroom off the combination dining room-kitchen, bolstered by every pillow in the house. His three children, all under four years old, peered at their father through bars at the foot of his bed, while a Presentation nun made certain her patient did not overeat.

All of the survivors sucked down the measured ounces of water the nurses doled out, but one of them passed on the warm milk. With a smile, he asked his nurse to bring him something stronger.

"Haven't had a drink of that stuff in a year," he said, downing a shot of whiskey. "It certainly tastes good now. Get some word to Mary, my wife, as quick as possible. Poor woman, she believes I am dead. God knows I have faced death in its most terrible form, but I am alive and well and that is something."

Thomas White called immediately for his family.

"I want my wife and children," he said. "I feel that I have been dead and brought to life. Won't I be glad to see them!" He said the group owed their lives to George Eddy and Walter Waite—that without them they might have all perished in the flames.

Outside, the crowd was cheering and jostling to get a peek inside the train windows. Those survivors who were strong enough hollered out to them, answering questions about their ordeal.

Quartaroli scoured the crowd for a glimpse of his loved ones. He saw friends waving and heard his hometown friend, Eleuterio Panizzi, say, "You have done well." He couldn't believe there were so many people outside. Suddenly he spotted his brother, Paradiso, and his wife, Erminia, and his sister-in-law and all those dear to his heart.

Erminia begged to come into the coach to talk to Quartaroli and care for him, but the soldiers barred her. The doctors didn't want wives anywhere near their husbands until they were sure the men were ready to leave the hospital car. Finally, a guard took pity on Erminia and let her inside briefly.

Quartaroli held his wife, savoring a joy he never thought he'd experience again. Neither of them had expected ever to see each other again.

There was one miner, however, who was in no hurry to see his wife.

"I've been gone for seven days," he said, asking that doctors keep her away. "I can apologize better to her at home."

William Clelland's wife soon arrived with their baby and was allowed inside. He grinned at the sight of them. The nurses offered food, but he was more interested in a cigarette.

"Never mind the eats," he told a fireman, "but slip me the makin's, kid."

While Clelland talked freely with reporters about their fight to survive, he refused to discuss his religious teachings.

"We made the most of our situation," is all he would say.

Later, Walter Waite talked of the ordeal below, telling reporters of the heroism of his fellow survivors—John Barnoski, John Brown, Ruggeri Buonfiglio, William Clelland, George Eddy, Daniel Holofzak, Federico Lenzi, John Lorimer, Giacomo Pigati, Salvatore Pigati, Frank Prohaska, Fred Prohaska, Antenore Quartaroli, George Semich, John Semich, George Stimez, Frank Waite, Thomas White and Francesco Zanarini.

"Those men were heroes and acted every inch the part of the men they were," he said. "Everyone lived so that the other man might live and every man was ready to die for the sake of his comrade at any moment. When Holofzak grew too weak to stoop to drink, he had to lie on his face to moisten his lips.

"I tell you that when a little water filled into a hole, there wasn't a man but craved it infernally. But the stronger men frequently passed their turns to let the old man drink."

It was an ordeal too horrific for John Brown to chance repeating. He vowed he'd never set foot inside a mine again.

"Until my dying day I shall never enter a mine again," he said.

"The experiences down there were terrible. The last few days seemed like a horrible dream and I scarcely know what happened. All I can say today is that I am alive and well, after having passed through the awful ordeal. It was a miracle. God alone knows the awful pangs of hunger and the sufferings of thirst which every man experienced during those eight days."

After they'd eaten some soup, the men were anxious to get into the buggies, carriages and other vehicles they saw pulling up near the tracks to drive them home.

Like the others, Quartaroli kept asking for solid food, but all the nourishment doctors allowed was a little hot broth. Finally, at 7:00 P.M., they told him he could go home.

He stepped down from the train, and a man rushed up to offer him a ride in ten minutes. Quartaroli thanked him for his kind heart, but declined. The house of his brother-in-law, Domenico Cresto, where Erminia, their baby son and Quartaroli's brother Paradiso waited, was only three hundred meters away and Quartaroli could walk it quicker.

He thought he would never get there, same as that Saturday morning a week ago when it seemed to take forever to get to work. Before he was at the door he was wrapped in the arms of his loved ones, convinced no one in the world could imagine his joy.

He scooped up his son and breathed in the sweet milky smell of the six month old he never thought he'd see again.

Daniel Holofzak, sickest among the survivors, also refused a ride. He said he had walked home from work every day of his life and he would walk home today as well. He made it, barely, and collapsed into his bed.

Mine officials dashed off telegraphs ordering the Illinois mine inspectors back to Cherry to take charge of matters when fire broke out again at the mouth of the shaft. The Chicago firemen and rescue teams persevered with renewed vigor while Giacomo Pigati sat at home, surrounded by family and friends as he read aloud the farewell letter he had written to his wife. He too vowed his coal mining days were behind him, saying he would work anywhere or do anything except mining.

Officials professed as much joy as the survivors' families.

"I would give up ten years of my life for this day," W. W. Taylor, the general superintendent, told reporters. "For one week I have worked here day and night, with only a few hours sleep, attempting to get a rescue party in the mine. The company has spent thousands and we do not regret a single cent. What is all the money compared with the life of a single man? The news that some of the entombed men were alive came to me as a great ray of light out of the darkness."

Hope that others might still be alive spurred rescuers on. Volunteers worked desperately to dig through a cave-in that blocked access to the third vein. There were at least one hundred miners trapped there and each second could be critical to saving another life.

"There are other resourceful leaders among the missing and they, like White, Clelland and the others, may have led their men to comparative safety," state's attorney Eckert said. "The search is now for the living."

CHAPTER TWENTY-SEVEN

Sunday, November 21, 1909

A ll night and throughout Sunday, relay teams of firefighters sandbagged the air course south of the shaft, hoping to starve a new fire at its mouth. Captain Kenny led the water hose vanguard, surfacing for short rests only when fire and smoke overcame him.

Inspector Newsam still held out hope of finding more alive.

"Scotchmen are the most resourceful miners in the world," he said, "and there are twenty-one of them down there, dead or alive. I can see no reason why they should not have found some refuge, just as did those who came up yesterday."

The women continued their vigil at the mine, not yet prepared to give up their loved ones for dead.

"The men they brought up yesterday could not have lived more than a few hours longer," said one. "If they don't come up today, they'll come up dead."

While firemen slowly subdued the flames, telegraphs and cablegrams flew back and forth, carrying the tumultuous news from Cherry. Early Sunday, President William Howard Taft dispatched a reply to the first telegram Mayor Connelly sent the night before:

> *Your telegram of yesterday announcing that twenty living men have been rescued from the Cherry mine did not reach me until this morning. You add that 150 more are believed to be alive. I sincerely hope that your judgment may be confirmed.*

William H. Taft
President of the United States

Until the Cherry catastrophe, mining had been strictly a state matter. Now, within a month, President Taft was expected to recommend that Congress create a federal bureau of mines dedicated to promulgating methods for preventing similar accidents. Geological Survey scientists had already sent the president an outline of work the government had completed toward that goal, with suggestions for a systematic, comprehensive implementation.

These reports included a compendium of directions for handling explosives used in mines; an investigation into the causes and prevention of coal dust explosions; experiments in oxygen helmet use to explore mines filled with noxious gases, with special reference to rescuing entombed miners; and a digest of state laws and those of European countries regulating the operation of mines.

Sunday was a day of quiet rejoicing and public sorrow. Church bells tolled throughout the day, announcing funerals for eighteen miners. Services had to be held outside, since the coroner advised not to bring the bodies into the churches. Some victims were laid to rest in trenches dug in the new cemetery, Catholics on the east side and Protestants on the west. Others were driven away to family plots in the neighboring towns the men had called home.

Before the graves were covered over, clergymen hurried back to the mine to administer to other survivors. They waited in vain.

Late in the afternoon, firemen and volunteers discovered twelve more bodies and brought them to the tent and, again, women seeking loved ones battled the soldiers. As each coffin was filled and taken from the morgue, an empty one was set up in its place.

Once the fire was tamed enough for rescuers to get past it, teams worked at fever pitch to clear cave-ins and obstacles to reach any survivors behind them. Despite the liberal use of four hundred pounds of chloride of lime and three thousand bichloride of mercury tablets brought down as disinfectants, the stench of decomposition and the black damp made breathing difficult.

Black damp nearly killed mining engineer John Collins as he crested a huge pile of earth and stone to peer into a tunnel. A fellow rescuer climbed the debris to drag the unconscious Collins by his feet to safety. Revived, he reported the tunnel was littered with hundreds of dead men and mules and said black damp was so thick there it meant instant death for anyone attempting to enter.

The Geological Survey scientists were astounded that the survivors had been able to live more than a week in air bad enough to extinguish oil lamps, which occurs when the percent of oxygen in the air falls from its usual 20 percent to below 16 percent. They found it even more extraordinary that carbon monoxide had not saturated the men's blood and killed them, since they'd been holed up so long without fresh air and concentrations of carbon monoxide just outside their chamber had reached upwards of 5 percent.

A door the survivors had removed to use as a barricade probably helped save their lives. They'd had no time to rehang it in the crosscut when black damp drove them deeper into the mine on Monday, most likely when the fan was started up. The inspectors, who'd returned to Cherry, suspected the open doorway caused air currents to short-circuit in the crosscut, keeping a small amount of relatively good air at the head of the entries, at the same time creating enough air pressure outside the survivors' crypt to prevent fresh air from forcing black damp through the cracks in the crypt walls when the fan was restarted on Thursday.

The geologists' helmet work at Cherry demonstrated how, with every second crucial, oxygen tanks enabled rescuers to penetrate the gas- and smoke-filled mine days sooner than they could have without protection. The scientists were certain this would help convince mine owners of the need to purchase oxygen equipment and to train men to use it as the laws required in Austria, Belgium, France, Holland, upper Silesia, Prussia, Russia and Saxony.

That afternoon, superintendent W. W. Taylor went into the mine to assess conditions but saw no hope of digging away the tremendous cave-ins to search for more men before the following day. Although workers soon found thirty-seven more bodies, the tremendous crush of morbid curiosity seekers descending on Cherry for a second Sunday made removal impossible. *The Chicago Daily Tribune* estimated the crowd of gawkers at twenty thousand.

"We can see bodies. Piles of them," miners reported, surfacing after eight-hour shifts. "They're all dead."

"But they could be living back there, couldn't they?" an old man asked.

"No chance," a miner said. He paused, noticing the old man's hands beginning to tremble. "Why sure," he said quickly. "Didn't the others come out? Don't you worry, he'll be up soon."

Labor leaders from the United Mine Workers of Illinois had been making their own quiet investigation into the catastrophe, and called a meeting for the following day. Furious at the lack of progress, they accused mine officials of dilatory tactics and several offered to go into the third vein themselves. Illinois union president Duncan McDonald and his attorney, Seymour Stedman, interviewed miners to determine whether the deceaseds' estates or families had any cause of action against the St. Paul Coal Company.

"We are preparing to push this investigation to the limit," McDonald said. "We believed we had a good basis for action when we started and we are sure of it now."

Labor's concerns about industry dangers were long-standing. The U.S. Geological Survey reported 22,840 men killed and 50,000 seriously injured during the past seventeen years, statistics four times worse than those in Europe, and climbing steadily even as the European rates declined.

The Chicago Federation of Labor voted to join the Illinois United

Mine Workers Union's investigation and to send federation president John Fitzpatrick to Cherry. They adopted resolutions demanding that Governor Deneen thoroughly investigate the disaster and call a special legislative session to consider passage of an employers' liability law. Union secretary Frank Hayes, who'd spent the week at Cherry, pledged all $700,000 in the Illinois union's treasury to protect miners' rights and urged labor members to run for office and help pass laws that would place human life above dollars.

"Legislators have to this time failed to consider the human factor in making laws for miners. They have considered the question as a business one and have clung to the commercial idea. The men must come, not from the ranks of the lawyers, but from men who know what it is to work and see their comrades killed—killed because human life is the cheapest commodity in the market."

John J. Brittain stood up and called for a strike against every single St. Paul Coal Company mine until the owners agreed to pay satisfactory damages for the tragedy at Cherry.

During the day women from the Illinois Home Missionary Society arrived to relieve those who had been aiding the families all week. Ironically, one of Cherry's most urgent needs was for coal fuel. The mine's entire output had been shipped, leaving scarcely enough coal available, even if the families had any money to buy it.

But Red Cross director Bicknell was looking beyond the immediate needs of the widows and orphans. He knew philanthropy from Chicago and across the country would eventually dwindle, and proposed dividing the relief funds over several years and establishing a board of trustees to oversee distribution. He and United Charities of Chicago's Sherman C. Kingsley discussed using *Chicago Tribune* Fund monies to pay off the dead miners' home mortgages so that families who wished to stay in Cherry could "fit them up" as boardinghouses to support themselves. A number of the bereaved had already talked of returning to family in their native countries.

Early in the evening, rain began splattering down on Cherry, sending everyone running for shelter. For the first time since their tragedy began to unfold, relatives and friends deserted the shafts. Only a few reporters lingered in the downpour.

CHAPTER TWENTY-EIGHT

Monday, November 22, 1909

Working double shifts, thirty volunteers trailed the fire-fighters' hoses in a race to clear debris trapping about one hundred men. Fifty-two hours and eleven obstacles later, they found only a pile of abandoned picks, shovels and work clothes. Bosses familiar with the area's miners predicted they were deeper in, alive—one had survived a long entombment in another mine.

During the night, several rescuers in the second vein east reported hearing cries for help coming from behind the rock fall. Others insisted the strain was playing tricks on their minds.

Teams shoveled out rock falls through the night, yet hundreds of tons of earth still stood in their way. Before dawn, they broke through one area to find twenty-nine bodies heaped and tangled behind a trap door. In their pockets, Dr. Malm and his assistants found messages to their families, scribbled on papers used to make blasting cartridges, on the edges of newspapers and on sheets torn from time books. There was cash too—two hundred dollars on one victim. Since few miners had bank accounts and boarders had no hiding places in the small, crowded houses where they lived, they kept their life savings where it felt safest, in their pockets.

*   *   *

Midmorning, rescuers' hearts stopped at scratching sounds behind a wall. Though the noise proved only the scurrying of rats, it spurred them on. If rats still lived, men could too. But before noon, they discovered twenty-three more bodies scattered along a corridor, some burned, some asphyxiated. Three bodies were still warm and exultant rescuers caused pandemonium by shouting, "They are alive!" Doctors guessed they had been just twelve hours earlier, but others said the new fires just warmed their bodies. Coroner Malm ruled they'd died within the past twenty-four hours.

By now volunteers and firemen were taxed to their limits. The work was difficult, the odor was unendurable and numerous fires and hidden pockets of black damp continued to plague them. Twenty-five explorers nearly perished when fire erupted in a tunnel, trapping them four thousand feet from the hoisting shaft. The fire was extinguished and the volunteers were rescued.

Later, volunteers chafed when a foreman blocked their entry to several second vein tunnels. Perhaps stirred up by that day's scathing newspaper editorial—"They Saved the Mine, But Lost the Miners"—they became incensed, threw down their shovels and called a strike. When officials explained that black damp hung thick enough in those tunnels to kill them instantly, and that the only safe way to increase ventilation in the mine was to shovel through the cave-ins, they called off their strike and began shoveling.

The largest group taken from the second vein, thirty-seven miners, was found huddled approximately four thousand and five hundred feet from the hoisting shaft. Some were sitting, some were lying flat on their faces, all were asphyxiated. Several had died cranking makeshift paddle fans they'd built from roof timbers. Notes written to their families indicated they had still been conscious on Monday.

John Leptak, a twenty-six-year-old Slav, wrote to his wife and two-year-old daughter, Mary, at 6:00 P.M. on Sunday the fourteenth.

> On Sunday, 15 minutes after 11 o'clock, there were in the last entry 70 of us men, and now we are only 30. The rest died. I am still alive and waiting, my dear wife, for God to come. I bequeath my wife $200; the funeral expenses $100, and to the girl, my daughter, $200. So my dear wife, we are still living a little bit, but we are suffocating. You do as you know

best and live as you can with God.

The longest missive recovered was a heartrending diary written by the young man who'd been trapped with his brother, just hours away from proposing to the girl he loved.

Celina Howard's and Mamie Robinson's vigils were over. Sam Howard and his underage brother Alfred were among the dead.

The day brought another particularly cruel twist of fate. A week in cold depths breathing noxious air had taken its toll on Daniel Holofzak's asthmatic lungs. The oldest survivor was given back to his family barely forty-eight hours. He died in his own bed, leaving his wife and eight children, one to eighteen. At twelve, John became the man of the house, too young to support the family and with brothers still babies just one and three.

To the dismay of Edgar T. Davies, chief state factory inspector, and his assistant, Barney Cohen, two of the day's dead were little trapper boys. Davies told *Tribune* reporters that Illinois mine owners would be immediately ordered to remove everyone under sixteen from their mines. In 1903 and 1904, shortly before the St. Paul Mine opened, Illinois had passed child labor laws that pulled twenty-two hundred boys aged eleven to fifteen from the mines. Davies said most age affidavits for the fifteen hundred children presently employed in Illinois mines "weren't worth the paper they were written on." Owners were being notified to reexamine every one.

By evening, crews had explored every area in the second vein except the fire-blocked northeast section and the east galleries, still sealed off by a series of rock falls. With the stables, pump room and east bottom caved in, mine engineers feared clearing that east bottom fall would cause the shaft to sway, endangering lives. Instead, officials decided to hack a new passage through the coal, circumventing the fire and exiting just behind the fall. It was perilous, it took days, but it worked.

Experienced miners throughout Cherry condemned the state inspectors' handling of the situation. Even the firemen charged there were unnecessary delays in the rescue efforts. National Guard captains Hall and Latimer asked the governor to declare martial law to facilitate the rescue work.

"Something has been the matter," Captain Latimer said. "There have been more cooks than there was broth. That is the reason we thought it would be best for the troops to take the entire charge. We are now acting under the order of the sheriff.

"I hope they will hurry the work and rescue those miners if they are still alive. But there have been too many bosses. That is the trouble."

Governor Deneen refused the captains' request.

Duncan McDonald, Illinois's United Mine Workers Union president, again returned to mine officials to protest unwarranted delays in reaching men on the third vein. He accused "scientific men and their theories" of thwarting the efforts of experienced miners to save their fellows and demanded to be lowered down the air shaft in a bucket so he could see for himself if black damp was present.

McDonald's visit, editorials charging that mine owners favored property preservation over lives and the discovery of the still-warm bodies prompted officials to force an opening into the third vein. They assured McDonald they'd send men down late in the day and hoped to rescue living men before daybreak, believing the strong current of fresh air and the tons of water poured down to douse the fires had increased third vein miners' odds of surviving.

Despite the cries against delays, union officials were outraged to discover mine bosses were coercing some men into working more than thirty-six hours nonstop, without food. One volunteer, subsisting only on sandwiches and coffee, was prevented from coming up top until he collapsed after digging sixty-four hours with virtually no rest. When he was refused food at the Pullman car where other volunteers were eating, Coroner Malm gave him two dollars. He used it to rent a nearby hotel room and sleep.

Besieged with media requests for information, H. M. Wilson, chief engineer with the U.S. Geological Survey in Washington, D.C., wrote J. W. Paul in Pittsburgh for an immediate briefing.

> *This will be a confidential report and should clearly show the embarrassments or otherwise under which you labored in view of your lack of authority, and possession of the same by the operators and state inspectors. So far as I can judge, you, Rice and your assistants are entitled to practically all the credit that is coming, both by opening up the mine earlier than would otherwise have been done, and for the saving of such lives as have been rescued. Unfortunately, at present it does not seem practicable to announce this in other than general terms.*

State inspector W. W. Williams and Pittsburgh geologist George S. Rice took charge of the difficult foray into the third vein. The auxiliary cage, hung from the southeast cage, dangled fifteen feet below the second vein landing, the highest safe level the rock fall allowed. With no ladder available, Archie Frew, Bundy's successor as mine manager, and volunteers Bernard Daugherty and Robert McFadden had to slide down rope to climb atop the auxiliary cage and drop into it.

Rice conducted final tests for gases, found none and just before midnight the men went down. They jumped into water waist deep and waded to the overcast, an opening high above floor level believed impenetrable by black damp and water. They found only a few dinner pails, indicating men had tried to survive there but had later fled.

On ascent, the lower cage got stuck in the shaft. With 38-degree temperatures, water sheeting down from open shaft rings and a strong breeze, the three got so chilled they climbed one hundred vertical feet up slippery buntings to reach the landing. Firemen up top fashioned a sling and pulled them up, one by one, through a hole in the cage seat. They reached the surface as cries came of new fires in the second vein. While volunteers tried catching sleep on cots and blankets in the boiler house, the Chicago firemen spent all night battling the newest blaze to hinder rescue efforts.

CHAPTER TWENTY-NINE

Tuesday, November 23, 1909

With the fire finally subdued, rescuers tried broaching the second vein's east galleries via an abandoned road, but found it caved in.

While search crews spread out over three quarters of a mile, firemen attacked blazes now breaking through several spots in the shaft lining. Smoke billowed twenty-four feet off the floor, suggesting that fire was cresting over the humongous fall. Momentary panic rippled through the vein as firemen hollered into the mine to evacuate and rescuers scrambled for their lives.

"We are now putting all our efforts into fighting a fire which is threatening the main shaft," superintendent Taylor told reporters. "We are absolutely certain there are no living miners in the tunnel. We want to make the shaft safe before we attempt to get out the bodies. It is better to protect the living than to recover the dead."

Once the hoisting cage was dislodged from the shaft, three volunteers went back to explore the third vein. They found scores of bodies, piles of which they couldn't reach because of the flood water. Officials decided to install a pump and pump line to drain out the water, a project that would take days. In the interim, they sent for a skiff from the Illinois River seven miles away.

More victims were discovered above the water line, on ground higher than the shaft on the northeast bottom. They'd hung a canvas barricade and used pieces of rail to fasten down a curtain and close themselves in against black damp. Their notes indicated that they too were still conscious on Monday—before the ventilating fan pushed black damp through their canvas stoppings.

Following a meeting of his union, Duncan McDonald told W. W. Taylor that the United Mine Workers would take full responsibility for the lives of any members who volunteered to search for men, provided they were given free access to the entire mine. Taylor said he'd allow any risks approved by the state inspectors. Soon, Richard Newsam, who'd been in charge since the disaster began, collapsed from exhaustion. Inspectors picked Hector McAllister to replace him, but McDonald telegraphed Governor Deneen, demanding the governor make that appointment instead.

Volunteers had become scarce, driven from the mine by incessant danger, oppressive odors and hideous sights. Mining company officials were forced to offer premiums to entice workers. When they found willing men, they withheld details of conditions in the tunnels and entries and of the continuing collapses.

In town, young Mamie Robinson sat in mourning, rereading the diary found with Sam Howard's body. His writing had grown increasingly indistinct toward his final entries, but Mamie ran her fingertips over occasional passages where he'd pressed the pencil so heavily into the paper that it had cut right through.

Midday, the postmaster came to the tiny Robinson house, bringing Mamie the small package containing her diamond engagement ring. Tears spilled from her eyes as she slipped it on.

"He was brave and good and we are proud of him."

✳   ✳   ✳

Back in Number 83 in the Long Row, widow Jessie Love also received a special postal delivery—a short letter from her brother, Bobby Deans. Postmarked Chicago, this first communication since he'd slipped town said he was leaving there at once with no idea where to go next, but that he would eventually return to Cherry. She was convinced he'd been kidnapped by mine officials.

"He was given money and forced to leave me without any means of support," she said. "The night of the fire he was taken to the Cherry Bank, where he remained for six hours, until after midnight, with representatives of the St. Paul Coal Company. He gave them a statement of what occurred in the mine immediately before and after the fire started. My brother got out of the mine after dropping half-conscious to the floor of the level, but was in no manner responsible for the fire. From the first, he was told that he had better leave the city before he got into trouble on account of the part he had in starting the fire.

"He never left the house from the time the fire started until Thursday night, as he feared for his life. He told me he was warned that unless he left Cherry, he would be taken to a tree, tied there and horsewhipped. He also was told that foreign cutthroats would attack him with knives and kill him.

"Rosenjack was taken away directly afterward," she added. "John Cowley, the mine engineer, has also left the village. Bob went away without saying a word to me."

Meanwhile, Coroner Malm said he intended to take all the time necessary to investigate every angle of the tragedy, including allegations by McDonald and others that mine officials had forced key witnesses to leave town.

CHAPTER THIRTY

Wednesday, November 24, 1909

Antone Laodigiana pushed through the circular tunnel with three other men, calling, "Anybody alive in here?" For more than an hour they waded through water three- to four-feet deep, then, five hundred feet from the hoisting shaft, they climbed a ridge and nearly stepped onto one hundred and sixty-eight bodies huddled together. Some had their heads rested on folded arms as if sleeping, others were lying across one another and some were sitting against the wall. All had most likely climbed there to flee the rising water and black damp.

One victim sat upright, holding three pieces of slate marked with the numbers 23, 45 and 92—increases as miners joined the group, or the number left clinging to life as black damp claimed their comrades? Messages were scratched on other slate shards torn from the ceiling and walls: "*We are trying to save ourselves. We have been waiting for someone to rescue us. We are—*"

"*We are here to die together,*" was penciled across a toolbox lid, with numerals following. Laodigiana thought it read 168. "I'm not sure. The writing was wavering as if it had been written by someone who was mighty weak."

Like Sam Howard and other second vein victims, these men had made paddle fans to stave off black damp. Theirs resembled steamboat paddles about three feet in diameter, built from drill machine parts and toolboxes the men had torn apart. The dead lay heaped below the fans. One man's hand was up, holding the fan.

"I think he died as he was turning it," Laodigiana said. "Another had a bucket in his hand. He was flat on his back and must have died as he climbed the ridge. The bucket was half-filled with black water that he must have gone some distance to get."

These miners had even begun to wall themselves in. Their barrier, a few feet high, stood abandoned midconstruction.

Officials lowered the skiff brought in from the Illinois River and rowed it across the vein to collect the victims. More were found in a grotesque heap at the bottom of the burned-out air-shaft stairwell. Firemen said they hadn't been dead long, but mine officials told reporters that decomposition had already set in.

No one expected to find such large numbers of men in the third vein when only one hundred and eighty-one miners worked there. Officials speculated that some second vein miners fled down into the mine when fire cut off their escape route, and that others, overcome by smoke and exertion while they climbed the burning staircase, had fallen backward into the bottom of the mine. The discovery of these newest victims sent many Cherry miners into angry protest, claiming that black damp would never have killed them if the ventilating fan had not been reversed shortly after the fire began.

Up top, workmen dismantled the ruined Clifford-Capell fan and loaded its heat-twisted blades onto a freight car bound for Milwaukee to return it to the manufacturing plant for repair.

Meanwhile, officials hesitated to reopen any second vein tunnels where they'd managed to keep fires extinguished for several hours, fearing that the slightest breeze would rekindle them.

*   *   *

George Rice soon discovered something deadly to all of Cherry accumulating in the mine. The geologist found pockets of white damp or carbon monoxide—enough to blow up the mine and the entire town above it. Still, officials scoffed at rumors they would seal up the mine before nightfall for fear of an explosion. Their primary concern, they said, was fire once more raging out of control on the shaft's south and east sides, encroaching on the shaft itself.

To save it, they cut holes in the lining above the second vein and poured water behind it, then boarded up the shaft's south and east sides just short of the cage and built a stopping near the air shaft bottom, hoping to subdue the fire burning between the two shafts. The maneuver had limited success. Accelerating smoke and steam rising behind the shaft lining changed courses to gag and suffocate crews west of the hoisting shaft.

Then the situation worsened. The distinctive, strong smell of burning coal filled the air and everyone knew the coal face itself had caught fire, producing extremely dangerous gases.

Shortly after midnight, the state mining board president, state mining inspectors, fire chief, rescue station geologists and coal company representatives held a conference. After exhaustive discussion, they unanimously agreed that everyone remaining in the mine was dead, and that the only hope of ever retrieving their bodies was to seal up both shafts before fire destroyed them. Cherry would have to wait out the fire, no matter how long it took.

Three hours into Thanksgiving Day, workers began to seal both shafts for the third time. Working through the night by lantern light, they used steel rails and concrete, inserting a two-inch pipe in the main shaft's cement cover to allow frequent monitoring of the shaft's temperature, pressure and air quality.

Every now and then, the men momentarily ceased their work, overcome by the sobs of another woman.

* * *

Support personnel began trickling out of Cherry on Thanksgiving—mine experts from other states, nurses, representatives of charitable organizations and, later, half the troops. Governor Deneen kept Company K for a time, until threats to dynamite open the shafts stopped circulating. Only six nuns, four nurses, a handful of mine officials and experts remained. Every few days the experts tested shaft temperatures, finally concluding it would be months before they could open the shaft.

The St. Paul Coal Company, however, was intent on reopening the mine as soon as possible, fearing that it might never be worked again otherwise. Survivors were already calling the $700,000 main shaft "hoodooed."

On November 30, 1909, more than six weeks after it was first ordered, the new electrical wire arrived at the mine.

CHAPTER THIRTY-ONE

December 1909

The mine company disbursed the last wages owed on pay-day, December 1. The next day, Coroner Malm finally re-convened the inquest jury—W. I. Kendall, deputy coroner and foreman; Peter Delphin, Cherry's marshall; John A. Stenstrum, barber; John C. Thompson, lumberman; Timothy McDonald, farmer and Joseph Neidetcher, alderman. Mrs. Harry P. Phelps, Malm's stenographer, and Chicago court reporter Neil Satterlee recorded the proceedings.

Dr. Malm presided, allowing full interrogation privileges to the Illinois Mining Investigation Commission and the Illinois Inspectors of Mines, represented by Glen W. Traer; and the United Mine Workers, represented by attorney Seymour Stedman.

Also attending were United Mine Workers Union president, Duncan McDonald; commission members J. H. Walker, Charles Burch and Bernard Murphy; Graham Taylor and H. H. Stoek, independent members of the commission; J. W. Miller, coal operator and commission member; Thomas Hudson, state mine inspector of the second district, which encompassed the Cherry Mine; and Hector McAllister, state mine inspector of the first district.

Seymour Stedman began, introducing the mine's charter into evidence. It was owned by the St. Paul Coal Company, an Illinois corporation organized in October 1902, capitalized for three hundred and fifty thousand dollars and divided into thirty-five thousand shares. Railroad president A. J. Earling owned three thousand four hundred and ninety-six of them, with Burton Hanson, F. G. Ranney, H. K. Williams and H. G. Hangan each owning one share.

Mine superintendent James Steele was the first of sixty-two witnesses to be questioned about everything they had seen or done during the fire. He reported repeated attempts to obtain replacement wiring, first through the Cherry Mine's clerk Frank P. Buck, then Granville's clerk Hugo Lindig. Lindig testified he'd requisitioned the electrical cable on October 14, and again two weeks later.

Driver Charles Thorne testified that he'd left the hay cart twenty-five or thirty feet from the air shaft and that the blaze from hanging kerosene torches never came closer than eight to ten inches from any wood roof or timbering.

Mine clerk Frank P. Buck's testimony was evasive at best. He insisted ignorance of the identities of mine company officers, directors or shareholders, or that railroad president A. J. Earling had any connection with the mine. Yet, he admitted to carrying out several of Earling's orders soon after the disaster, but could give no explanation for following the directives of someone with no authority over him.

Mine carpenter R. L. Daugherty said he'd seen men fleeing the mine for two hours after the fire started. He told jurors it generally took one hour for all the miners to exit at day's end.

Q: If these men had all been notified at the starting of the fire, do you think they could have been out?

A: Yes, sir, I think so.

John Chedister, the mechanic, was questioned about the bell signal confusion that contributed to the heroes' deaths on the cage. He'd tested the pneumatic bell several days after the fire and it did not work. He repaired its pipes, which had filled with ice, and also had to replace the cylinder and plunger. He said the trap door he'd installed between the rails on the second vein was set on a hinge that a third vein miner could open with the slightest touch, but admitted a coal car sitting over the trap door would have left a miner only a seven-inch opening to crawl through.

George Eddy recounted the early hours of the fire and the week spent underground. He told jurors there was but one exit sign, ROAD TO THE ESCAPE SHAFT, written in English only, on a board nailed to a timber midway in the second vein. He said the mine had just two water spigots, one at the main shaft and one at the stable.

Two key witnesses were notably absent from the proceedings— Alexander Rosenjack and Robert Deans.

Although Coroner Malm had requested Rosenjack post bond after the fire and he'd agreed, Malm had been too busy with the heroes' bodies that first Sunday to pursue it once Rosenjack assured him he would return to testify. Malm didn't know if searches for Deans and Rosenjack were made, despite contacting Sheriff Skoglund and Spring Valley Deputy Sheriff Hicks attempting to locate the two.

State's attorney Lawrence M. Eckert testified that Rosenjack had phoned his Princeton office a few days after the fire, telling his stenographer he was at the nearby American House and would keep her advised of his moves. Eckert found Rosenjack had registered as John Smith and refused to sign his name, then left Princeton the following morning. He was next reported in Cherry, drawing pay from mine clerk Frank P. Buck before heading to LaSalle. Eckert searched LaSalle all day without finding him. A billiard hall proprietor told him Rosenjack had played there all day and part of the night and that he "wasn't looked upon with much favor" after he'd bragged to patrons about who he was and that he had a gun.

Back in Cherry, Eckert learned from Rosenjack's friend, young Fred H. Buck, that he was enroute first to Chicago's Saratoga Hotel, then to Peoria. Eckert and Buck couldn't find him in Chicago and without funds to hire detectives, Eckert never pursued the Peoria lead. Eckert believed Rosenjack was absent out of fear, based on threats overheard as Rosenjack restrained the crowd after the fire.

> A: . . . I heard people on the sideline say he ought to be hung and shot, and things of that kind.

Fred H. Buck testified next, saying first that he'd last seen Rosenjack in Cherry on the Sunday following the tragedy. Asked if he'd seen him back in Cherry later that week, he said he "couldn't say what day it was that I last saw Mr. Rosenjack." He admitted receiving a letter in which Rosenjack said he felt safer staying away for a while, a letter Buck said he had destroyed.

Frank Mehovich, who boarded with Rosenjack, said he'd first discovered Rosenjack was gone when he didn't show for supper November 15, and that Rosenjack's trunk and clothes were still in the boardinghouse as recently as a week ago. He said Rosenjack's brother, August, who was also a coal miner, lived in Pennsylvania.

State's attorney Eckert, recalled to testify regarding Bobby Deans's whereabouts, said he'd seen him only once. Crossing paths at the coal company office, he'd asked Deans where he lived, but when Eckert went to speak with him, he'd already left town.

Deputy Sheriff Hicks was grilled about his efforts to locate Rosenjack and Deans. He said he'd gone up to LaSalle and Oglesby looking for Rosenjack, but had made no effort to find Deans, nor asked assistance from any other sheriffs or police in the state.

> Q: Do you consider that a fulfillment of your duty in an important case like this?
>
> A: I didn't know he was really wanted so bad. I understood, and I was talking to Rosenjack myself, that he would be here for the trial, as the coroner stated. . . . I haven't made as strenuous an effort to find him as I might have done. The coroner

gave me the subpoena for him, and I didn't go very far with
it; that is as far as I have done.

Unlike Deans and Rosenjack, engineer John Cowley did face the
jury. He recounted the events of November 13, from the time he
first smelled "something burning like tar" about 1:15 P.M. Deputy
coroner W. I. Kendall tried to impeach Cowley's testimony with the
statement he'd given on November 14, pouncing when Cowley recounted his confusion on hearing a seven-bell signal, a fact he'd
omitted previously. Kendall zeroed in on that seven-bell reference,
using it as a hammer to pound away at Cowley's entire testimony.
He asked if anyone had coached him, if mine officials had come to
him for a statement, if he'd gone into the train car to talk with them.

Cowley denied being coached or inside the train, but said he'd
given W. W. Taylor a verbal statement in the engine house when the
general superintendent came to him. Traer then asked if anybody on
top had authority to give him orders to raise the cages.

A: No, sir. . . . Only the bosses at the bottom. Mr. Bundy was the
only man that had authority to give me orders.

[He agreed he took a chance raising the cage that last time.]

Q: But you thought that was the thing to do, to take chances at
that time?

A: Yes, sir, when I seen that smoke was rolling out of the mine;
I thought it was time to get that cage away.

After the martyrs were taken from the cage, he ran seven or
eight cages down at intervals, ringing bells. Then his buddy took
over, running twelve to fifteen more without rescuing anyone
else.

On the stand, second vein cager William "Billy" Richards said he
only hoisted two cages of coal after the fire began. He repeatedly de-

nied telling Albert Buckle, Domenico Cresto or anyone else they could not go up but had to go on working. Although as cager he was always the last man out of the mine, he said he'd left his post after sending the explosives out because it was impossible to remain in the smoke and heat with fire just two hundred and twenty-five feet away. Asked how men had been able to go down into the mine long after he'd left, he attributed it to the reversal of the fan.

Richards admitted to being a foreman, yet disclaimed any responsibility to warn the men to flee the mine. He said his only authority was to order men off the cage if too many of them got on.

Martin Powers, the United Mine Workers Union check weighman, said it was impossible to keep track of every man who went down each morning because if a miner had "checks" left in his pockets from the previous day, he wouldn't stop at Powers's desk for more.

Before testimony continued, the joint commission formally requested state's attorney Eckert to convene a meeting of the county board of supervisors to request the necessary funds to bring in Deans and Rosenjack to testify.

CHAPTER THIRTY-TWO

Spurred by the testimony, Stedman directed his Chicago law firm to research manslaughter liability laws. Those associates and Duncan McDonald, meanwhile, apprised him of several individuals in Cherry who might be spies employed by the mine company.

On December 4, miner Robert Reed testified that he'd seen Rosenjack heading toward Cherry the previous night. Ladd buggy driver Mose Meek, hired to take Rosenjack to the boardinghouse to collect his trunk, testified that they were stopped by a man just outside Cherry. Rosenjack chatted with him, then directed Meek to return immediately to Ladd without retrieving his belongings.

Mrs. Jessie Love testified that she hadn't seen her brother, Robert Deans, "since the official came and took him away." Kendall asked if Deans had any money to stay at the Chicago hotel from which he'd written her. She told him she knew he had nothing.

Q: You are satisfied that somebody else must have furnished him the money and had him stay away?

A: Yes, sir, certainly they did. If it hadn't been for that he never would have left me.

Frank P. Buck was recalled. His testimony turned from evasive to belligerent. Six times in succession, he refused to answer whether he'd received any recent communications from Rosenjack. (See transcript excerpt, Appendix A, Article 3.) When Traer asked if he knew Rosenjack was in the carriage the night before, he refused to answer. Coroner Malm asked why. "Because I don't want to." Stedman asked what conversation he'd had with Rosenjack the night before. Buck said none, he hadn't seen him.

Walker asked if he'd heard from any other source that Rosenjack was in town, or if anyone had met him. Buck just smiled. Finally, he admitted knowing that someone had met Rosenjack in Cherry, but he refused to say who it was.

Walker then asked Malm to have Buck's son brought to the proceedings, requesting that father and son have no contact and no opportunity to discuss the questions. There was a pervasive belief that the mine company was coaching the employees called to testify.

Buck said his son could not leave the office before he returned, that one of them had to be there.

"Lock the office and bring him over here," Stedman ordered.

On the stand once more, Fred H. Buck readily conceded speaking to Rosenjack for fifteen minutes the previous night, and said when Rosenjack phoned him ten minutes before heading for Cherry, he'd told his father. He denied knowing there was a subpoena for Rosenjack and said he didn't tell his friend the coroner and commission wanted him because Rosenjack already knew it. Young Buck said he had no idea where Rosenjack was headed, only that he'd said he was afraid to show himself in Cherry. Buck admitted ordering the bank to give Rosenjack his pay, but couldn't say when he'd done so, and denied acting under any instructions from mine company officers.

Despite repeated questions about what he'd said to Rosenjack that made him turn back before retrieving his trunk, young Buck denied telling him anything that would have prompted that move.

Dr. L. D. Howe told of the heroes' rescue efforts and accused engineer John Cowley of "bull-headedness" in refusing to raise the last cage sooner and taking his time once he'd decided to hoist it.

A: ... he pulled it out about as fast as a snail would crawl ...

Dr. Howe also testified that he'd seen no one in charge during the crisis, while he and the others were risking their lives trying to drag out as many as they could save.

A: I saw no effort made. I saw none of the bosses on the bottom at all.

Cherry Bank clerk Charles Connolly testified that on the Monday or Tuesday following the fire, Fred H. Buck brought in a note requesting a twenty dollar salary advance for Alexander Rosenjack, which he gave to Buck. A week or ten days later, he filled another advance, this time from Rosenjack's bank account. He also said Robert Deans did not have an account at the bank.

John Cahill, another Cherry Bank clerk, said he'd received a note for money from Rosenjack ten days ago. Although he'd destroyed the note, he denied anyone had told him to do so. He also denied knowing of any arrangements for Deans and Rosenjack to leave town, and said no one from the coal company had talked with him or Connolly prior to their testimony here.

Before the session concluded on December 9, juror John C. Thompson told the coroner that without Rosenjack's or Deans's testimony, or satisfactory evidence that every effort had been made to locate them to testify, the jury would not announce a verdict. Dr. Malm adjourned the proceedings until 1:30 P.M., December 20, in hopes of securing Rosenjack, Deans and several other witnesses. On December 20, without taking any testimony, the coroner adjourned again until 1:00 P.M., January 4, 1910.

On December 21, Beatrice Galletti filed a petition to appoint Chicago's Northern Trust Company to collect and administer her son John's estate. She placed its value at $10,000, the amount of her wrongful death suit against the St. Paul Coal Company.

CHAPTER THIRTY-THREE

January, 1910

With still no signs of the missing witnesses, the coroner's inquest reconvened on January 4, 1910. Failing to appear were Alexander Rosenjack, Robert Deans, state mine inspector Thomas Moses, Burton Hanson, St. Paul Coal Company secretary and W. W. Taylor, St. Paul Coal Company president, who had assured Cook County Sheriff Christopher Strassheim that he would testify.

Alma Lettsome was the last new witness. He was asked if he'd heard any statement from Rosenjack as to how the accident occurred.

A: Mr. Rosenjack made a statement to me.

Q: What did Mr. Rosenjack say?

A: He told me to chop his head off—going down the track. We went down the track, after the disaster, together. We went into Depue together, and he sent a message to his father and I sent one to mine, and we both went in there together.

The coroner recalled Frank P. Buck. He admitted asking Danny Robinson to take a man to see if Bobby Deans was at his sister's home, but said he didn't know his name and wouldn't recognize him again. He denied calling for an automobile, knowing anyone who had or meeting with Deans or Rosenjack at the Cherry Bank.

Buck said he hadn't heard from either man since last testifying, but had heard rumors around town that Deans was back in Scotland. He admitted visiting Chicago twice since the controversy began, but said he saw neither man there. He continued to deny knowing who the officers of the St. Paul Coal Company were.

James Hanney was recalled as the final witness. He denied ever saying during the fire that he could have put out the hay cart blaze with his coat, and insisted he'd never heard anyone who was with him at the time say it.

> A: . . . I heard a whole lot of persons say it since—I never heard anyone say it, with authority—with any authority. At the time I seen it would have taken a lot of coats to put it out; it would take a whole lot of them.

The proceedings were continued to 1:00 P.M., February 1, 1910. Transcribed, the nine long days of testimony would add 731 legal-size pages to the three hundred Dr. Malm amassed during preliminary questioning. In addition to child labor law violations, an array of violations of the state mining laws had been exposed:

There was no separate and continuous escapement shaft running from the top to the bottom of the mine, within the meaning of the legislation.

In the absence of a legal escapement shaft, one hundred and eighty-one men were employed in the third vein.

There were no sign boards posted to indicate the routes leading to the exits.

Instead of only pure animal or vegetable oil, kerosene was used in the mine.

During the night shift, one engineer had to run between engine houses fifty feet apart to operate cages in both shafts, although law required that an engineer remain at each throttle while men were underground.

The state mining inspector, who was sworn to uphold the law, allowed the escape shaft to be placed less than three hundred feet from the main shaft.

The main passageway was obstructed with lengths of pipe.

Hoisting signals were not posted directly in front of the engineer at the throttle.

Explosives were stored inside the mine.

During the Bureau County Court's January session, Judge Joe A. Davis entered orders appointing the Northern Trust Company administrator of the miners' estates and set the wrongful death trial date for June 20. With nearly three hundred lawsuits pending against the St. Paul Coal Company, Streator Relief Committee vice president John E. Williams feared litigation dragging on for years, forcing the coal company into bankruptcy before most claims were satisfied. The former miner spearheaded a mediation plan, making overtures to the parties involved before inviting local and national United Mine Workers Union leaders and representatives of the coal company and the Streator Relief Committee to discuss settlement options in Chicago the second week in January. The coal company sent Williams a letter denying responsibility but nevertheless supporting his proposal for a settlement conference.

With no indication by early January that the mine would soon be unsealed, foreign consuls hired lawyers for their nationals with loved ones still entombed to protest the "unreasonable" lengthy closure and to demand that the mine be opened.

*   *   *

The coroner had not rendered a verdict by the time the United Mine Workers of Illinois published the findings of its independent investigation on January 15. The thirty-seven-page report enumerated the statutory violations brought to light during the inquest and concluded that the coal company was solely responsible for both the disaster and the disappearance of the two key witnesses. It called for an overhaul of industry practices and the creation of uniform mining laws throughout the United States.

The union also demanded that mine inspectors challenge age affidavits and strictly enforce child labor laws. All ten boys employed in the mine—Albert Buckle, Richard Buckle, Matt Francesco, Alfred Howard, Frank Jagodzinski, Alfred Kroll, Joe Leadacke, Andrew Packo, Albert Sandeen, and Edward Sandeen —had been hired on illegally before they'd turned sixteen. Four of them—Richard Buckle, Alfred Howard, Alfred Kroll and Joe Leadacke—had been killed in the fire.

CHAPTER THIRTY-FOUR

February 1910

It took the Milwaukee manufacturer two full months to repair the huge melted Clifford-Capell fan and return it to Cherry. Crews reinstalled and cased it while they waited for the mine to cool, but temperatures declined slowly. When checked on February 1, the hoisting shaft was 68 degrees, unchanged from January 29. Officials decided to unseal the shaft, concluding this must be the mine's natural temperature. Workers cut a three-foot-square opening in the shaft's concrete cover, directly above the north hoisting cage hanging just inches below.

Inspectors Webb and Moses donned Draeger apparatus to explore the second vein and found it basically the same as when the mine was sealed. They saw no smoke or fire and reported the temperature comfortable enough to work. Tests after a second trip to retrieve air samples confirmed that black damp still predominated the air.

Later in the afternoon, crews removed both shafts' concrete covers and started up the fan in reverse to draw air down the hoisting shaft and exhaust it up the air shaft, forcing out the black damp. Once it had run long enough to clear the air in the west runaround, two of the state mining inspectors took their lamps, went down and decided it was safe for men to enter with lamps, since a steady stream of fresh air was flowing through the mine.

Throughout the night, workmen cleaned out falls of broken roof timbers in the west runaround and reinforced brattice around the main shaft's east and south sides to block the fire. The work was slow and dangerous, but officials decided it was safest to employ as few men as possible to handle it. Their main goal was to clear the west passage, opening a second road leading out of the mine to give underground workers a sense of safety. Later in the week, the road was clear enough for pit cars to travel through it. Workers brought down a large steam pump to throw out third vein water.

On February 10, state's attorney Lawrence M. Eckert returned to Cherry to meet with bereaved families who'd filed wrongful death claims against the coal company. He read them the company's prepared settlement contract proposing settlements ranging from eight hundred dollars for childless miners up to twelve hundred dollars for those leaving the greatest number of offspring. Already alarmed by statements that they'd receive virtually nothing if their lawsuits forced the coal company into receivership, families were uneasy with Eckert's unexpected involvement on the company's behalf. He tried to reassure them that his intent was to protect their rights, but his makeshift headquarters in W. W. Taylor's sleeping car and the modest settlement offers suggested a suspiciously cozy relationship with the coal company. The survivors' response was an angry protest.

Aided by mules, volunteer crews spent all of February cleaning out the second vein and constantly repairing the pipelines that kept swelling from heat and bursting when cages hit them.

Cherry was locked in a recurring nightmare of grieving and funerals. Fifteen more bodies were discovered the second week of February. Four more came out during the third. Many were mummified and disintegrated the moment they reached fresh air. Horrified, relatives in the midst of identifying loved ones saw noses crumble from their faces and their heads and limbs fall off.

Three months had passed and still the fire refused to die. It smoldered behind shaft timbers, throwing off constant heat and smoke. But by February's end, most timbering and shaft linings were repaired and the air shaft staircase rebuilt. After finding sixty-five bodies in the north entry between February 27 and March 5, officials determined they'd recovered all second vein victims.

It turned out that the gunshots that farmers had reported hearing from below ground in the earliest hours of disaster were not signals from trapped miners after all. Workmen found the body of an older miner beside several dead youths. He'd shot all of them in the head and then sat, waiting to join them.

Among the scores of dead miners recovered in early March was eighteen-year-old Johnny Galletti. Following a small double funeral, Beatrice Galletti buried her eldest son alongside Elfi Carlo in the Ladd Cemetery on March 6, 1910.

Just two days earlier, state lawmakers had enacted Senate Bill 42, creating the Mine Rescue Station Commission of the State of Illinois, the first in the nation. It was mandated to build rescue stations both to furnish rescue teams trained to respond to mine accident scenes and to serve as training facilities to instruct state miners in mine rescue procedures and first aid.

Despite the modest offer Eckert had presented to claimants, self-appointed mediator John E. Williams was encouraged by his preliminary meetings with representatives of labor and the coal company. After tallying the various relief donations, he determined five hundred thousand dollars more would be needed for the Cherry families.

Though the four-hundred-million-dollar Chicago, Milwaukee and St. Paul Railway Company owned the St. Paul Coal Company, it had no legal liability for the Cherry disaster beyond the resources of its coal company, which owned the ill-fated mine. Williams calculated that if every judgment was affirmed and the coal company was either sold for full value, with no creditors, or forced into bankruptcy, each claimant would net out only about $1,000. He looked to English law in proposing a settlement, studying Parliament's Workmen's Compensation Act of 1906, which set the compensation for an accidental death at three times the employee's annual salary.

With an admission in hand of "a moral obligation" to the dependents by railroad president Arthur J. Earling, Williams sought the opinion of the Cherry Relief Committee. Every member favored mediation as the "best possible solution and the greatest precedent for the future."

Next, Williams drafted two settlement proposals, one based on the new English law, the other to be based upon recommendations from a commission to be appointed by the President of the United States. He and three top United Mine Workers officials took the two proposals to Earling. Though the railroad president favored the plan based on English law, as did the foreign consuls, he refused to pay out any more than two hundred and fifty thousand dollars.

Williams next called a general meeting of the widows, hoping to convince them to dismiss their lawsuits in favor of his proposed settlement. Next, he tried persuading Earling to pay out triple wages. Shuttling back and forth from foreign consuls to union officials, the mine company, widows and orphans, Williams distributed copies of the English legislation in a singlehanded effort to build a consensus between these disparate interests.

Negotiations repeatedly broke down, often within a hair's breadth of settlement, but Williams was undeterred. In the end, he achieved an agreement based on the English code, but not everyone was appeased. A majority of the claimants did drop their suits, but nearly sixty others decided to hold out for more.

In March, Paul Yerly of Spring Valley buried his twenty-year-old son, then sat down to pen a letter protesting the proposed settlement.

> . . . we have identified my son Joe at the Cherry mine. State Attorney Eckert told me that the counsel and yourself are to settle for the

widows for $1800 and the single men $500 but we do not want to settle for that . . .

Throughout March, workers at the mine alternated between dousing the fire and blocking it. They pumped out water, packed sandbags around the main shaft and reinforced brattices there to protect it from fire. For a time, the fire threat was so ominous, officials evacuated both men and mules. By the end of March, most of the water was pumped from the mine and carpenters had built a special cage to hoist out all of the rock.

On March 29, Richard Newsam and four of his state mining inspectors went down into the third vein. They plunged into two and a half feet of water and found most of the works around the bottom untouched by fire. When they ventured farther, however, they encountered huge rock falls closing off roads into the back of the mine where they expected to find more bodies.

It took crews a full week of rock shoveling before mine inspector Hector McAllister, mine manager Archie Frew and shift foreman John Fraser could climb over the remaining falls, broken timbers and other debris to look for other third vein victims. They spotted bodies scattered along a one hundred-foot area at the end of the north air course near the air shaft bottom, and crews began clearing a passageway to them. On Sunday, April 10, thirty-one more victims were found huddled together. Before they'd died, these men had constructed two fans from one-by-twelve-inch boards mounted on mine props. The fans measured four feet in diameter and turned with mine machine handles. One of the blades bore a final message, written in chalk: "All *alive*–2 P.M. , 14."

Workers took the fans to the mine company's office. By Tuesday, when W. W. Taylor ordered carpenters to crate them up and load them on a train to Chicago, hundreds in town had come to look at them. A crowd collected as the train pulled into Cherry and watched in silence until station agent C. W. Jacobs and the carpenters began to load on the huge crate. Suddenly, they charged the train with a roar, battling the carpenters, the sheriff, his deputies and anyone else who stood in their path.

Shrieking curses, a crush of women flailed their way through the front lines. They fell on the crate and attacked the wood with bareknuckled frenzy, ripping away the boards to get at the fans. Victorious, the women hefted the fans to their shoulders and paraded them through Cherry while the crowd surged after them. On the verge of a riot, they blockaded Main Street, forcing business to a standstill for more than an hour.

The women harbored the fans inside two of the widows' homes and refused to relinquish them. Throughout the night they took turns standing sentry at both homes' doorways and porches, prepared to defend their spoils with whatever strength they had left.

By April 15, twenty more bodies were retrieved from the third vein. Chief mine clerk Frank P. Buck said there were only five to seven men still unaccounted for. That same week the four state inspectors who'd been working in nonstop relay fashion since the mine was reopened on February 1 decided that unless fire broke out again in earnest, their work in Cherry was completed. On April 13, they departed for home.

St. Paul Coal Company officials decided to permanently abandon the second vein and to concentrate all future mining in the vast third vein. Over the next thirty days, men worked to close down the middle vein, ripping out everything of value from the interior workings there—pit cars, tools, tracks and timber.

By the middle of May the fires had been burning nonstop for more than six months. Despite constant water, they still sizzled deep in third vein coal ribs near pump room and stables.

On May 10, the coroner's jury finally rendered its verdicts.

. . . We, the undersigned Jurors, sworn to inquire into the death of Alex. Norberg, on oath do find that he came to his death by burns received while on a cage at or near the second vein, in the main shaft of the St. Paul Coal Company's mine at Cherry in said county, while engaged in an attempt to rescue the miners in said mine, during the late fire therein, to-wit, on November 13, A.D. 1909, at about 3:30 o'clock, P.M.

And we further find that said death was caused indirectly by a confusion of the signals regulating the movement of said cage.

Findings on the deaths of the trapped miners read differently.

We, the undersigned Jurors, sworn to inquire into the death of Thomas Bayliff on oath do find that he came to his death by suffocation in the mine of the St. Paul Coal Company in Cherry in said county, during the late fire therein, which said fire broke out on November thirteenth A.D. 1909, at about 1:20 to 1:30 o'clock P.M. and which said fire was caused by a pit car load of baled hay coming in contact with, or in close proximity to an oil torch in the second vein of said mine.

And we further find that said fire was caused by the careless handling of said car load of hay while in transit to the third vein of said shaft.

And we further find that there was a great delay in notifying the men in said mine of the danger by reason of said fire in time to insure their escape.

CHAPTER THIRTY-FIVE

The catastrophe at Cherry occurred on the heels of the Industrial Revolution and while the Progressive movement was pushing for labor reforms. The turn of the century had sparked a wave of improvements arising from the dual belief that the unregulated growth of industrial capitalism was eroding the quality of American life and the rights of the millions of immigrants crowding into the nation's cities. Progressives envisioned a new political and social democracy with the power and will to reform corporate monopolies and boss-ridden political machines. They sought to change wages, labor conditions and the general welfare of working people with legislative changes in the areas of minimum wage, maximum hours, child labor laws and safe working conditions.

In 1902, Maryland passed legislation designed to protect injured workers. By 1910, several other states were exploring the framework for similar laws, but the concept of a comprehensive worker's compensation act did not take firm hold until Cherry.

The polarization between labor and management in the Cherry settlement mirrored sentiments in the country as a whole. While the St. Paul Coal Company had paid out four hundred thousand dollars in settlements by mid-May, a number of widows still continued to press their lawsuits. As John E. Williams strove to win over these last holdouts, he and United Mine Workers attorney Seymour Stedman exchanged a heated barrage of lengthy, insulting letters.

In early May, Williams wrote Stedman, accusing his firm of assisting Johnson and Belasco, the law firm trying the remaining cases. He denounced Johnson and Belasco agent John Zukowski's repeat visits to Cherry, urging clients to hold out by telling them the mine company would pay them higher awards either to avoid the expense and trouble of a lawsuit, or because there were now so few claims left that the company had assets adequate to pay out full judgments in case of a trial.

Williams urged Stedman to influence settlement instead, insisting that these claims, added to the mine company's prior four hundred thousand dollars in debt and anticipated $75,000 expense to rehabilitate the plant, would force it into receivership or bankruptcy. His bigger concern, however, was that the claims would jeopardize nascent worker's compensation laws.

> *Shall it now be said that it failed in the Cherry case? Shall the reactionary employer be able to point to Cherry and say, "I told you so. The working men are unappreciative, ungrateful and thankless?" Shall we justify the critics of President Earling who predicted that any man would get the worst of it who tried fair dealing in a personal injury case?*

Stedman replied with a seven-page attack and a prediction that the Cherry affair would not result in passage of an employer's liability law.

> *. . . Mr. A. J. Ehrling [sic] must smile in his sleeve at your naive expression, especially when he considers how easily his company is being relieved of the whole affair and that the stockholders will not materially suffer.*
> *. . . I cannot weep over railroad tracks, steam engines and Wall Street gamblers and worse . . . I know of the railroading of two witnesses away from the scene of the accident, one was taken to Europe. It*

may be that Bobbie Deans paid his own way to Scotland—I doubt it. . . . You [say you] were "led to enter this affair as a mediator to settle a precedent." You flatter yourself. You have been a tool in the hands of the railroad company. . . .

Soon after, the mine company voluntarily raised to the mediation amount all settlements that were privately struck soon after the fire. On May 23, 1910, the Streator *Daily Free Press* reported that $400 checks had been written to Mrs. Mittal and Mrs. Cebulka and sent to their attorney-in-fact for forwarding. The two Hungarian widows had already signed release documents, settling in full for $1,200 before moving their families back to Europe.

CHAPTER THIRTY-SIX

S now yielded to spring rains and those to the summer sun, and the farmland surrounding Cherry began to grow lush once more. Seasons changed, sorrow remained. The dead had left behind 160 widows and 470 children, 407 under fourteen, thirty-three of them born since the fire. A three year old and one widow had died. Thirty-five widows had returned to Europe, twenty-two re-married.

From May into September, crews worked to clean out rock falls around both shafts in the third vein and then to rebuild and rein-force the mine with timber, steel and concrete. They permanently sealed off the second vein from the main shaft and drove a new entry through the coal face to house a water reservoir to furnish the third vein in case of future fire.

On June 15, Ernest P. Bicknell realized his vision of a permanent re-lief commission as the Cherry Relief Committee turned over its records and the remaining $281,538.13 to the Cherry Relief Com-mission. Its members, from the various organizations and commu-nities that had generated and held those funds, served gratis and throughout their tenure kept in close contact with the pension fam-ilies they served.

Since the coal company had made flat cash payments of $1,620 to every widow regardless of family size, Bicknell drafted a plan to ben-efit the children, using extensive data collected in Cherry by the

American Red Cross. A twenty-five dollar monthly pension was allotted widows with children under fourteen, increasing five dollars per child to a maximum forty dollars. All other widows, and orphans who'd lost both parents, received a lump sum payment—widows under fifty, three hundred dollars, over fifty, five hundred dollars. Death benefits paid by the Illinois United Mine Workers Union were $150, or approximately three months' salary; the national Knights of Pythias paid out seventy dollars and the local, fifty dollars.

Between the mine company and the relief funds, each victim's family ultimately received approximately $3,261.72.

Brothers Joe and John Bernardini, among the last out of the burning mine, received the best settlement from the coal company. Permanently crippled by their burns, each received sixty-five hundred dollars.

On June 23, the St. Paul Coal Company pled guilty to nine counts of child labor law violations and was fined a total of $630. On July 7, workers clearing an area just ten feet from the air shaft discovered a body buried beneath a roof fall. Nearly eight months after the fire began, the last victim was brought out of the mine and Dr. Malm recalled his jurors to render their final verdict.

CHAPTER THIRTY-SEVEN

On October 10, 1910, the Carnegie Hero Fund Commission awarded its silver medal to George Eddy, forty-eight, mine examiner and boss, and Walter Waite, forty-one, assistant mine manager, and to eleven who'd sacrificed their lives on the cage: John Bundy, fifty-three, second vein mine manager; Robert Clark, twenty-eight, miner; John Flood, forty-nine, merchant; Dominick Formento, thirty-two, merchant; Isaac Lewis Jr., thirty-four, liveryman; Andrew McLuckie, thirty-one, miner; J. Alexander Norberg, thirty-eight, third vein mine manager; James Speir, thirty-four, miner; Henry Stewart, twenty-eight, miner; John Szabrinski (Smith) twenty-nine, cage operator; and Charles Waite, forty-three, mine examiner and boss. Driver Joseph Robeza Jr., twenty-two, would not receive his posthumous silver medal until May 1, 1911. Miner John Suhe, nineteen, who also sacrificed his life in the seven rescue attempts was the only hero passed over for the award. His father was still in the mine and the Carnegie Commission at the time did not recognize attempts to rescue relatives as heroism.

Industrialist Andrew Carnegie established the medal in 1904 to recognize acts of outstanding civilian heroism in the U.S. and Canada. Both Eddy and Waite were awarded $1,000 in cash and the martyrs' widows received monthly grants of varying amounts.

The Cherry disaster spawned much needed legislation. In addition to creating the U.S. Bureau of Mines in 1910, Congress also passed national child labor laws. The Illinois legislature, convened by Governor Deneen especially for the purpose, immediately enacted stronger regulations, requiring mine owners to purchase and maintain firefighting equipment and workers in certain key jobs, such as hoisting engineer, to pass certification exams. They also appropriated one hundred thousand dollars in relief funds, and the three mine rescue stations they helped create were open by February 1911.

Contrary to Seymour Stedman's prediction to mediator John E. Williams, the Cherry disaster did impact the creation of worker's compensation laws in the United States. In 1911, the Illinois legislature passed that state's first liability act, allowing miners and their families to recover damages for injuries and deaths caused by their employers' negligence. This legislation was the precursor of Illinois's worker's compensation law. Modern worker's compensation laws, also designed to protect employers against bankruptcy, are now part of every state's statutory fabric.

In April 1911, the Northern Trust Company issued vouchers to divide up Johnny Galletti's estate among his heirs. His siblings were awarded $180 each as payment in full. Since the judge felt uneasy about widows handling their children's awards, Beatrice Galletti had to petition the court to appoint a guardian for her five minor children, then later petition that he be allowed "to invest for them in real estate" so she could buy them a house. She, however, refused to accept her $360 payment for her son's death. Judge Joe A. Davis wrote to her married daughter, Mary Corsini:

> . . . I have your letter in which you say that your mother does not wish to sign her receipt. I am sorry she is so foolish as she is just losing the use of her money. If she should change her mind, let me know. I will return the papers to the Northern Trust Company and tell them to hold her money for the present. If your mother does not make up

her mind to sign soon, then I must take some other means to close up the estate.

In August, the trust company filed a petition requesting Mrs. Galletti's share be paid to the Bureau County treasurer. She was subpoenaed to appear in court on September 23 to show cause why the funds should not be turned over to the treasury. She did not appear. The judge entered the order, fining her sheriff's fees of $3.05, which he deducted from the $360 paid into the treasury.

In February 1912, Judge Joe A. Davis ordered the guardian to reimburse Beatrice Galletti $877.53 for the home she built for her children, provided she first turn over title to the property to them.

Three years later, on July 20, 1915, she finally petitioned the court for payment of her share of her son's estate.

CHAPTER THIRTY-EIGHT

Even though many Illinois miners had little work during the winter of 1910 to 1911, more than sixty thousand donated to a union fund to erect a memorial at Cherry. Women and children too added their contributions, raising $2,500 to build the simple monument. On November 13, 1911, thousands swarmed into Cherry's Miner's Cemetery for the unveiling and wreath-laying ceremonies.

The thirteen-foot monument, crafted in Chicago of parian marble, is centered at the front center of the tiny cemetery. The figure of a grieving woman sits at its base below the inscription:

IN MEMORY OF THE MINERS WHO LOST THEIR LIVES IN THE
CHERRY MINE DISASTER, NOVEMBER 13, 1909. ERECTED BY THE
U.M.W. OF A., DISTRICT NO. 12, ILLINOIS, NOV. 13, 1911

The St. Paul Mine reopened at the end of 1910, providing an industry to Cherry until 1927. A 1922 miners' strike was resolved, but following an impasse in a subsequent strike in 1927, the company closed down the mine. By that time, mechanization could take coal out of Illinois's shallower southern coal mines much less expensively than miners could hack it out by hand from the deep interiors of northern coal fields. The company dismantled the mine, leaving only the boilers, tipple and little else.

In 1929, John Bartoli bought the mine property. It lay idle until

1930, when he fixed it up and formed the Cherry Coal Company with a few small investors. They pooled their funds, bought a hoist and with a crew of thirty began mining coal, mainly on a "demand basis." After the Cherry Coal Company ceased production in 1934, it leased the mine out for a year, then closed down operations completely in 1935. In 1936, the Chicago Bridge and Iron Company bought the tipple and other metal ruins for scrap.

Today, little remains. Most of the buildings are gone and the remnants of the concrete-covered shafts are overgrown with grass and weeds.

Since the seventy-fifth anniversary of the disaster, Cherry has hosted a special commemoration every five years and hundreds of Cherry's descendants return from across the country to honor the memory of the victims. While the event falls under the auspices of Cherry's mayor, mine survivor Ambrose Marchetti's son-in-law, Paul Rooney, and grandson, Jack Rooney, a local expert on the disaster, have been instrumental in upholding the tradition. Attendance at the memorial masses, parades, pancake breakfasts and cemetery ceremonies swells with each special anniversary and the tiny Cherry Library opens its doors the entire day for visitors to view its collection of disaster artifacts and photos.

The library's most recent acquisition is a meticulous, multilevel scale model of the mine, unveiled during the ninetieth anniversary observances. Created by Ray Tutag Jr. after studying mine maps and hundreds of disaster photographs, the huge model is complete with offices, engine houses, hospital and train.

William Maxwell, the third vein miner who'd collapsed onto one of the last cages out of the burning mine and sent rescuers back to save his fallen son, remained a miner even past retirement. It was soon after Maxwell moved to Michigan that John Bartoli bought the property and lured him back to Cherry to manage the Cherry Coal Company's mine. He was seventy-three.

On an October Saturday morning in 1930, almost twenty-one

years after he'd escaped death in that St. Paul Mine, Maxwell was cleaning up rock in the second south entry. Suddenly, a section of roof collapsed, crushing him to death under several tons of rock.

In recognition of his heroism, the St. Paul Mine Company named Walter Waite superintendant of mines.

For years Mamie Robinson wore Sam Howard's engagement ring. Eventually she married and raised a family in Arlington, Illinois.

Thomas White went back to the mine, but never did regain his preordeal energy and vitality. Sore eyes, a pasty, prematurely aged appearance and the occasional sharp pain in his lungs while he worked were reminders of his week trapped in the crypt.

While most of the Galletti family remained near Cherry, John Tintori and Attilio Corsini moved on to other coal mines in Illinois before taking their families to Detroit in the 1920s to find work in the auto plants.

Peter Donna and Alexander "Scottie" Deans were the longest-living survivors of the Cherry disaster. Donna never again set foot in a mine and called the tragedy "the biggest bunch of carelessness I have ever seen." He died in 1977 at eighty-three. Deans lived out his life in Arizona, where he died in 1990 at the age of ninety-seven. His brother Bobby Deans, who had fled to Scotland, never returned to the United States.

The whereabouts of Alexander Rosenjack remained a mystery until Ambrose Marchetti's grandson, Jack Rooney, tracked him down through some genealogical sleuthing in 1999. From Rosenjack's great-nephew and family genealogist, Rooney learned Rosenjack had left Illinois for Detroit, where he worked as a streetcar motorman. Family members said his eyelids had been damaged in the disaster.

Rosenjack spent the rest of his life in Michigan, living for a time in Jackson before settling in Battle Creek. He died there in 1957 of a cerebral hemorrhage at the age of sixty-nine.

From 1916, until his retirement thirty years later, he worked for the city of Battle Creek.

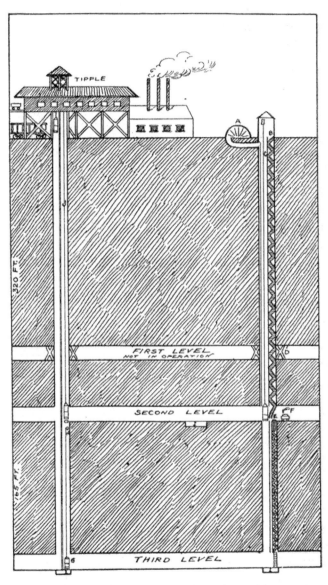

Cross-section view of the Cherry Mine shafts and bottoms. Underground mine tunnels snaked for miles from this area.

CHERRY MINE DISASTER—

VICTIMS.

Check No.	Name.	Occupation.	Wages.	Age.	Nativity.
547	Amider, Alfio	Miner		18	Italian
291	Agramanti, Foliani	..do		40	..do
510	Alexius, Joseph	..do		28	..do
240	Atalakis, Peter	..do		34	Greek
247	Atalakis, G	..do		39	..do
131	Adakosky, M	..do		18	..do
Co....	Armelani, Chas	Trackman	$2 56	32	Italian
Co....	Armelani, Paul	..do	2 56	33	..do
86	Burke, Joseph	Miner		31	Irish
155	Bauer, Milce	..do		43	German
110	Brain, Oliver	..do		40	Scotch
25	Burslie, Clemento	..do		34	Italian
289	Bolla, Antonio	..do		24	..do
108	Bastia, Mike	..do		28	..do
274	Brown, Thomas	..do		51	English
170	Bolla, Peter	..do		32	Italian
573	Bawman, Frank	..do		28	Belgium
538	Bawman, Lewis	..do		31	..do
536	Barozzi, Antone	..do		26	Italian
228	Bruno, Edward	..do		33	..do
210	Bredenci, Peter	..do		30	Lithuanian
191	Budzon, Joseph	..do		30	Polish
169	Boucher, Jerome	..do		39	Belgium
272	Bakalar, Geo	..do		25	Slavish
17	Bayliff, Thomas	..do		31	English
498	Bernadini, Chas	..do		26	Italian
208	Bosviel, Adolph	..do		33	....
294	Budzom, Chas	..do		30	Polish
447	Bertolioni, Tonzothe	..do		22	Italian
569	Benossif, J	..do		34	..do
579	Butilla, August	..do		32	..do
309	Bordesona, Joseph	..do		35	..do
Co....	Betot, John	Trackman	2 56	40	Lithuanian
Co....	Brown, John	Cager	2 56	33	
Co....	Buckels, Richard	Spragger	1 40		German
Co....	Bruzis, John	Timberman	2 56		Lithuanian
Co....	Bundy, John	Mine manager			..do
597	Costi, Angelo	Miner		23	Italian
489	Ciocci, Peter	..do		24	..do
479	Canov, Canivo	..do		33	..do
451	Cioci, Canical	..do		22	..do
415	Costi, Lewis	..do		22	..do
37	Camilli, Frank	..do		36	French
585	Casserio, John	..do		26	Italian
231	Castoinelo, Chelsto	..do		27	..do
36	Cagoskey, John	..do		56	Slavish
196	Chebubar, Joseph	..do		32	Austrian
572	Casollari, Elizio	..do		29	Italian
470	Conlon, Heary	..do		21	French
203	Cohard, Henry	..do		34	..do
97	Cipola, Mike	..do		40	Slavish
105	Clark, Robt	..do		28	Scotch
129	Carlo, Elfi	..do		28	Italian
436	Casolari, Diminick	..do		40	..do
530	Cavaglini, Chas	..do		45	..do
570	Compasso, John	..do		33	..do

Victims of the Cherry Mine disaster, including details regarding
their survivors, ages, nationalities, positions and wages.

NOVEMBER 13, 1909.

VICTIMS.

Married or Single.	Children—Name and Age.	Residence.	Remarks
Single............	....	Cherry........	....
..do............	....	..do........	....
Married..........	Toressa, 3; babe, 2 weeks.......	..do........	Widow and two children..........
....	....	....	No particulars...................
			..do....................
Single..........	....	Cherry........	....
Married..........	Albert, 5; John, 3; Edith, 2 mos........................	..do........	Widow and three children........
..do............	Richard, 8; Marco, 7; Albert, 6; Rachael, 4; Caroline, 2....	....	Widow and five children.........
..do............	Joseph, 2...................	Cherry........	Widow and one child............
..do............	Mary, 18..................	..do........	..do...........
..do............	Beatrice, 10; Winnie, 6......	..do........	Widow and two children.........
..do............	Sidney, 6; Rolando, 3; infant........................	..do........	Widow and three children........
Single..........	....	....	....
Married..........	Marico, 6 mos...............	Cherry........	Widow and child...........
..do............	....	....	Widow...........
..do.....:......	Dowardo, 6.................	Cherry........	Widow and child...........
Single..........	....	....	....
Married..........	August, 6..................	Cherry........	Widow and child...........
..do............	....	....	Widow...........
..do............	Josie, 9; Antone, 8; Teressa, 2..	....	Widow and three children..........
..do............	Annie, 2; Mary, 1............	Cherry........	Widow and two children.........
..do............	Satislar, 3; Joseph, 2........	..do........	..do...........
..do............	Amelia, 17.................	..do........	Widow and one child...........
..do............	George, 10 mos.............	..do........	..do...........
..do............	Rosie Pearl, 18; John Lincoln, 1...................	..do........	Widow and two children........
..do............	Child, 2 wks...............	..do........	Widow and child...........
..do............	Clatilda, 15; Bertha, 15.......	..do........	Widow and two children........
..do............	Infant..................	..do........	Widow and child...........
Single..........	....	....	....
..do............	....	....	....
..do............	....	....	....
Married..........	Annie, 9; John, 5; Sophia, 4; Mary, 2.....................	Cherry........	Widow and four children..........
Single..........	....	..do........	....
Mother..........	Albert, 15; Lottie, 11..........	..do........	Mother and two children........
Married..........	Alfred, Amy, William, Florence, Herbert, Ethel, Lincoln, Edgar...............	Cherry........	Widow and eight children..........
Single..........	....	..do........	....
..do............	....	..do........	....
Married..........	....	....	Widow and two children in Italy...
Single..........	....	....	....
Married..........	One child..................	Cherry........	Widow and one child...........
Single..........	....	....	....
Married..........	Line, 3; Mary, 10 mos.......	Cherry........	Widow and two children..........
..do............	John, 16; Andrew, 11; Mike, 7...	..do........	Widow and three children........
..do............	Joseph, 7; Mary, 6; Phillip, 3; John, 1.....................	..do........	Widow and four children..........
Single..........	....	Seatonville....	....
..do......	....	Cherry........	Supporting three sisters; Minnie, 18; Laura, 10; Dora, 5.................
Married..........	Henry, 7; Marcal, 4; Paul, 3....	..do........	Widow and three children..........
..do............	Mike, 9; Annie, 8; Andrew, 4...	Streator........	..do...........
Single..........	....	Scotland......	....
..do....	....	..Cherry......	....
..do............	....	Italy........	....
Married..........	Jennie, 13; James, 11; Samuel, 8...................	..do........	Wife dead; three children... ......
..do............	Annie, 6; Frank, 5; Mamie, 4; infant 5 mos.................	Cherry........	Widow and four children .. ..

Victims—

Check No.	Name.	Occupation.	Wages.	Age.	Nativity.
Co...	Debulka, John	Driver	$2 56	27	Slavish
Co...	Dovin, Andrew	Miner		49	..do
35	Donaldson, John	..do		46	Scotch
7	Dovin, George	..do		18	Slavish
38	Demesey, Fred	..do		29	French
58	Dumont, Leopold	..do		33	Belgium
269	Detourney, Victor	..do		36	..do
151	Denalfi, Francisco	..do		30	Italian
461	Durand, Benjamin	..do		26	French
236	Dunko, John	..do		22	Slavish
Co...	Durdan, Andrew	Timberman helper..	2 36	....	
Co...	Davies, Jno. G	Trapper	1 13	17	
416	Elario, Miestre	Miner		24	Italian
241	Fiko, George	..do		18	Slavish
487	Floses, Peter	..do		23	Italian
554	Erickson, Chas	..do		55	Swede
Co...	Erickson, Eric	Timberman	2 56	39	..do
153	Farlo, John	Miner		30	Italian
47	Fayen, Peter	..do		40	French
370	Forgach, John	..do		34	
Co...	Fo mento, Dominick	Grocer		32	Italian
Co...	Freehirg, Ole	Timberman	2 56	35	Swede
Co...	Francisco, John	..do	2 56	48	Austrian
Co...	Francisco, August	Driver	2 56	23	..do
Co...	Flood, John	Merchant		49	Irish
204	Governor, Jno	Miner		42	Belgium
258	Grehaski, Andrew	..do		49	Slavish
197	Guglelm, Peter	..do		34	Italian
528	Garletti, J	..do		29	
531	Guidarini, Jno	..do		41	Italian
586	Gialcoizza, Angone	..do		33	..do
493	Garabelda, Jno	..do		35	..do
486	Gulick, Joseph	..do		34	Austrian
575	Gwaltyeri, Jalindy	..do		28	Italian
14	Garletti, Jno	..do		19	..do
119	Geckse, Frank	..do		20	Austrian
189	Grumeth, Frank	..do		24	German
80	Gibbs, Lewis	Timberman	2 56	34	English
114	Halko, Mike	Miner		28	Slavish
221	Hadovski, Steve	..do		28	..do
184	Howard, Samuel	..do		20	French
66	Hudar, Jno	..do		45	Slavish
206	Hynds, William	..do		25	American
262	Hertzel, Jno	..do		39	German
290	Halofcak, Dan	Miner		45	Slavish
	Rescued Nov. 20; died 48 hours after.				
216	Harpka, Joseph	..do		52	Austrian
413	Hainant, August	..do		25	French
Co...	Howard, Alfred	Trapper	1 13	16	..do
161	James, Frank	Miner		43	Scotch
483	Janavizza, Joe	..do		....	
Co...	Jamison, James	Driver	2 56	20	

Continued.

Married or Single.	Children—Name and Age.	Residence.	Remarks.
Married..........	Infant.....	Cherry........	....
..do.............	Annie, 16; Emma, 14; Margaret, 13; Joseph, 11; Susie, 9; Frausley, 7; Albert 4; Caroline, 3....................	..do........	Widow and eight children...........
..do.............	Flenan, 21; John, 15; James, 10.....................	..do......	Widow and three children.........
Single...........	....	..do.........	....
..do.............	....	..do.........	....
..do.............	....	..do.........	....
Married.........	Victot, 12; Julia, 9; Eddy 7.....	..do.........	Widow and three children........
..do.............	John, 6 mos....................	..do.........	Widow and one child............
..do.............	Marsalle, 2....................	..do.........	..do..........................
....	Infant....	..do.........	..do..........................
....	....	....	No particulars.................
Single...........	....	..do.........	....
..do.............	....	Cardiff......	....
..do.............	....	Austria......	....
..do.............	....	Italy........	....
..do.............	....	Cherry.......	....
..do.............	....	Cherry.......	....
Married.........	....	..do.........	Widow, no children.............
..do.............	John, 8; Albert, 5; Andrew, 3; Louisa, 1....................	..do.........	Widow, four children............
..do.............	Mary, 4; John, 1............,	..do.........	..Widow and two children........
Single...........	....	..do.........	....
Married.........	Peter, 22; Matt, 15; John, 13; Zony, 12; Mary, 10; Willie, 8; Veronica, 7; Jennie and Joe, 3.................	..do.........	Widow and nine children.........
Single...........	....	..do.........	....
..do.............	....	..do.........	....
Married.........	Clara, 18; Martha, 16; Theodore, 14.......	Cherry........	Widow and three children........
..do.............	Boy, 16; boy, 12; boy, 3; girl, 20; girl, 18; girl, 9...............	Streator......	Widow and six children.........
..do.............	Mary, 8; Annie, 4.............	Cherry.......	Widow and two children.........
..do.............	Aldo, 11; Amelia, 9; Annie, 6; Antonia, 3...............	..do.........	Widow and four children.........
..do.............	Minnie, 6; Phillip, 2..........	Cedar Point....	....
Single...........	....	Italy.........	....
Married.........	Johanna, 10; Josie, 5; George 1 mo......................	Cherry........	Widow and three children........
....	....	..do.........	....
....	....	..do.........	Widow mother and six children....
..do........:....	....	....	Widow and two children in Austria.................
Single...........	....	..do.........	....
Married.........	....	..do.........	Widow, no children........
..do.............	Child, 6 mos..................	..do.........	Widow and one child..........
Single...........	....	..do.........	Mother....................
Married.........	Annie, 14 Mary, 12; George, 6; Susie, 4; Lizzie, 2; John, infant......................	..do.........	Widow and six children..... ...
. do......	Marguerite, 2.................	..do.........	Widow and one child...........
..do.............	Mary, 19; Susanna, 18; Teressa, 14; Louisa, 11; John, 7; Martha, 5; Hanna, 3; August, infant...................	..do.........	Widow and eight children........
Married.........	Mary, 18; Annie, 16; Susie, 13; John, 12; Pauline, 10; Maggie, 7; Steve, 3; George, 1.........	Cherry........	Widow and eight children.........
..do.............	....	Austria......	Widow and seven shildren........
..do.............	Dorica, 1.....................	Cherry.......	Widow and one child.........
Single...........	....	..do.........	....
Married.........	Daisy, 13.....................	..do.........	Widow and one child.............
....	....	....	....
Single..........	....	Oglesby......	Father..................

Victims—

Check No.	Name.	Occupation.	Wages.	Age.	Nativity.
186	Klemiar, Thomas	Miner		55	German
4	Kanz, Jno	..do		42	Austrian
127	Kussner, Julius	..do		30	German
144	Klaeser, Jno	..do		41	..do
170	Klemiar, Richard	..do		24	..do
182	Kometz, John	..do		53	Slavish
72	Krall, Alfred	..do		15	Polish
73	Krall, Henry	..do		36	..do
94	Kroll, Alex. S.	..du		23	..do
61	Kenig, John	..do		42	Austrian
197	Klemiar, Geo	..do		56	German
48	Korvonia, Joseph	..do		33	Austrian
56	Kovocivio, Frank	..do		38	..do
508	Korvonia, Antone	..do		21	Russian
444	Kutz, Paul	..do		33	Lithuanian
Co...	Kliklunas, Dominik	Driver	$2 56	24	..do
171	Love, James	Miner		26	Scotch
26	Leyshon, Chas.	..do		24	Welch
288	Lukatchko, Andrew	..do		35	Slavish
193	Leptack, John	..do		26	..do
492	Lonzotti, John	..do		16	Italian
468	Love, Morrison	..do		31	Scotch
467	Love, John	..do		34	..do
472	Love, David	..do		24	..do
533	Leynaud, Urban	..do		37	French
512	Lonzetti, Selcomo	..do		32	Italian
567	Lallie, Frank	..do		21	..do
Co...	Lurnas, Mike	Timberman	2 56		..do
Co...	Leadache, Joseph	Trapper	1 13	16	Lithuanian
Co...	Leadache, Frank	Driver	2 56	20	..do
Co...	Lewis, Isaac	Liveryman		33	
133	Leadache, James	Miner		40	Lithuanian
91	Mumetich, Hasan	..do		20	Austrian
128	Miller or Malner, Lewis	..do		19	..do
134	Miller or Malner, Joseph	..do		39	..do
174	Miller, Edward	..do		33	
305	Mokos, Joseph	..do		43	Slavish
102	Meicora, Joseph	..do		36	Austrian
32	Mohahan, James R	..do		62	Scotch
60	Mills, Edward	..do		44	English
280	Mekles, Tonys	..do		54	Austrian
549	Merdior, Arthur	..do		26	Belgium
599	Marchiona, Frank	..do		32	Italian
331	Marchiona, Archie	..do		52	..do
327	Maceoha, Jno	..do		26	Slavish
263	Mills, Arthur	..do		29	English
101	Mittle, Jno	..do		37	Lithuanian
139	Mayelemis, Frank	..do		27	..do
24	Masenetta, Anton	..do		25	Italian
34	Malinoski, Joe	..do		26	
63	McCandless, Robert	..do		27	Scotch
95	McGill, Jno , J	..do		17	..do
551	McCrudden, Jno	..do		25	..do
552	McCrudden, Peter	..do		48	..do
200	McMullen, Geo	..do		24	..do
172	Mazenetto, Jno	..do		18	Italian
546	Mani, Joseph	Miner		56	..do
Co...	Mayersky, Jno	Timberman	2 56	39	Slavish
Co...	McLuckie, Andrew	..do	2 56	31	Scotch
Co...	McFadden, Andrew	Driver	2 56	42	

Continued.

Married or Single.	Children—Name and Age.	Residence.	Remarks.
Married	Joseph, 6	Cherry	Widow and one child
..do	Kathrine, 13; Killian, 12; Marguetrite, 7; Mary, 4	..do	Widow and four children
		..do	
..do	Teressa, 10; Peter, 7	..do	Widow and two children
Married		..do	Widow and no children
..do	Mike, 19; Mary, 17; Susie, 14	Streator	Widow and three children
Single		Cherry	
Married	Eugene, 17; Selma, 12; Bernard, 9; Edmund, 4	..do	Widow and four children
..do		..do	Widow and no children
..do		Austria	Widow and six children
..do	Charles, 14; Earnest, 10	Cherry	Widow and two children
..do	Joseph, 9 mo	..do	Widow and one child
..do		..do	
Single		..do	
Married	Barlico, 3; Powis, 3	..do	Widow and two children
Single		..do	
Married	Jeanette, 4; Christina, 2	Scotland	Widow and two children
Single		Wales	
Married	Amin, 12; Andrew, 6; John, 4	Cherry	Widow and three children
..do	Mary, 2	..do	Widow and one child
..do		..do	Widow
..do	Morrison, 9; Jeannette, 3	Scotland	Widow and two children
..do	Morrison, 10; Katy, 7	Cherry	..do
..do	..Morrison, 4; John, 2	Scotland	..do
..do	Bertha, 13; George, 3; Maroo, 6 mos	Cherry	Widow and three children
..do		Italy	Widow and two children
Single		..do	
..do		..do	
..do		Cherry	
..do		..do	
Married	Robert, 8; Lola, 6; Isaac, 2	..do	Widow and three children
..do	Katie, 22; Josephine, 17; Annie, 10		
		..do	..do
		..do	
Single		..do	
Married	Mary, 17; Joseph, 7; Annie, 6; Eva, 4; Frank, 2	..do	Widow and five children
..do	Edmund, 7; Raymund, 5	..do	Widow and two children
..do	Mary, 17	..do	Widow and one child
..do	Joseph, 3; Cecil, 2; Mary, 3 mo	..do	Widow and three children
..do		..do	..do
..do	Edward, 9; Philip, 7; Alma	..do	..do
..do	..do	..do	
Married	Anton, 5	..do	Widow and one child
..do	Olga, 1	..do	..do
..do			Widow
..do		Old county	Widow and one child
..do	Doris, 6; Harold, 2	Cherry	Widow and two children
..do	Mary, 7; Annie, 6; Susie, 3	..do	Widow and three children
Single		..do	
Married			Widow and two children
Single		Scotland	
..do		Cherry	
..do		..do	
..do			
Married	Marie, 11; Peter, 8; Kathrine, 4; Margurite, 2	..do	Widow and four children
..do	George, 2; Infant	..do	Widow and two children
Single			
Married	Katie, 20; Mary, 4	Cherry	Widow and two children
..do	Annie, 13; Susie, 11; Emma, 8; Joe, 6; George, 2	..do	Widow and five children
..do	John, 10; Jeannette, 5; James, 3; Andrew, 2; Wm. Tayter, 2 wks	..do	Widow and five children
Single		Spring Valley	

Victims—

Check No.	Name.	Occupation.	Wages.	Age.	Nativity.
)o....	Mazak, Jno	Timberman	$2 56		
)o....	Matear (or Mactear), Wm	..do	2 56	30	
)o....	Norberg, Alex	Mine manager		37	Swede
)o....	Norberg, August	Timberman	2 56	34	..do
1	Ossek, Donaty	Miner		32	Austrian
209	Ossek, Martin	..do		36	..do
157	Ondurko, Matt	..do		26	Slavish
541	Olson, Chas. P	..do		50	Swede
273	Palmiori, Albert	..do		50	Italian
227	Prusitus, Perys	..do		39	Lithuanian
118	Prusitus, Peter	..do		38	..do
182	Pavoloski, Jno	..do		27	..do
198	Pressenger, Joseph	..do		38	German
239	Prich, Joseph	..do		38	Austrian
476	Pearson, Alex	..do		30	Swede
488	Perono, Dominick	..do		32	Italian
226	Papea, Chas	..do		33	French
542	Pearson, John	..do		37	Swede
558	Perbacher, Peter	..do		49	Austrian
318	Packo, Andrew	..do		37	Slavish
513	Pete, Ben	..do		35	Austrian
0....	Pshak, John	Timberman	2 56	42	Slavish
0....	Pauline, Antona	Driver	2 56	26	Austrian
10	Repsel, Martin	Miner		36	..do
57	Repsel, Joseph	..do		29	..do
19	Rodonis, Joseph	..do		33	Lithuanian
64	Rolland, Victor	..do		18	
83	Rittel, Frank	..do		37	Austrian
299	Richards, Thomas	..do		21	Welch
414	Ricca, Cegu	..do		30	Italian
504	Riva, Joseph	..do		27	..do
423	Raviso, Joe	..do			
321	Ruggesie, Gajjamyo	..do		25	Italian
)......	Rossman, Robert	Trapper	1 13	17	German
)......	Ruygiesi, Frank	Driver	2 56	21	Italian
)......	Rimkus, Joseph	..do	2 56	27	Lithuanian
)......	Robeza, Joseph	..do	2 56		
55	Sopko, Cantina	Miner		24	Slavish
22	Speir, James	..do		34	Scotch
44	Stettler, Harry	..do		24	German
71	Sandeen, Olaf	..do		50	Swede
85	Seitz, Paul	..do		34	Slavish
111	Shermel, Antone	..do		36	Austrian
132	Stark, John	..do		35	..do
62	Stanchez, Frank	..do		30	Polish
473	Stefenelli, Dominick	..do		39	Italian
474	Sarginto, August	..do		25	..do
253	Siamon, Andrew	..do		24	Slavish
482	Semboa (or Sereba), J	..do			
495	Smith, John W	..do		46	Scotch
225	Sublich, Charles	..do		32	Lithuanian
245	Suho, John	..do		17	Slavish
181	Suho, Mike	..do		44	..do
194	Suffen, John	..do		39	Austrian

Continued.

Married or Single.	Children—Name and Age.	Residence.	Remarks.
Married		Cherry	Widow and three children
..do		..do	Widow
..do	Mae, 6; Dorothy, 2	..do	Widow and two children
Single		..do	
Married	Benat, 8; Mary, 3; Albert, 1	..do	Widow and three children
..do		..do	Widow
..do	Mary, 6; Verna, 5; Annie, 4; Matt, 2; John, infant	..do	Widow and five children
Single		Cleveland, O	
Married		Italy	Widow and seven children
..do	Perys, 8; Tony, 6; Mike, 2; infant 11 mo	Cherry	Widow and four children
..do	Pete, 8; William, 7; Blaygue, 6; Frank, 4	..do	Widow and four children
..do	Rosie, 6; Mary, 2; Susie, 10 mos	..do	Widow and three children
..do	Hilda, 6; Annie, 4; Walter, 3 mos	..do	Widow and three children
..do		..do	Widow
Single		Old country	
Married	Mary, 6; Joseph, 4; Annie, 2; Peter	Cherry	Widow and four children
..do	Lucy, 4; Kathryn, 6 mo	..do	Widow and two children
Single		Sweden	
Married		Austria	Widow and six children
..do	Andrew, 16; John, 14	Cherry	Widow and two children
Married	Annie, 12; John, 10; George, 8; Mary, 4; Lizzie, 14 mos	Cherry	Widow and five children
..do	Antone, 1	..do	Widow and one child
..do	Martin, 8; Lucy, 4; Barbara, 3; Antone, 1	..do	Widow and four children
..do	Joseph, 2	..do	Widow and one child
..do	Peter, 15; Mary, 9; Mabel, 8; Joseph, 6	..do	Widow and four children
Married	John, 12; Martin, 9	Cherry	Widow and two children
..do		..do	Widow
Single		Italy	
Single		Cherry	
..do	Teressa, 13; Andrew, 10; Hannah, 8; Marguerite, 4 John, 2 wks	..do	Mother and five children. Father and mother not living together
..do		..do	
..do		..do	
..do			
..do			
Married	Alexander, 12; William, 11; Jennie, 9; George, 7; James, 5; Elizabeth, 1	Cherry	Widow and six children
..do	Herman, 2; Maria, 4 mos	..do	Widow and two children
..do	Roy, 17; Edwin, 15 Jennie, 12; Evelyn, 6	..do	No widow
..do	Hattie, 3; Edward, 1	..do	Widow and two children
Single			
Married		Cherry	Widow and three children
..do	Josephine, 2; Helen, 3 wks	..do	Widow and two children
..do		Cherry	Five children
.do	Andrew, 6; Martin, 4; Mary, 2 mos	..do	Widow and three children
..do		..do	Widow
		Cherry	
..do	Arthur, 18; Roy, 12; Phyllas, 4	..do	Widow and three children
..do	John, 4; Charlie, 2	..do	Widow and two children
Single		..do	
Married	Tony, 9; George, 4	..do	Widow and two children
..do	John, 9; Annie, 5	..do	Widow and two children

Victims—

Check No.	Name	Occupation	Wages	Age	Nativity
146	Sukitus, Joseph	Miner		30	Russian
308	Steele, Peter	..do		24	American
312	Sarbelle, Julius	..do		28	Italian
282	Stearns, James	..do		40	American
135	Seitz, Edward	..do		28	German
301	Scotland, William	..do		32	Scotch
251	Shemia, Jno	..do		40	Austrian
Co....	Stewart, Harry	Laborer	$2 36	28	Scotchman
Co....	Szabrinski, Jno. (known as John Smith)	Cager	2 56	29	Lithuanian
Co....	Stam, Antone	Timberman	2 56	44	
89	Staszeski, Tony	Miner		33	Polish
16	Sestak, Jno	..do		25	Slavish
52	Tinko, Joseph, Jr	..do		28	..do
212	Finko, Joseph, Sr	..do		51	..do
315	Tinko, Steve	..do		24	..do
Co....	Tinko, Andrew	Spragger	1 40	17	..do
Co....	Teazone, George	Timberman	2 56	28	Italian
516	Talioli, Eugene	Miner		38	..do
537	Tonnelli, Emilia	..do		30	..do
313	Turchi, Nocenti	..do		31	..do
431	Tosseth, Frank	..do		29	..do
478	Famashanski, Joseph	..do		28	..do
503	Tamarri, Pasquale	..do		25	.do
Co....	Tonner, John	Trackman	2 56	47	Scotch
596	Ugo, Filippe	..do		28	Italian
29	White, Geo	Miner		54	English
113	Welkas, Anthony	..do		31	Russian
Co....	Waite, Chas	Mine examiner	3 04	42	English
Co....	Wyatt, Wm	Timberman helper	2 36	35	..do
149	Yurcheck, Antone	Miner		47	Slavish
211	Yacober, Frank	..do		32	German
477	Yannis, Peter	..do			
Co....	Yagoginski, Frank	Driver	2 56	34	Polish
Co....	Yearly, Joseph	..do	2 56	20	
5	Zliegley, Thos	Miner		27	Slavish
148	Zekuia, Joseph	..do		33	..do
497	Zacherria, Giatano	..do		40	Italian
265	Zeikell, Pat	..do		28	Austrian

Concluded.

Married or Single.	Children—Name and Age.	Residence.	Remarks.
Married..........	Joe, Annie, Mary...:............	Russia.........	Widow and three children.........
Single..........		Streator........	
Married..........		Cherry.........	Widow and infant.................
..do............		..do...........	Widow and one child.............
..do............	Henry, 5; Albert, 4; Willie, 2; Lewis, 2 months................	..do...........	Widow and four children..........
..do............	James, 9; William, 5; Andrew Craig, 3 months..............	..do...........	Widow and three children.........
..do............	Mary, 12; Annie, 12; Susie, 9; John, 7; Andrew, 4; Emma, 2...................	..do...........	Widow and six children...........
..do............	Henry, 7; Wdlter, 5; Helen, 4; Robert, 1 month............:...	..do...........	Widow and four children..........
..do............	Eale, 2...................	..do...........	Widow and one child.............
Single..........		Spring Valley..	
Married..........	Antonia, 2 weeks..............	Cherry.........	Widow and one child.............
Single..........			
Married..........	Joseph, 6; Tony, 5; Mary, 3; Andrew, 2; George, 2 months.....	do.....	Widow and five children. ....
..do............	Louis, 26; John, 14; Paul, 12....	..do...........	Widow and three children.........
Single..........		..do...........	
..do............		..do...........	
Married..........	Brogo, 6; Mary, 4.............	..do...........	Widow and two children..........
..do............	Angel, 5; Dominick, 3; Annie, 2; Katie, 2 months.........~.....	..do...........	Widow and four children.........
..do............	Stella, 6; Jennie, 4; Charlie, 2; Amelia, 6 weeks............	..do...........	Widow and four children.........
Single..........		..do...........	
Married..........	Armendo, 2...................	..do...........	Widow and one child.............
Single..........		Old country....	Widow................
Married..........	Rachael, 17; Rose, 15..........	Cherry.........	Widow and two children..........
..do............		..do...........	Widow..............
..do............	Stanley, 10................	..do...........	Widow and one child..........
..do............		..do...........	Widow and two children..........
..do............	Joseph, 4.................	..do.:.........	Widow and one child.............
..do............	Ruth, 14; Eva, 12; Annie, 9; Thomas, 4; Norris, 4.........	..do...........	Widow and five children..........
..do............	Mary, 17; Annie, 12..........	..do...........	Widow and two children..........
..do............	Barbara, 11; Frank, 8; John, 6; Mary, 4.................	..do...........	Widow and four children..........
Married..........	Frank, 16; Mary, 13; Margurite, 11; Agnes, 5; Hannah, 3.......................	Cherry..^......	Widow and five children..........
Single..........		Spring Valley..	
Married..........	Annie, 13; Mike, 11; John, 10; Mary, 8; Emma, 5; Joseph, 3; George, 3 mos........	Cherry.........	Widow and seven children.........
..do............	August, 8; Jennie, 2; infant.....	..do...........	Widow and three children.........
..do............	Antone, 3; Rudolph, 2; infant...	..do...........	Widow and three children.........

By Mr. Stedman:

Q   I haven't asked you yet what it was. You have now admitted that you had some.

A   I refuse to answer the question.

Q   How recently have you received anything ?

A   I refuse to answer it.

Q   On what grounds ?

A   Because I don't think it concerns this thing at all. I don't think my business and Rosenjack's has anything to do with this; that is the reason.

Q   Was it of a business character, - these letters were written in reference to ?

A   I refuse to answer.

Q   Was it of a private nature ?

A   I refuse to answer.

Q   How recently have you received letters from him ?

A   I refuse to answer.

Q   Have you communicated with him over the telephone ?

A   No, sir.

Q   At any time ?

A   I don't think so. I am not positive.

Q   Are you refusing to answer as a matter of protection to you personally ?

A   No, sir; I am just refusing to answer on general principles. I don't think Mr. Rosenjack would be hurt, or anything of the kind, if he was here.   That is private business. If you folks want Rosenjack you will have to get him.

Excerpt from chief mine clerk E. P. Buck's evasive testimony at the coroner's inquest, under questioning by attorney Seymour Stedman.

ACKNOWLEDGMENTS

The contributions of several key people formed the backbone of my research. Their shared passion about this story spurred me on.

My cousin, Lester Corsini, was the first to flesh out the disaster story for me. Since detailing his father's and uncles' experiences at Cherry and loaning me his disaster photo collection and Antenore Quartaroli's Italian diary years ago, Lester has spent countless hours recounting family stories and poring over documents and photographs with me.

Jack Rooney, whose grandfather, Ambrose Marchetti, also survived the disaster, is as passionate about this story as I am. Since childhood, Jack has endeavored to keep the victims' memories alive and has been instrumental in planning the anniversary commemorations. Throughout the many years we have corresponded, he has been generous both with his time and his knowledge.

Without Judy Giachino I would have never been in contact with the numerous Cherry descendants who have shared their family stories with me. Judy's online Delphi forum provided us the opportunity to meet and correspond.

Over a number of years, Jane M. DeMarchi, of the U. S. Department of Labor, Mine Health and Safety Academy in Virginia has provided a wealth of information from the MSHA files.

When my husband and I made a research trip to Cherry, Edward E. Caldwell paved the way. He lined up appointments and research materials in Cherry and in Princeton, Illinois, organizing our time and streamlining our schedule to maximize every minute. Ed has also given generously of his knowledge and through our shared interest in this story has become a friend.

Special thanks to Charles Bartoli for his guided tour of the mine property, and to Carol McGee, Bureau County Genealogical Society, who helped me retrieve and research priceless primary documents, including the bound onion-skin carbon copy of Coroner Malm's inquest proceedings.

Each of my initial readers—Peggy Hoffmann, David Katz, Ilene Katz, Ron Kranz, Fran Kranz, Claudia Scroggins, my husband, Larry Katz; my literary agent, Ellen Levine, and CAA agent, Matthew Snyder—offered invaluable suggestions early in the writing process.

My editor, Rosemary Ahern, was exacting and insightful in posing her revision queries. I couldn't have handpicked a more perfect partner to help shape this book.

Thanks also to each of the following, many of whom claim a relative among the Cherry miners—The Ladies of the Lounge, Jan Greenberg, Marianne Willman, Ruth Ryan Langan, Mitchel Katz, Steven Katz, Joanne Tintori Rodzik, Leslie LaFoy, Tonya Piscitelli, Carolan Kviklys, JoLynne Woznicki, John Tintori, Krista Carra, Leo Bracciano, Cheryl Weiss, Pamela David, Nora Roberts, Mary McBride, Kasey Michaels, Jill Churchill, Jasmine Cresswell, Fayrene Preston, Kay Hooper, Maggie Osborne, Marianne Shock, Virginia Martinsen, Martha Pleiss, Caroline Waldron, Ph.D.; Charlotte Hughes, Elizabeth Buss, Larry Greenberg, Jennifer Thompson, Atria Books; Barbara Hansen, staff and volunteers, Bureau County Historical Society, Princeton, Illinois; Eileen Pinter, Cherry Library; Mary Louise Bergishagen, Maria Danno and the West Bloomfield Township Public Library reference librarians, Michigan; Angie Cooper, Coal City Library District, Illinois; Joanne Meroney, Lois Osborn, Matson Public Library, Princeton, Illinois; Mark W. Sorensen, assistant director, Illinois State Archives; Janice Wamhoff, Coroner, Bureau County, Illinois; Thelma L. Blount, United Mine Workers of America; Bureau County Clerk's Office, Princeton, Illinois; Ray Riggs, West Bloomfield Fire Department, Michigan; Francie LaCamera, Illinois State Library at Springfield; Fr. Sebastian, St. Bede's Academy, Peru, Illinois; Russell M. Magnaghi, Ph.D., Northern Michigan University, Marquette, Michigan; Walter F. Rutkowski, Carnegie Hero Fund Commission; Paul Rochlen, John Tintorri, James Cornelius and John Hoffman, University Library, University of Illinois at Urbana; Lisa Oppenheim, Illinois Labor History Society; Gladys Parochetti, Zita Guerrini, Rosemary Shellhorn, Mary Rooney, Paul Rooney, Bob McCook, Mary McCook, Paula Brown, Joanie Johnson, Richard Joyce, Mary C. Miller, Mikki Judge, Mary M. Smith, Jim Steele, Karen Steele, Bruce R. Steele, Ray Tutaj Jr., Frank Tarasko, Judy Day, Noreen Griffin, M. Renee Gundersen, Pat Lawrence, Veronica Mehrpay, Mike Suhe, Jerry Nichols, Dave Philippe, John Philippe, Katherine Natta, Joe Natta, John Beatty, Matt Phalen, Billy Pigati, Linda Tolodxi, Frank Arduini, Charles Sarture, Cornelius J. Hollerich, Arthur Saltzman, Dean Scarsbrough, Adam Piscitelli, Sandra Sonnino, and to Buster, for his devoted company until "the end."

Finally, thanks to my late grandmother, Catherine Tintori, for repeatedly telling me that my grandfather survived the Cherry Mine disaster. I remembered.